PATTERNS OF THE WHOLE, VOLUME ONE:

HEALING & QUARTZ CRYSTALS

A JOURNEY WITH OUR SOULS

Patterns of the Whole, Vol. I

Healing & Quartz Crystals

A Journey With Our Souls

John D. Rea

Two Trees Publishing
Boulder, Colorado

Copper grid for treatment & the following crystal patterns—the Star of David, cluster pattern, twelve-pointed star, digestion pattern, sleeping pattern and the relationship pattern—are from *Exploring Atlantis, Vol. I , II & III,* copyright © 1982-85 by Rev. Dr. Frank Alper and are discussed with permission of the author.

Exerpt from *My Mother's House by Collette.* Copyright © 1953 by Farrar, Strauss and Young. Copyright renewed © 1981 by Farrar, Stauss and Giroux, Inc. Used with permission of Farrar, Stauss and Giroux, Inc. Diagram from Optical Crystallography, 4th Edition, by Ernest E. Wahlstrom. Copyright © 1969 by John Wiley & Sons, Inc. Used with permission of John Wiley & Sons, Inc.

First published in 1986 by:
Two Trees Publishing
1272 Bear Mountain Court
Boulder, Colorado 80303

Cover photo: John Rea (with the help of Bill Farrell & PhotoWorks)
Artwork (except logo): Jay Jacoby

Printed in the U.S.A. by Braun-Brumfield, Inc./Ann Arbor, Michigan.

ISBN 0-938183-01-X
Library of Congress Catalog Number 86-40223

Additional copies are available from the publishers.

This book is dedicated to my wife, Alayna.

You are guided to know what you are to be.

**The Souls of All are here to help you
once you acknowledge your right to grow
over time in your universe.**

Contents

---

* *Capitalized italics are subheadings in the chapters.*

Acknowledgements

I would like to acknowledge the role my wife, Alayna, has played in the writing of this book and in my growth. She has been a channel for her Soul at a conscious level as long as I, though our gifts are slightly different and complementary. She would have been my healer had she not become my wife and healer, and her steady guidance, encouragement and sharing are a blessing that fills my life. We are truly partners in all we do, including this book and its contents. I have done the actual writing—and the actual channeling—but in many ways this is a cooperative effort between us.

I would also like to acknowledge the role of Rev. Drs. Frank and Helene Alper as I have come to acceptance of my Soul and ability to channel at universal levels. Their work has been fundamental to me, both for this book and for my life as well. Dr. Frank Alper is a conscious channel whose work is to awaken many teachers of God, the shepherds of humanity—which is what we all are. Frank teaches about crystals himself, and I recommend his books on this subject and many others.

Further thanks are in order to LeAnn Meyer, whose help in editing has been invaluable, and to Gurudas, especially for his practical suggestions.

Notes on Authorship

Off and on for years I have been a songwriter and writer, largely as a recreation, and for years I've had inspiration from within for what I wrote without knowing its source. I simply thought of it as creative inspiration, being creatively active. A decisive change has taken place in the past few years as I have become more and more receptive to my own Soul and the receiving of spiritual assistance in general. I believe this is a change that will happen for increasing numbers of people in the years ahead.

All my life I have been guided and never knew it, really. Occasionally, through faith or intellectual speculation (rather than direct experience), I would guess that God might be with me as he might be with all creatures. Most of the time I felt I was alone.

There is a change that comes most gently, most quietly, one small step at a time, until the cumulative impact hits and a flower bud emerges from the stalk that once seemed bare. So it is with me. I am now conscious of my guidance and receptive to what is for my highest and best good. I feel my connection to my Source. So it is and so I believe it will be for increasing numbers of people in the years ahead. None of us are ever really alone.

This brings me to explain, if I can, something about the authorship of this work. I, John Rea, am the writer. But the identity of the actual author is a bit more complex. It is so with all authors, but few of them are aware of it. Inspiration is a magical thing. Most authors would accept that there is something about inspiration they don't understand. There are times when an author writes and nothing comes out that works. And there are times when everything flows as from a source that is bottomless and faultless, encompassing the whole of what is taking shape, even when consciously there is no such perception in the writer, perhaps until after the fact if at all. This "inspiration" is a source that is not at all understood in our time. For its source, in turn, is our own Soul in varying degrees, directed through our own conscious and unconscious filters and biases, our own objectives and conditions for what is acceptable to us.

These conditions often limit what comes through, for our Souls will never violate our free will. We are in charge of what we write, even if the source of it is not always our personality-level expression.

What I am describing in the inspirational process is more universal than one might think, for it is a part of all processes in life, in all that might benefit from direction and guidance: when to apply for a particular job, when to give a friend a call, how to respond to an ailing child. All walks of life and activities are subject to such guidance, such inspiration. They need not be at face value "spiritual." They need only be the honest activity of human beings adapting in the best way they can to their lives on earth.

I would like to say here that the gift I am speaking of, sensing the guidance of the Soul or sensing the best course for our lives—this gift is usually experienced more fully by women in our time. It is a natural consequence of not taking yourself too seriously to be open to guidance or intuition. You do not always need a rational or intellectually conscious understanding of "why" all the time, if you are more humble and simple about your life. Women, in our time, more often retain the good, common sense and innate intelligence that is responsible for receptivity to true inspiration at the level of our actions and daily affairs. Men usually reserve their inspiration for their peak events or expressions, or else their "work", as it is thought of by many. For men see their work as something outside themselves, something which defines their natures, whereas women usually see themselves for what they are more gently.

If it seems extreme to you, the separation of characteristics I am giving here for men and women, that is well, for it is indeed the case that in our time the distinctions that have existed in the past and still remain are growing blurred, and true wholeness comes to many, be they male or female in expression in this life on earth.

I would like to give you an example of inspired connection in another walk of life besides my own.

My father, before he died, shared with me several times the process by which he did his best work as an attorney. He would study a case for hours, sometimes days, interviewing, considering all the possibilities in law, in case history, and in his own legal experience until he had as complete a picture as possible of what was going on. Then he would sleep on it. He usually did his best work in the early morning before dawn, he used to say, because at that time, very often, he would awaken with a complete idea of the best direction to take in the case. He said he knew it seemed strange, but it was as if someone were helping him, even talking to him quietly there in the early morning as he worked alone, rapidly making notes of the general points to be emphasized legally. Sometimes, he said, it was almost as if he were taking dictation, so fast did the ideas and language come to him. Even when he couldn't understand at first the sense of his inspiration, if he trusted it and allowed it to develop as he took notes, then later it would prove correct. Though this first inspired understanding of the case might seem an unlikely one, when it was researched in the directions indicated and followed through in briefs, in negotiations and in the courtroom, it invariably turned out to be the correct one.

My father remembered to his last days, with amazement, the incredible intricacy and elegance of the legal directions he was guided to follow, through the most complex and involved of situations.

"There were lawyers who were smarter than I, and lawyers with better memory of the points of law and the case histories, but the ideas I've received in the earliest hours of the morning are like something from another source. They have always turned out to be true in the end, through all the twists and turns I could never have foreseen. And I wonder sometimes where they come from, and I have to say, in my inmost thoughts, they must come from somewhere beyond myself, maybe from God." In such a way he spoke about his inspiration.

My father was not one to mention God very often, except in jest. For him the thought of God being involved in his inspiration was a wild leap into the unknown, given almost reluctantly.

I would like to describe for you a little about the nature of my own source of inspiration, or of guidance. For it is in this that I differ from most authors, at least at the level of what we are conscious of and understand. The authorship of most of what I write has become my self and Soul in relationship. In all probability, this is a transitional phase. When I channel directly from Spirit—from my Soul and other Spiritual beings—I am increasingly attuned to my Soul on many levels, increasingly attuned to who I really am. This seems to be a part of a transition we all may share as human beings in this time, becoming gradually as one with our Souls, our Divine or High Selves, and then in time as one with God. In potential this is what we already are.

For me, what seems to be going on is a process of choice and attunement: choice to pay attention at all to another level of reality, attunement to notice and allow what is happening to be in balance and alignment at many levels. I must admit that at present it happens while writing, channeling or just listening—though less and less each day—that I am out of alignment with my inner source just slightly. As an example of this, I might be following the momentum of where an idea or phrase seems to be going and continue in a straight line instead of taking a turn my inner guidance would lead me to. Or I might enjoy what is being taught me so much that my enjoyment becomes a wish to stay on the same subject overly long, thus impeding the flow and proportion of the communication. In these times I carry the momentum I create until I remember to check in again with my Source.

What I am describing is a moment to moment sort of thing. Only little things seem involved, subtle compared to most of what we deal with in life, but still very noticeable; for each time they occur I must notice once more I am out of phase just a touch and must pick up the thread of connection once more. This being out of phase has a significance. Each moment carries with it the free will expression of every level of myself: emotions, thoughts, actions and reactions all are up to me. Yet each moment all these things are up to a source inside myself if I stay tuned and notice what is best, if I allow myself to "channel" at all levels what is coming from the highest aspect of my Being. In this channeling mode I may act on what comes through, evaluating, as it were, all that comes to me before it happens, or I can allow the flow of action (or of thought, emotion, speech or writing) to come from my Source directly, alignment allowed through and through. As the alignments of the different levels of myself become more complete, the strongest flow of all becomes the grace of God to all. This grace is directed from my Soul at frequencies at one with God because my Soul itself is one with God on the levels it exists at rest, or the level it knows best. It is an easy thing for a Soul to do. What is difficult is letting the free will expressions on other levels evolve or grow to the point of acceptance of the Self or Soul, allowing it to integrate with them and direct them from "on high," as it were.

There is a principle that the highest expression of ourselves is in fact our Source, is in fact our attunement with the Father/Mother God of all, at-one-ment with our perfect harmony of expression for the highest and best good of all.

Does this all seem strange to you? I hope not. I am the author of what I write, and yet I am aware of a greater intelligence working through me, quite consciously, and it is the natural extension of my own common sense—the place in me that truly knows with a certainty that is not of this world when I trust myself in balance with all. As I am guided in what I write, say or do, things happen for the most part effortlessly, without expenditure of energy in the slight perplexity and indecision that once accompanied my work. In my writing or channeling now there is often little or no premeditation as to what will unfold. At most times I am a bit surprised at what comes out myself, recognizing it as an integration of my own wisdom and a greater wisdom than I am conscious of from the level of my seemingly limited personality, my current expression in time and space. My Soul and my Creator know enough to guide me. This I know and trust more and more all the time.

The guidance of my Soul is not my only guidance, I might add. The nature of this process of channeling, once it becomes fully activated within, is to allow communication with any level of expression one wishes. It is my intention all the time to work with the level of expression and the being or beings that best reflect my own energies at the present time, in the way that is for the highest and best good of all. By this I mean as well that I am working with those whose natural function it is to guide me—my own Soul and those whose energies are familiar to me. In addition to my Soul and the aspect of me that is one with my Creator, I will often work with and channel different angels or master Souls, who are as one with me in light and love for all. Such sharing is always beneficial, for it is in order to so exchange with all, that we may love our brothers as we would love ourselves.

It is not because of any inability on the part of my Soul that I do such sharing. For my Soul is of the nature of God itself, and only out of ignorance and Self doubt have I ever accepted those outside myself as wiser and better than the inner Source who teaches me—this Source who is as one with God. There is no limit on Soul in harmony with its Creator. Each and every Soul has a capacity for self-acceptance and grace, and each and every one of us is able to express our Souls as we come into mastery of self.[1]

---

[1] You see, at times we shall capitalize these words; at times we shall not. The meaning differs with use, as self (small "s") and soul (small "s") denote those states of self and soul (our inner, emotional natures) that are themselves as subject to dissolution and error; whereas our Selves and Souls are not. For all things below are as above, as Hermes Thrice Great would teach to Greece and Rome, before your time, out of the ancient ways of Egypt.

As to our use of capital letters in a slightly broader context, we wish to be able to use capitals to signify the levels of our existence that are divine at times when special emphasis towards God in His or Her unending nature might prove helpful to our meaning; and we wish to use lower cases for the selfsame words at other times, to de-emphasize a bit the effect of separation resulting from such usage, which can prove harmful to our growth if we but think ourselves unworthy of such grace, the oneness with our Souls—and God in time as well. Such separation explains for us in former times as well as now, the gap between our Souls and selves. But we are one in ways we often fail to grasp, at levels of our Souls and God, at all the times we share as one.

For me the reason for sharing with other energies at any level is the exchange of love and blessing at the level of Soul with one and all, as we each express a totality, yet each express a perfect aspect of God Himself/Herself. We are patterns of the whole as well as complete unto ourselves. And we function for the highest good of all when we share our truth in love with one another, and thus give each other opportunity for growth.

I might add that I do not trance channel, or allow an energy to take over my voice or conscious occupancy of my body at any time. I allow a conversation to take place in my inner silence, either totally in thought, or directly in writing or in speech. I allow an exchange of energy, light and love as well. But I choose not to allow less than full consciousness to exist in me while channeling or sharing with subtle or spiritual levels of expression from my Soul. I am responsible for all I think, say and do, responsible to set the conditions for my life; and it is appropriate for me to remain in full consciousness so that I may play my full role as awakening child of light and love. This is a choice I make from out of my own sense of what is in order for me, what is appropriate. For another some other course might be equally appropriate, and we are both blessed in what we choose. May we be guided in our choices from the highest level of our truth.

Something for me to point out to you is that the process I have been involved with in writing this book has changed in the course of writing it. It was at first a process I envisioned, of writing a chapter and then channeling a chapter, so that my involvement might be balanced with that of my Soul. This rapidly changed to another process, that of becoming one with my Soul as I worked. After a certain point, it became appropriate for me to realize that all true inspiration came from my Soul as one with God as I allowed it to flow through me as personality. It became more and more artificial and difficult to pretend to myself to be separated from this source of inspiration. Now I would never choose to separate myself from who I am at the level of Soul, anymore than I might shut off my mind or brain in its functioning on my behalf when I think. This is the progress that has happened for me in the course of writing this book. The abilities of my Soul are mine now to a greater and greater degree all the time, especially in the areas of expression I have worked on: the speaking, thinking and writing in alignment with my Soul. And the energy contact with my Soul is rapidly changing my abilities to relate to others with the full energies of my Soul, at levels that include the far-reaching love that all Souls possess as gift of their Father/ Mother God in perfection.

A last thing to say about this is that I am not a being of love and light all the time. I share an ordinary existence with my Soul, my wife and my friends. But I am able to transfer the responsibility to my Soul more and more for what I do; and this is a gift of balance on another level than the one I had envisioned when starting this book. The responsibility for balance is mine, at the level of my personality expression, but more and more, as with balancing on a bike, the process of personality responsibility and balance becomes as second nature, an opening to the Soul; and this enables us to share in undivided energies clearly more and more. The giving from my Soul becomes a process that takes place through me, as healing function long awakened starts to work through who I am. This is the healing vibration of love for all, that comes from Souls of all of us, as one expression of the light and love of God.

So much of what we need is the love of our own Souls, you see. So much of what makes us whole, what completes us, is the acceptance of our Souls. This is what I have been taught through my contact with Soul in many forms, including many teachers, and helpers I knew nothing of. And this is what my Soul has to teach to others through me.

This is a process my wife, Alayna, shares with me, for she is similar in her abilities to work with Soul of all through her. And we share this in a way that blesses all when we are with our Souls in truth.

God bless you in love and light from all our Souls together.

Introduction

A Channeling On Crystals

From the Souls of All In Us

There was a time when crystals were in use all over the world, in the lands of Atlantis and Lemuria, and in the kingdoms of the Dahomey (in Africa) and of the Etruscans. The early Egyptians used crystals in their pyramids. And the holy men of the Americas—among the Hopi, the Navajo, the Cheyenne, the Cherokee, and other tribes up to the present time (as well as the ancient nations of the Americas in times before)—all knew the uses of crystal that were given to their peoples, to honor and respect, to use wisely. For these quartz crystals that you play with as rocks from a hillside are hidden codings of the secrets of life and death. They are the fathomless depths of knowledges that far surpass your own. They are communion with the nature of the divinely inspired hierarchies of Watchers and Friends who have fashioned your planet since its inception, who have guarded it from all harm not of your making, and who watch over you even now.

Each little crystal is a "Star Wars" drama in its own right, complete with a complexity that George Lucas might appreciate if he could see it in Technicolor and Panavision. And the inventions of your time pale beside the inventions that were powered with crystals, through crystals, by crystals—in programmings that you would find more akin to the behavior of living systems than the operation of machines of your time.

For you are akin to these living systems we mention in conjunction with crystals. You are programmed in ways beyond your calculations for this time zone era. You are encoded with the networks of living light that make up the language of creation for your universe. You are a pattern in the whole fabric of creation that has an exactness your science can bring you an appreciation of. It is an exactness that operates on frequencies of light and love that you would find in your experience more akin to feelings of wonder and awe, blessing and sharing, knowing and assimilating, enjoying and protecting, and lighting the way for others as they walk their path—more akin to these qualities than the more narrow range of frequencies that are within the traditional scope of your science. Yet the laws of operation for divine science are within the scope of your scientists' understanding if they but knew more of the order of things as they occur for all.

We have come to teach you more of the benefits of working with quartz in its crystalline form. We are light workers like you, here in service to the Divine. We are a gift to you in love and light. We are your own Souls giving to you in this way. We are frequencies of light and love beyond the understanding of your current age, yet we are within your experience through the work of channels, such as the one working here, and through the conscious growth of your own selves, akin to the children of the Sun, Moon and Stars as you are.

You are the ones who guide the destiny of this little planet. And it is time for you to awaken to the working and blessing of your own natures, your own True Selves. For you are blessed as the Children of His/Her Creation in light. And you are blessed as the Children of His/Her love and delight, for is it not written, "You are my Child, in whom I am well pleased?" And you are indeed the Child of a Lord of Love and of Life itself, Creator with the tools of infinite structure and design, Simple Child of the greatest wisdom and heart everlasting. And you are more loved than you can know in these bodies of time and space limitation, blessed in expression at all levels in which you find yourselves for the glory of God and of Woman/Man.

—The Soul of the Channel, from the
Father/Mother level of Creation, in
the Name of Christ (or the Universal
Love aspect of God)

It is important for us to say a few things before we begin this excursion into the properties of crystals, so that many things can become clear from the start. We are not involved with crystals as a means in themselves, though we love them as creations of the Divine. We are involved with crystals in as much as they further our growth as spiritual and grounded human beings.

In this book we are channeling the truth of our own Souls, as is the case with all the work that each of us does in True Guidance in harmony with all. With you, our readers, we are conscious co-workers in the divine plan more and more, as so many sages and saints have said, and thus we each are at work creatively with whatever we are given, allowing us each to be both expressions of the whole and the unique expression of that whole for which God intended us. Thus it may very well be that you find yourself adjusting and adapting what is given here to fit your own expression of the whole. And this is wonderfully in order for all. It is in order for us in turn to give you information that is not too detailed and worked out. Over and over the author has had to check himself in his own exuberance to sort out the details of many things. For too much detail is not needed. Each of us will receive slightly different details, and the whole in which we express ourselves will be represented through many. Love and respect for one another in the abundance of our sharing is the greater goal behind the skillful means of the information and techniques that any one of us is given. For as a child we come to the Lord who made Heaven and Earth. And as a Child (the Child in each of us) does the Father/Mother of All find harmony within us.

Lastly, there is no thing in Heaven you do not already know yourselves if you will look within and find it. "Ask and you shall receive, knock and it shall be opened unto you." There is nothing I will tell you that you cannot verify for yourselves in the wisdom of your own heart and mind. The truth is a mirror of the whole within each of us. And the wisdom of the highest, most hidden levels is before your eyes. Trust yourselves to know the Truth when you find it. Allow the truth to emerge from your own understanding, for this is the wisdom that is available to you from your own Soul as well as mine. Your experience is as vast as mine, and you tap it with your common sense to guide you. You confirm what you discover in this life by exploring what is reasonable to your common sense understanding, your sense for truth, for sharing, and for the integrity of others; no real secrets to it. So it is with your work with crystals and spiritual growth in general.

So God bless you on your quest for growth through the workings of light and love, and through the workings of crystals too, for as long as such may prove relevant for you. Walk in this thy Father's Light, Amen. And blessed be our Mother.

Chapter One

Quartz Crystals:

An Overview

This chapter will be a brief summary and overview of quartz crystals and the areas of information that are possible to explore with them. We will go into greater detail later. We will also include something of our own background with crystals, that you might learn from our experience somewhat.

A Few Preliminaries

We would like to take you step by step along the ways of using quartz crystals to accelerate your growth in the way that is in order for you at the present time. We will share with you from the level our Souls as well as our hearts, and we will give you what we ourselves have learned in this area of expression, the access to our Souls through the heart. This is a definite way we walk with crystals. For you it may be appropriate to walk in another way, and in this you are blessed as well as us.

We might add that the methods we will use in this work are those that have worked for us, and we will use direct, first hand experience with the crystals as a vehicle for your growth and alignment to who and what you are at different levels of truth. Through such first hand connection many things of a subtle nature will become clear for you in time as well as on the earth you live. Thus you remain who you are, and yet you grow with us through your crystals. Is this to your understanding? We hope it is, for this is the method we will use throughout this book, beginning with the simple and working up, so to speak—until you find yourselves exposed to our truth. For the nature of crystals is as the whole, and we are of that whole, you and I, together as one in the love of God, in all kingdoms of nature and beyond.

Crystals In Nature

Natural quartz crystals were formed in quartz veins and pockets that pushed into earlier sandstone deposits roughly 100 to 350 million years ago. The geometry of these formations is exquisite and intricate, and aligns with the magnetic fields of the earth. Crystals are different in each major deposit in the world, the main minable deposits being found in Arkansas, Brazil and Madagascar, with newer deposits opening up in Columbia as of the date of this writing.[1]

Natural quartz crystals came out of the ground as you see them, without being faceted, broken off or altered by mankind, except inadvertently in mining. If the crystals are found in matrix they are usually kept that way. The breaks you see on individual crystals were sometimes the result of mining, but much more often they were caused by earth changes long ago, and most of them are at least partially healed by new crystal formation at the base of each.

There are those who say there are no accidents in this world: each crystal has a purpose in the form in which it is found that awaits discovery. Just as each tree or animal in nature differs from its archetype and has its own quality, so too with each quartz crystal.

Only man-made crystals are uniform and identical. In nature they are of infinite variety, like oak leaves or animals; they are one of nature's crowning works of art. No two are alike.

---

[1] Note: For the sake of brevity, we will often refer to natural, clear quartz crystals simply as "crystals," although strictly speaking, crystals are actually the orderly formations of the latticeworks of many minerals and elements besides quartz.

Crystals in Tradition

Traditionally, quartz crystal was said to harmonize and align human energies (thoughts, emotions and consciousness) with the energies of the universe, and to make these greater energies accessible to man.

In earlier times, when all things were thought to be conscious parts of a greater living consciousness, quartz crystal was thought to synchronize man's consciousness with that of the heavenly bodies and the hierarchies of angelic beings, visible and invisible.

Crystal was a sacred power object to the American Indians, Tibetan monks, Druid priests, and the priests and kings of Christian Europe as well. It was the stone of the White Light and of the First Ray, the Philosopher's Stone of the mineral kingdom, just as Saints and Holy Men were said to be the Philosopher's Stone of the human kingdom. It was also the stone of all possibility, available to many due to its widespread distribution over much of the planet. This was a part of its great popularity and its usefulness.

"Scrying", gazing into crystal points and crystal balls, is a part of our heritage from fantasy and legend: to see past and future, gain visions and learn information unavailable to the ordinary faculties in a crystal of wonder are a part of old Celtic tales, Oriental magic, Alchemical romances and fantasies based on the old traditions, such as Tolkien's *Lord of the Rings* or *The Silmarillion*.[2]

Candle gazing through a crystal quartz point or ball suspended or resting at eye level for a few minutes before meditation or prayer was a practice common throughout the world, in such diverse areas as the Far East, the Middle East, Africa, pre-Christian and Christian Europe, and in the Americas as well. It was said to bring clarity and calmness to whatever endeavor it preceded, as long as it was used with good purpose, tempered by moral judgement and common sense. This technique is one we will elaborate on later.

---

[2] J.R.R. Tolkien, *The Lord of the Rings* (New York: Ballantine Books, Inc., 1965), and *The Silmarillion* (Boston: Houghton Mifflin Co., 1977).

Since earliest times it has been known that different types of natural quartz crystal have different qualities when held or worn. We will take up a few of these now by way of example, with properties we find most accurate, and go into more detail subsequently:

Rose quartz was said to have a calming influence, to promote health, harmony, loving relationships and peace.

Clear quartz was said to be the total of all colors of the rainbow, good for clarifying the mind and bringing energy and light to all man's endeavors, including the workings of his physical and subtle bodies.

Amethyst was said to be a great purifier: it transmuted baser to higher energies, and it was good for the heart and blood. It calmed the whole being and allowed greater acceptance and trust in times of stress. (We might add that it also offers an attunement to the divine feminine on the Violet and/or the Silver Ray of expression.[3])

Natural Quartz Crystal Today

In modern times, quartz crystal and other crystals have been discovered to have unique piezoelectric properties that make them usable in energy exchange mechanisms with many practical applications for our world, such as oscillators, semiconductors, transducer applications and the like. They are essential for the electronics, optics, aerospace, communications and precision-instrument technologies upon which our modern way of life is based. Although synthetically grown quartz crystal can usually be substituted for the natural material, and a

---

[3] This quality of silver light is more as a projective energy than as the color silver *per se*. It is thus a mirroring that is accomplished, of the aspects of Soul and self that are required through the various programmings that are possible with it. This mirroring is an aspect of silver in your industries as well as homes, for silver has long been the perfect "mirror" when placed behind glass, even though it is too expensive to be used by your world very often. The aspect of silver involved with crystals of an amethyst hue is the inner aspect of mirroring for your self and Soul as one with God, if this be to your understanding, rather than the color silver itself.

related, fused silicon semi-metal or very pure "glass" is the basis for computer technology, there are many applications for which the natural material of the finest clear grades is useful or necessary. "Silicon Valley" in California, a center for our computer and space age technology, is named for quartz and fused quartz, or pure "glass," whose chemical name is silicon dioxide—meaning that one silicon atom to two oxygen atoms is the proportion of elements universally found in pure quartz compounds.

There are many other fields in which applications for crystal or silicon technologies are being found: laser technologies, including the LCD (Laser Compact Disc)/stereo applications; fiber optics; acoustics; and increasingly medical applications as well. Synthetic fused quartz and quartz crystal may prove essential for many solar-power applications in the near future. And the applications that exist as the basis of scientific instrumentation and possibilities for research in these and many other fields are virtually endless, based on the abilities of crystals to be so precisely calibrated as to sound and light and simple space considerations.[4]

---

[4] For example, crystals are used in research and industrial applications to calibrate gold, since the oscillating properties of the crystal can be precisely measured, the so-called resonating frequency established for any given slice of crystal depending on its length and mass, and thus the weight of any metal evaporated on its surface can be precisely measured due to the shifts in frequency that are observed.

Another example would be the ways that crystals can diffract light of definite or measured frequencies to exact angles of refraction, thus allowing prismatic separations of wavelengths of light for calibration of what light is allowed to pass through a quartz lense into an enclosed chamber or area of observation. Thus the effects of exact frequencies of light are available to all who would experiment with the world around us, whether it be with the atmosphere itself, certain isolatable gases (for discovery and identification purposes, or merely for varifying results of interactions), or with elements of any substance known to man.

An example of what could be done with crystals would be the use of thought waves to broadcast sound and light. This is but one of the applications that might be made use of, were we to guide you in your work past the obvious restrictions you have placed upon your growth through wars and other wrongs upon your earth. This is not a technology currently available to humanity.

Both man-made and natural quartz crystal have unique properties to amplify, bend and synchronize many types of energy —light, electricity, magnetic fields, and perhaps more subtle vibrational fields we are not yet equipped to measure. Kirlian photographic work by many people shows significant changes in the energy fields of those using or wearing natural quartz crystal. Practitioners doing work with polarity therapies, kinesiology, Rolfing, massage, acupuncture and acupressure, visualization, affirmations, breath therapies, Ayurvedic medicine, hypnotism, counseling, past life regressions, sacred ritual, aura balancing, therapeutic touch, laying on of hands, radionics, herbalism, aromatic and bath therapies, diet, exercise, homeopathy, flower essences, negative ion generators, magnetic therapy, chiropractic, color and sound therapy, colonic therapy, naturopathy, nursing and traditional medicine, have discovered uses of crystals to be effective in their work. We ourselves have had successful experiences using crystals with many of the above therapies or forms, and/or advising others in using them.

Today there are large numbers of people learning to work with quartz crystals through their own discovery, books and the teachings of others. Workshops on the use of crystals— and other gems and minerals—have been popular for some time, presenting the teachings of many theatres of expression and many backgrounds of mankind, from new methods of scientific experimentation to the practices of the current wholistic health movement; from the traditional, native medicine ways of North America to the shamanistic practices of the Amazon (and ways of many other indigenous peoples on this earth); and from the traditions of our Eastern cultures, some long gone, to the cultural uses of quartz crystals in our more Western past, also some long gone. Today, some of the old ways with crystals are to be found anew, as these in part are Atlantean ways that find a ready market in this time as well as long ago. They are a resonancy of the past that was encouraged for your growth in same, yet still today must bear releasing for some Souls to reach another level of expression.

Such ways are all a part of the lore of crystals we would share with you as best we may, in the little time allotted to us, for practical and other considerations. Yet we will specialize a bit, as you shall see. For we are guided by our truth, though we have known the ways of others many times before as we incarnated through the lives of personalities in every age of humanity, every race and creed/religion that your world has known. For we are of your Soul. And we are you together, everyone. And we bring you wisdom of the Soul along a path of our own choosing, blessing for your Soul.

We would give you the advice to take such workshops and seminars as you are drawn to, but know that they are not entirely what applies to you. For you are free to choose your way from all you hear and come to know from others still as well as self. And we are blessing you in your discovery on your own and still with others. There are more such workshops all the time. There are more ways to awaken to your Souls than we can dream of individually, from the level of our lives on earth.

We ourselves teach seminars on the use of crystals and other gems, as well as work with Soul. Our sense is that most of this work, from ourselves and others, is valid for this time. It meets a need that is present in people of many walks of life, to know more about directions for their conscious growth in Soul as well as selves' own new expressions of the conscious whole. For Soul and self are one in this, and both have much to do—through the natural gifts we all have as human beings and beings of energy, light and love.

We ourselves have learned from many people in order to broaden our work and make it as relevant to ourselves and others as possible. And we now suggest you do the same, if so you may be guided for your growth.

Our Own Early Experiences with Crystals

When we began experimenting with quartz crystals and other stones, six or seven years ago, we made no assumptions about the effectiveness of healing techniques being taught and practiced with them. We had initial experiences we sought to explore and expand on through further experience and through learning all we could from others.

After a period of early, isolated discovery, we began to work with several small groups, not all of whom were connected with one another. As our circle of awareness expanded in this field, we found that there was considerable interest and experimentation going on through people of different traditions and background, using crystals for meditation and conscious awakening, and for healing oneself and others. We found little that was published; it seemed that many were working in relative isolation. As we took an interest in what was being discovered, we found a groundswell of activity arising spontaneously and powerfully, in many places.

At about that time, (1980-82), at a personality level I was trying out involvement with mining crystals and marketing them. I met and heard of many people working with crystals who might not have heard of one another. These were people I sold crystals to, or so I planned that it might be.

In Arkansas, the primary source for quartz crystals in this country, people involved with mining crystals felt real bewilderment and excitement over the new explosion in the "crystal consciousness" or "crystal healing" market. They would shake their heads in disbelief and even laughter, then put their minds to how to take advantage of the rush they felt was on, just as their daddies had experienced such a rush—though from a different cause—back in '36 through '39. That was the time of the great crystal rush before the war, that mapped out most of the mines and continued through the years of '41 and '42 when the Army Corps of Engineers set itself to drill the mines to find what sure deposits might exist, what quality of crystals too, in case the wartime need we had (for bomber scopes and sonar, and the like) might soon expand or be cut off from all outside supply.[5] Now once again, backwoods Arkansas miners couldn't deny that a new and promising market for their crystals had emerged. And I was trying to work with those miners as best I could to find what work with crystals might be mine.

"Why, I remember when we used to bulldoze them points," said one to me, the oldest miner in the area and probably among the ones who had been at it longest. "I remember watching old John Moody bulldoze hundreds of them candles, the long, skinny ones, under. We was after the clusters, you

---

[5] At that time hundreds of local miners and farmers were put to work in mining exploration and discovery that the Corps of Engineers designed. These were the parents and grandparents of those who do the mining now.

know. Them Europeans only was interested in them clusters. And I remember thinking when I got home, 'There must be some use for them points.' They was pretty too, you know. And next day I told him, 'Hold it, John, I'll give ya 50 cents apiece for them points if they ain't beat up too bad.' They was all the long, clear, skinny ones, ya know. Hand size, the way people like. And them baskets of points I bought offa John Moody, they sat around for 'bout a year or so, before I sold 'em off, or gave 'em up, I don't know which."

Just by way of background, the crystal business itself is not really involved very much with the uses that we will describe for you in this book. Ninety percent of all clear crystals by simple tonnage are simply crushed for the scientific purposes we have already mentioned. A small remainder are of specimen grade, actually saved as such. And most of these go to markets that one might describe as specimen markets or collector markets, for Europeans especially. In Europe there is a cultural bias towards having crystals or mineral specimens on the mantel-piece or in the living room for decoration, and thus the nicest clusters of crystals are sold abroad for this traditional market. Americans in the United States have never really appreciated this use for crystals very much. The way crystals have been mined, then, has generally reflected these markets, in that the clusters usually were saved, the bulk of the material was allowed to be crushed, and the single points or single crystals left intact—until recently—were often thrown away or sold for very little on roadside stands, simply because there were more of them than people wanted. This has changed somewhat, but still it is a fact that most crystals are crushed, and most clusters are sold in rock shops or in Europe (especially the nicest ones). This is not really important information, it is simply interesting as background on my own involvement, which was, I thought, to help create the newer market, the emerging market for the uses of crystals we will be discussing in this book.

In my early crystal experiences, I was exposed at least somewhat to the process of mining crystals, and to those who did the mining. At one open-pit mine, I watched people throw crystals around like beer bottles, between swigs of the actual stuff, dropping some and keeping some—the dropped ones mostly in the baskets set for crushing because they broke or chipped when dropped, the undamaged ones in baskets kept for show, to sell as specimens for the few that might be interested. And it was few people too, they told me—and just as few crystals saved—compared to all the crystals they would find that could be sold for crushing to the electronics and processing companies who bought from them.

I watched also as people dug with pokers in the red clay soil, for crystal clusters and crystal pockets, with almost surgical skill; and I heard their tales of working late at night by the light of the sparkles that rose from crystals they crushed with the scraping of their big bulldozers or heavy lifts (for crystals let out sparks at night when crushed: mechanical energy converted to electrical spark and light—the piezo-electrical effect in action).[6]

It didn't take long for me to learn I was better suited to selling crystals than mining them. And better suited to learning about crystals and teaching others than I was to selling. This process was a painful one and short for me: two short years and I was gone from Arkansas for good, except for occasional, kindly visits I might still take. Nonetheless, I learned a lot, mostly the ways of fools, and I learned to never mind the ways of others when it comes to ways of self and Soul, for we are guides to who we are, and no one else can lead us.

And all the while, along the way, as I found new information or a new technique, I would explore it with myself and others for simple understanding. A group of us would try it out for size. This period was a transitional one for me. To discover through my Soul was still far off, it seemed. So I felt in feelings of unworthiness that I was only half-way conscious of at my personality levels of expression. And yet,

> My Soul knew all along just what would be
> To heal the Soul's expression on this earth through me.

---

[6] In a nutshell, piezo-electricity is this conversion of one form of energy to another, as in the mechanical pressure of the bulldozer converting to a spark of light and electricity within the crystal being crushed or squeezed. A related property of quartz and other substances is piero-electricity: the ability of quartz to convert heat to electrical energy in a similar way.

Since that time I have recovered much of what I am. And I place my early crystal discoveries in a context that lets them naturally fill a useful purpose in the stages of growth I have known. They have been integrated in my expression, if you will, and they are a tool for helping others. They are but one tool among many to help us discover who we are, that we may outgrow all tools and stand alone as the beings of light and love we are. Yet they are useful in the transitional phase we are currently in. For a short but significant time, many forms of communication, education, healing and blessing are in order for us as we explore and awaken to who we are. And the meaningful applications of quartz and other crystals are limited only by our own beliefs, and limits we place on ourselves.

Such applications include healing uses, meditational uses, communication uses, and many small, specific uses, such as putting a quartz crystal in drinking water (in glass, stainless steel or porcelain containers but not in plastic or aluminum), using them with plants, trees and gardens for strengthening, balancing and complementing Nature's efforts, and using them as mirrors of who we are and need to be at Soul and personality levels as well.

Care and Cleaning of Crystals

There were traditionally many ways taught to care for crystals. Cleansing was an aspect of such care, along with traditional methods of charging or setting crystals in motion for definite purposes, and traditional ways to honor the intrinsic qualities of crystals, such as setting them in the moonlight periodically. Or in the sun. Or exposing them to ceremonial energies or places, or exposing them to prayer from the heart. Sacred ceremonies,[7] healing clay baths, and sea salt baths are the ways we have heard of cleansing crystals most often, though any act of intentionality to clean your crystals, such as

---

[7] Some examples from Native American tradition are smudging with sage in a Sacred Way and/or placing the crystal in a Sacred Circle of the Four Directions and calling on the Keepers of the Four Directions, the Spirits of the Ancestors and beings who would help us, to cleanse them in a Sacred Way. Similar practices come to us from Europe in many Christian, pre-Christian and esoteric Christian traditions.

washing them in water or wiping them off with the intention to clean them will help. As one option, we were guided to use the sea salt method, either burying crystals in dry, aluminum-free sea salt overnight if they were really in need of cleaning or just putting them in a wet sea salt bath between uses that don't involve great amounts of detoxification or release.

It is our feeling that when a crystal is first acquired it is a good idea to clear it of unwanted influences by cleaning it. And then it is important to charge or have it blessed—"programmed", if you will—so that it can best serve the purposes of enhancing the growth of those using it. If sea salt is used, there are a few other guidelines to follow. Make sure the sea salt is aluminum-free and not rock salt. At a health food store or in the health food section of a super-market such sea salt is available. Read the label and/or ask the store personnel if you are unsure about ingredients. If the salt comes in bulk, the ingredients will be on the bulk bag. Some health food store sea salts still contain aluminates (to keep the salt from caking); the magnesium anti-caking additive that most sea salts use as an alternative is okay.

Another point: sea salt used for cleaning crystals can usually be used only once, and it is a semi-toxic substance after it has been used in this way. Exercise care in disposing of it. Better still, get someone to cleanse the sea salt for you, through their energy work or prayer; and learn to do this for yourself as well.

It is a good idea to cleanse your crystals regularly, perhaps seasonally or more often if your crystals are used a great deal, or if you feel moved to do so.

Cleansing crystals is a subject that there is a lot of differing opinion about. One thing to mention is that it is good for you to learn to judge for yourself, based on what seems true for you and what you experience for yourself. There is a place in each of us that knows, especially tempered with a good dose of common sense and a good feel for objective versus subjective realities. Don't let others, including us, put a straight jacket of beliefs on you. Run things through your own experience and common sense. That is what we have done, and that is what you should do, too. Have fun at it! For freedom requires that we be good at choosing what is true for us, out of our own inner knowing and good judgement.

We might point out that one reason for the divergence of opinion on the use of crystals is that we are now getting a sur-facing of many different traditional ways of using crystals, both from what is still being taught in living traditions today, and what is stored in the past-life experiences and learning of all of us. There have been many different ways of using crys-tals on this planet over the past millennia, many different as-pects of our being and our bodies that were being emphasized and developed by these different practices and traditions. None of them are lost to us. Some of them were more limited and limiting than others. Some were aspects of what we might call the balance to our truth, rather than our truth. Yet all of them are true from at least one point of view; all are patterns of the whole that have their own integrity, as the seeds of our growth. Each of us is a universe to explore, with our own unique lessons and purposes, as aspects of the Whole of our Creator, and as holographic, perfect parts of the mosaic of humanity that are complete, beautiful and full of purpose both individually and as patterns of the whole. So it is with the les-sons we learn in life, and so it is with the different traditions of crystal use among men—past, present and future.

In the exploration of ways to use crystals, may you be open to the ways that are true for you. Don't be afraid of any, and, one more time, use your common sense.

Just to conclude our introduction to caring for crystals, of the many other practices we have heard regarding care of crystals and care of their users, common elements in all appear to be respecting the gifts crystals offer us, being careful with thoughts and desires when around them, being loving and attentive as a way of staying balanced when around them, and exercising the Golden Rule in regard to the effect we may have on others when using crystals: specifically, caring about the integrity and freedom of one another.

This is a time when it is best for all methods or tools to en-hance our real growth, from the point of view of all levels of our being.

A Final Note

It was once believed that quartz sand added to a garden brought the energy of the stars into the soil,[8] and that something similar was true for human beings: quartz crystal helped bring the energy of the stars and the Soul into expression in humanity. May it be so today as well.

---

[8] Rudolf Steiner, the great European philosopher, practical teacher and spiritual teacher, recalled this when he gave lectures to farmers and biochemists on ways to regain the fertility of the soils that were fast being depleted in the early part of our century. For further insights of this nature see Rudolf Steiner, *Agriculture: A Course of Eight Lectures* (London: Bio-Dynamic Agricultural Association, 1974), and Herbert H. Koepf, Bo D. Pettersson and Wolfgang Schaumann, *Bio-Dynamic Agriculture: An Introduction* (Spring Valley, New York: The Anthroposophic Press, 1976).

Chapter Two

Beginning With Quartz Crystals,

A dialogue with Soul

There is a beginning sequence to working with quartz crystals that all frameworks for their use would find acceptable. This is the sequence we would like to channel to you today.

First take up your pen and write what you know about crystal use. What people have told you since crystals first interested you. Now realize that what you have written is the set of instructions you have already given the crystals in your possession, both with limitations and with direction. For you to "know" something about a crystal is for you to accept a definite limitation about a crystal. And this is inevitable.

The limitations we set ourselves are of this same nature: with each understanding we have about who we are, we accept a shared responsibility for both our abilities and our limitations. We do this in order that we might live in a limited world, created with definite freedoms and with definite limitations. We do this in the name of functionality. And it is definitely in our interest to be able to function. So we accept some limits, we resist others, and we grow within this framework we have set up for ourselves. So we function with crystals as well.

Any belief you have about an object conditions the way it responds to you. With a crystal this response is supersensitive and instantaneous. To psychic vision different things look different to each of us as they order their appearance and nature to fit our ideas about them.

So be very careful what thoughts you bring to a crystal. Enjoy yourself with it. And you will see the enjoyment is its stable gift to you, should you allow this to be the case. Laugh and play with a crystal, knowing that is what it is for. For you have a choice about what its role for you shall be. It is you alone who can set the conditions for what a crystal will become for you. And yet in this you are never alone at all. For we are with you as well. And we guide you in a wisdom of happiness that you would think must spring from flowers, the happiest things you can see with eyes of physical expression, so happy is the joy we share with you.

Next we would like you to think of a crystal in your possession. It is not the physical crystal so much as the quality of being, in the crystal, that is the object of this second exercise. Notice what it is about this crystal you like. Is there a feeling you associate with it? If so, focus on this feeling as we describe a process for you to duplicate.

Many years have passed since we first did this process with you, the reader, the first time. Yes, we mean you, the reader. You have been guided to do again what all of humanity has done in the past with crystals: attune to the crystal lattices of light that are akin to you on many levels; attune to the quality of light harmonics that move at electro-magnetic frequencies within your being in time and space. Open up to the feeling of being in tune with your crystal. Now accept yourself as worthy to interact with the purest light you can imagine. Accept the light that echoes in the windows of perception that are harmonic with your crystal. You will feel a blessing in this light. For what is coming through for you is in perfect order for your Soul, and this light has a healing quality for you as a result.

You have already worked with your crystal successfully as you allow it to "treat" you inside your own being. As you grow in acceptance, you will allow it to treat you in a myriad of ways you can only guess at now. They will be ordinary ways, when finally you come to them. For by the time they are experienced, all things have already been accepted by you for your growth. Otherwise you would not experience them at all.

Acceptance is the key to experience of yourself as well as crystals. Enjoy yourself as you share what you learn and feel, with yourself and with all who are ready for what you have to offer. For in sharing we cement what we have learned into our own frameworks for functional growth. That is why it is such a good idea to teach what you learn almost as soon as you learn it. It becomes your own all the more readily.

A third exercise to enjoy is to approach the crystal as a window in time, to imagine, if you will, that you are looking through this window at something you have already experienced in your life.

Notice the things that are familiar to you in this "remembrance." You have purposely picked some incident, place or thing—or someone, if you will—that you have been guided to choose. Otherwise you would not have picked it.

There is a gift for you in looking back through the window of your crystal at some particular memory in times past that holds some charge for you, that has arisen almost unbidden to be the choice for this exercise. Simply rest with yourself, feeling what this memory is like for you, as you imagine it coming to you shining through the window of your crystal. Allow it to be what it is, no more, no less. Ordinary perhaps. Perhaps more. You are letting the crystal help you attune to the frequencies of your past, stored as they are in the resonancies of your experience. The crystal will awaken these memories more vividly for you if you allow it to. Thus you will integrate more fully what has happened. You will be in tune with that past experience, and you will find it naturally becoming more harmonic, more naturally integrated into the overall resonancy fields of your experience as a sum total pattern of being. This exercise is a tool for you to share with others. Through it you may explore the things that need forgiving, and the events of your life that need more understanding and integration. You have in the crystal a tool for psychiatric work par excellence, if you use it for yourself or for those you may be guided to help.

This is enough of an introduction to your work with crystals. By doing the exercises we have given you, you will find yourself already attuned to a wide range of inner work with crystals as tools. You will have much you can share with others. And you will be ready to experience more with an understanding for what you are already able to do. Remember, you are no stranger to this work, no matter how strange these things may seem in your immediate, present incarnation. Trust your Soul to be your guide. Know the Two are One. We bless you.

Chapter Three

Choosing Crystals for Yourselves and Others

Very briefly, we would like to give suggestions for choosing crystals for yourselves and others, as so many times this is grounds for confusion and questioning in the many people that we meet who buy their crystals from us or from others. There is little enough to it, once you know that. But in the meanwhile, a few gentle words of encouragement might do nicely.

The first thing to know is you can't make errors in your choices. Crystals all love their roles with you, and none are evil or unkind to you. Occasionally, perhaps, a programming in a crystal might preclude the uses that you put it to, but this is comparatively rare, and in these times, when all things are needed to guide you to your Source in truth, the crystals volunteer quite willingly to assist you in all you do for growth.

Is this to your understanding? Good. We hope it is, for we would have you simplify the process for yourselves, not grow in confusion, so to speak.

The next thing to say to you is this, that crystals all bear your inspection with perfect equanimity, some remaining dormant, others activating themselves for you, as simple response to who you are. They are your friends, every one, and they love your attention. They appreciate your sympathies as well, from darkest cloud of longing, or blank despair, to open-hearted love in God: all are good to them, for they are whole.

"The Dark Side of the Force," Dear Gertrude

We write with tongue in cheek the following "true tales" about your times in recent past. All is bright and merry within the world of crystals, unless you harm them with your will, which hardly happens any more. Your older times were times of dreams. You have them still inside of you. Thus we pattern what we say on these old dreams, that you may see them so for what they are. And humorously, then, we say to you that crystal use in older times was like the stuff of fairy tales somewhat: "evil deeds" of men were done with glowing crystals, "dark and true." Can you see these pictures in your minds? We hope you do, for we are here to tax your souls with pictures of these dreams for you to see their meanings once again: in darkest caves and crannies, where men designed the deaths of others with their swords of magic fire, guiding crystals to do naught for them but silly things and evil deeds, so fell and dark were they. This can no more be the case, for since 1892 "the Lord is come to earth," you see: a pattern of completion. A singular year, 1892, yet one that marked beginning of the dawn, we have to say again. The kicking and resistance started next.

Our language here is purposely that of fairy tales and magic dreams. We laugh a bit in words like these describing fears that haunt your past, and religious ways of blessing men who did "fell deeds" in times of yore. You have to see the blessing through these sayings you hold dear, of "comic" heroes from your past who work with crystals "evil deeds." You have to see the blessing here, of deeds that give a gift to man/woman: the gift of learning what to do and what to say in face of pressures and of loss; the gift of in a later time appreciating more what went behind (what was forgotten, if you will), as days of yore are really food for growth in all of you and us as well.

The new awakening giving birth to Soul in you, at the personality level, has begun to dawn for humanity. So it is that the darker possibilities of growth for you, the learning through subtle junk that hurts all others, is no longer permitted along your subtle byways of expression. So near to you is Love in this, that only you can know inside yourself that this is true, these words we speak, that "the days of darkness" are no more with reference to your Souls. And so in inner light and trust the goblins are no more.

The awakening has brought great upheavals to your world, we know. This is as it should be. "The last full measure of devotion," as it were, to all that has gone before, patterns of the past no longer needed in your growth but still lingering in the hopes, dreams and fears that scare you in your dreams-come-true on earth—these have walked the earth in your more modern times. The twentieth century has seen a measured, steady growth in wholeness, through all the wars and pain of death and fear. The great cries of anguish and alarm have awakened you to Light on Earth, in many ways. And now we bring you your own Souls that you might see the truth in what we bring, that since 1984 the dawning of your new race is here at last with you, as the energies of your new age are put in place through you and us, and we awaken still the heart of God in all mankind to know the truth of God supreme in all we do for you on earth.

This means, quite simply, that you are safe with crystals as in no other time on earth. "The evil that men do," for you is confined to the world outside yourself, so to speak, in another dimension of Soul we would say. The physical world itself, the ordinary way of living, is the field of play for evil or mistakes, rather than the inner fields of play, the energy attention and light attention ways that men have struggled to attain to gain their ends with others. These realms are swept clean, we say, except for smallish ends of work unfinished that have to do with each of you and deeds you need to do for your Souls in wholeness. Again we say, the evil that you see in life is simple, interactionary choice of all mankind, free of the shackles of "darker things," accumulated through the ages. The darker things are gone to where they need to be for healing. And you and all mankind are left to heal yourselves, in simple choice of freedom, with yourselves and Souls together.

Thus it is that the choices of picking crystals are simple now that nothing really wrong for you can happen if you want this to be so. (We mention what you want in this, for it is still possible for others to affect you if you give them choice to do so, more than we intend for you at any given time; inimicable results may still seem possible in the short run of things, though all things conspire to make you whole in God.)

The crystals that you pick are largely cleared themselves, reflecting the tendency of humanity today to be cleared as well, for the Soul to work at so-called psychic levels of interaction.

Thus it is the tendency of crystals to be influenced by Divine resonancies of freedom calling out for you and them, influencing you and them through freely chosen pathways of expression. Thus they, the crystals, and their source, would choose to help you with their lives in God, and only tend to take on less than perfect resolutions as they mirror back for you yourselves, that you may grow through them.

Is this too complex for you? We hope it is just an introduction to the whole of what you do with crystals, condensed enough for you to know that you are safe to use them as you grow in truth.

Choosing Crystals

The next thing we would say to you is that there are few considerations for you to notice before you choose a crystal. Choose as you feel guided, knowing that the choices open for you are only good ones. You can't go wrong. Some crystals are better suited to your growing than are others, but only to the extent that they naturally would suit you out of pre-conditioning they receive at creation of their own energies. Once you buy a crystal and adapt it to your use, the crystal you have chosen suits you perfectly as you allow your Soul and other helping hands to program for you the intentions of guidance that your crystal uses to bless you with its healing light The new energies you feel from it are best for you, otherwise they wouldn't be there for you. This is the result of programming at the Soul level, as we shall soon instruct you to do for yourselves.

We shall give instructions in this book for you to know the way to program crystals in certainty that they will work as is intended by your Soul, to heal and bless you with their light and peace. This is the reason you have chosen to use crystals, you see—the blessing that they offer you. And if you choose a crystal that you like, you are buying something that safely can remember all it needs to know to do its job, even though you little know yourself at conscious levels the way it does its work. This way we hope to teach you of in time, at least beginning in this book. For now, let it be sufficient to tell you to pick a crystal by how it feels for you.

An Opportunity for Choice

Choosing crystals is an opportunity for choice, you see: a chance to practice simple discrimination as you choose the one for you, or one for another, as with this you need only think of the person you intend to get a crystal for and feel a compatibility in the crystal that you choose for them. This is possible at subtle levels you only begin to notice now. And still you can't go wrong, really, for as you choose, so the one you choose adapts to you or another almost at once.

Another thing about this choosing is that you are guided in it, though you know it not. Little coincidences in life are guided choices from on high, as it were, guided choices of your Soul. And usually you will be able to notice which one your Soul would draw you to.

As we help people with their selecting over the years, we see that all are able to select the ones for them, so to speak, the crystals they attune to readily. Thus a choice is made that leads to Soul, for as you choose in accord with your Soul, so again the next choice is made easier, and easier again, until at last you find yourself in simple agreement with your Soul in all, and so you find yourself.

We say this not to give you an idea you are choosing for all time, that you are not to make mistakes, for there are no mistakes with Soul. There are only choices that we grow to make, and making, learn to grow some more.

The simple choice of a crystal is easy. What is hard is to accept yourselves in choosing, that you allow yourselves the freedom to make mistakes with choice. For with all choice there are mistakes, no getting around it. And with all choices there is growth for self in Soul; there is growing toward the light of what is true for you, learning what is not true by the chance of simple choice in life, by which you freely come to Soul.

So we give you a few suggestions for choosing crystals. Know that you are choosing for yourself in this, no other, and know the rest is up to God.

What we shall do in this book is give you confidence to work with crystals in your lives for growth. The rest is up to you.

Chapter Four

Programming Crystals:

Feeling Crystals As They Are, And What They Do For You

Remember, a crystal will be limited by the beliefs you have about it and yourself as well. It will function as best it can for self as well as others, but it will be limited for you as you accept yourself as less than you might be in truth. This is a simple thing to explain for you, but it is not so simple for you to act to change the way you sort your reality to fit the world you choose to see from time to time amid the expectations and anticipations you have for self and Soul along the way you walk in life. Freeing you from these, your close-held, cherished structures of old belief—this is something that is worth the effort of your Soul to do through you as you allow your growth to rapidly unfold for all as well as you.

A crystal can be given any blessing first, you see. And you allow it functioning room, a chance to grow, so to speak, as you allow yourself a chance to breath in freedom of the truth you share with God and Soul together. Your Soul is willing benefactor of your life once you esteem yourself as much as God loves you.

A crystal will be limited by the belief structure you have in general, for it will not override "programming" you already carry. If, for example, you believe you are a bad person, the crystal will accept this belief for now, perhaps only gently suggesting to you from time to time, if it is so programmed, that you are limiting your own growth with such a belief. And a crystal will accept not only your beliefs about how it works, it will also accept, to a large extent, your belief systems about how everything else works too. If you think there are no levels of angels working with you, or fail to take this possibility into account in your work, the crystal will oblige you with an acceptance of this as a possibility. It will honor your free will, so to speak. The angels themselves may watch you in your work, but they too will never intervene unless you ask them to. And then they will help, not intervene.

So it is that once you believe your crystal can be programmed for perfect protection from all outside influences that are not for your highest and best good, then the crystal will allow you ample room to give it this programming instantaneously. And once such programming comes from a divine level, it will work completely.

This "divine programming" we would like to describe for you at length in future chapters. It is sent by God to program—or prepare—the growing light of God, or Child, who grows in you on earth. It is a programming of intentions that are received by you all the time without your knowing it through crystals of this world, in God as well as in the gift of God, the energies of the Divine Mother who rules your planet with Her love.

We would like to teach you about programming your crystals with a little story.

The Best Intentions

There are wonderful singers in this world who can heal with their voices, activating the wholeness in those who listen to them and soothing the traumas we have stored in our being, perhaps without knowing it. A particular woman, whose name I won't mention, is a lead vocalist for a group of musicians who are interested in whales and natural places of great beauty, and the ancient ways of our world that can teach us of an innocence from former times that we might once again recapture in our lives. This singer channels healing in a powerful voice for all who are drawn her way. She came to my hometown not too many years ago. Many people were deeply affected. Her songs had a quality of love and belonging, and a tenderness. For the most part they were songs she had written herself, and I was so moved by them that after the concert I underwent several releases of energy that came from recalling a space in my own heart that was like the space she had offered us all. This was her gift to me. And I was very grateful.

The next day I was thinking how nice it would be if I could have this singer's quality around all the time. I tuned into her Soul as best I was able to at that time (which my Soul informs me was well enough), and I asked that the "best of her energy might be recreated [not taken from her in any way] in my home through my crystals." This is what I thought to myself in programming my crystals. In return I asked that the crystals treat her (as she was tired that night, and her voice had been strained), under the direction of her own Soul, in the way that was for her highest and best good, in God's will, in the Name of the Best in us all. That was that. I did this programming and then forgot about it.

At that time I was doing a lot of programming with my crystals, and I just went along my merry way—until several days later I began to notice a very pleasant experience. At least it was pleasant at first. I became aware more and more of a feeling of completeness and well-being. When I went to sleep I felt a warming going on—an amethyst, purple, ruby, rosy kind of feeling I liked a lot. It was very healing and completing. A little like being with a lover.

I might have suspected something was going on, but I didn't. I just enjoyed what was happening in ignorance.

The next night the same thing, only stronger.

The next night I almost didn't sleep. That night began with near ecstasy, a real intensification. When I couldn't sleep, I began to try to get the feeling to go away. It wouldn't. Instead, it grew. And it grew.

The next day I was tired from lack of sleep, but the amethysty feeling was still there, like rubies and amethyst combined, or like heart energy and grounding energy growing too strong too quickly for me to adapt to.

I couldn't figure out what was happening. It dawned on me about midday that something was going on that was coming from my crystals, something I had programmed to work with me irrespective of time and space, no matter where I might be. I couldn't figure out what I had done to be getting such powerful energy, energy that I could tell would make the next night more sleepless still.

I consulted with a healer friend who was in touch with her own guidance (for this was a time before I had met my wife, Alayna; and also a time before I was consciously connected to my own guidance). She confirmed that I was being influenced by something my crystals were programmed to do, but what? She suggested I either figure out what, or take my crystal set-ups apart (they were in various configurations at the time), and put them in sea salt.[1]

I had too many crystals to look forward to the prospect of moving them all, and besides, there had to be a simple explanation for my difficulties, there had to be. So I sat down and made a list of all the programmings I had recently put in crystals, on the assumption that I myself was probably responsible for my own difficulties. About the third thing I thought of for that list was the singer who had affected me so powerfully. I had asked the crystals to carry "the best of her energies."

That was my difficulty. There was nothing wrong with her energies. There was nothing wrong with the way I had sent the crystals' energies to her, for I had placed them in the hands of her Soul for the highest and best good.

The problem was that I had indeed recreated the best of her energies in my own house—permanently; and they were influencing me without any checks or safeguards on them other than that they were a duplication of the "best" of her energies.

When I realized this, I went into the room where the main configuration of crystals was (something I wouldn't have to do now), and I added to the crystal programming in my whole house, "may the best of her energies be in my house only to the extent they are for my highest and best good under God's

---

[1] Note: If you are having trouble with a crystal, you can always put it on top of sea salt. This will ground out most of its energies from affecting you or anyone else (perhaps as high as 80%). If you bury the crystal completely you will ground out its vibrations completely. Not a bad thing to know if you have any large crystals. And you will clean the crystal while you are at it!

will, in the Name of Christ. Not too strong and not too weak, please."

Instantly there was a change in the whole house, and instantly there was a change in me. A pressure on me was released. I was fine. The divine marriage, underway inside me for almost a week, was at last placed in its proper place in my life, to arrive when it would be appropriate for my growth.

To explain a little better what had happened to me, there is an incompletion in us all in order that we might function in partial expression until we work out the difficulties we have been given to face in any particular life or cycle of lives. While this "working out" is taking place, and even beyond that—until we are ready to be completed in our total expression—we are left less than total in our energy patterns. Thus, one person, let us say a male, might express the blue and indigo aspects of the spectrum, or perhaps blue-turquoise and gold, even though all people are expressions of all energies at least to some extent; and another person, a female, might express a different range of energies. The healing singer's energies were a complement, in many respects, to my own. There was too great a pressure towards completeness when I programmed my crystals in such a limited way to radiate the best of her energies. I was being completed before my time, so to speak. I was ready to pass into divine bliss—for the first few days. But then I became activated too fully, too fast under the pressure of total expressions that the crystals got from both my own and her energies. Whew.

As soon as I changed the programming to reflect the highest and best good for me as I had already done for her, everything was fine.

I would have lost a good story and saved a few hours of sleep had I programmed the crystals correctly in the first place. At this point, I'm glad I didn't. May all our mistakes end so happily in the long run. I suspect they shall.

As a postscript, I might add, because this singer knew nothing of the blessing I had sent her way, her Soul thanked me and released the energies without using them. All of us have free will expression, in this case the right not to be affected from outside ourselves without our knowing about it and giving permission that it may happen. Our Souls receive the blessing whether the actual personality level of a human being does or not. Our Souls may or may not actively use the blessing; but an exchange has been received and given, and the blessing returns to the giver a thousand-fold, whether it is needed by the other Soul or not.

This is the law of exchange from the level of God and our Souls for all upon earth, though most on earth do not know of its existence it seems.

Alignment With Life

Next we would make use of what we have told you about crystals thus far to guide you in a meditation of attunement with them, for it is through attunement that you may initially gain access to the process of programming that can have such decisive results upon the crystal's ability to work with you and those you would help.

Begin by closing your eyes. Imagine yourself as a cloud of light, drifting in the darkness of the void of space in all eternity. This is an image that will bring you closer to crystals, believe it or not, for we will guide you further in a moment.

Allow yourself to drift in space in this way for several moments. Experience the effects of being a cloud of light, of being programmed to reflect light, if you will, but more, being programmed to accept all that comes to you in harmony. So it is with crystals at their formative level.

Now we suggest you let the sun penetrate your darkness, the void wherein you drift, and allow its light to enter you entirely, enter the cloud you are imagining yourself to be.

Through this experience you will find what a crystal feels like when it becomes suffused with the light of the sun in your own world.

Can you feel anything from this simple experience? For a few moments, tell yourself what you have noticed, or tell another you share this experiment with, for by sharing we recognize factors that by ourselves we might have missed.

Now, again in your imagination, open your eyes and see the world through your crystal of cloud: notice what a cloud of energy might notice in the world around you, again, solely in your imagination. Yes, please do this yourself at this time.

Can you feel how you take it all right in? How you are super sensitive to all that happens around you when you are empty in the way a cloud of light might be? This is the way a crystal experiences all of life. We have guided you to see this so that you will notice and appreciate the process by which a crystal becomes programmed so readily. You do not have to strain to program a crystal. The crystal will notice more than you about what you are trying to do. It will respond to the dominant expression of your energies, as we have already hinted at to calm your fears.

Suggestion For Noticing Yourself

We would suggest you try to program your crystal in the following way at this time:

First, look about you and notice anything you see you are especially interested in. When you have done this quite casually, close your eyes once more and guide your attention to the cloud we have given you in your mind's eye. Allow yourself to notice the way the cloud feels inside itself, noticing the impression of the thing or object you have chosen to admire quite briefly in your look around yourself.

You will see that the impression is incredibly strong of what you have noticed so casually. You may even taste or smell the object you scanned with your mind's eye as well as your physical eye, without knowing you were being so thorough in your appreciation of what was present.

Do this exercise for yourself a few times: again, notice something outside yourself, close your eyes, notice the way you experience the object without opening your eyes, while imagining yourself within the energies of your "empty" cloud of light. This is the way you actually are, as well as the crystal. You have just clouded over your own appreciation of things more thoroughly than need be, out of misplaced need for protection. At a later point, in a few chapters, we will point out to you simple ways to protect yourself so that you may notice in safety the world around you with as much absorptive ability, if you will, as the cloud of light in which you have dwelt in your imagination so far in these exercises.

Experiencing the Senses as They Really Are

Next we would like to guide you through a further experience of light and love as it pertains to crystals, for purposes of attunement to their inner nature.

Close your eyes once more and listen within. An inner attentiveness that accompanies the act of listening is most helpful for the following exercise.

Close your eyes to all outside influences except your tongue. Notice what you hear on the tip of your tongue. (Yes, please do this exercise for yourself.)

It is an incredible feeling, is it not? It is an expansion of your awareness for you in ways we have known about all along, but you were asleep to. Your tongue can hear. You can experience it, in part. Notice the sensation you still possess, from this little excercise. We have expanded your consciousness a little bit, in a harmless, necessary way; for one day you will need the attentiveness of your whole body, performing the functions of your ears and eyes and nose and throat (in tasting, in case you hadn't guessed). The five senses. They are more than they appear to be. We will not dwell on this overmuch, but know that your crystal is not so limited to the awareness of the localized senses as you through your assumptions of self, developed through evolutionary stages, if you will, but rather programmed through the process of progressive shutting down or closing off the senses of the whole of the being of one's body over time. We are trying to give you our perspective from the level of our Souls, to allow you more attunement with this Self of yours, which you know and trust and are in fact awakening to before you know it.

The Form of What You Are

We would guide you in a further exercise to taste the feel of being a crystal for yourself, for crystals are not so limited as you. They are left to their own devices in God, so to speak. They rest in what they truly are, rather than in what they imagine and assume themselves to be.

To continue: place yourself on a couch, or other easy place to lie down and relax. Drift in the comfort of your own mind for a moment, and allow the following words to affect you in a way that is purely beneficial. For we are guided at this time to give you experiences that will benefit you in the long run.

Notice the feeling of the light around your body. We would guide you to do this in the following way. Close your eyes and sense the space above and below yourself—indeed, all around your enclosed space, as it were, the space you think you occupy. Now study this space a bit. Feel it as well as imagine it, for in feeling it you will sense it accurately. Now allow yourself to relax into this cloud of space around you and in you.

Is this not the same cloud we have been using with you already? Is this not the cloud you have imagined drifting in the void of space? For this is what you are as well as imagine. In fact, you imagine what you are at all times. You only think these things are outside yourself. If you had lost yourself somehow, you would find yourself again through this: that you are what you imagine yourself to be. Think of something, and you are as you imagine it to be. For if you could not imagine something, you would not be able to be it. Another way to say this is that you cannot think of anything that you yourself are not.

So we will guide you now to turn your attention to an actual crystal. Look at it twice, rather quickly, and then close your eyes once more. Notice what you feel from within your cloud of starry light, still drifting in the void so as to minimize extraneous input, if you will. But a cloud nonetheless. Feel the impact of the crystal on your cloud. Pretty nifty, huh?

We would accept for you the charge of watching over your Souls once you have accepted yourself. In the meanwhile, look at this crystal as a friend to self, small "s." Because as friend, it will point out for you the way you actually are. It will trick you in this, if you are not familiar as yet with its intentions and our intentions as well. We are here for your growth and nothing more.

Kiss yourself in the mirror if you will, for you are done with the next phase of our introduction of crystals for you. We will continue in chapters ahead to teach you how to program your crystals in more detailed ways, for it is programming you have already been doing from within your cloud, as it were. The impressions you experienced there were programming of the most basic and yet sophisticated order. The programming of reality. Eventually we will guide you with some more specifics, to program your crystals in more detail, in the ways it is possible to do. For now, the programming you have been doing already in this chapter in simple, basic exercises is exactly the same as the programming you will do for yourself when next we meet in God, so to speak—perhaps a little more consciously and more fully for what you intend to do with yourself, but otherwise the same process exactly, involving yourself with your true impressions in God. The time we mean, when you are with your Souls, is when you are clear of your intentions of a limited nature on earth and are free to explore your Souls as you really are in truth. The intentions will change, but the process will stay disarmingly simple, if you will allow it. It is the process you are already a past master at, but do not know it. Simple living in integration with self and Soul as one.

We will teach you this and more if you will let us. For you already know this inside yourself, and so it is easy to discover it again for you as well as for ourselves, in integration with the whole of life.

Chapter Five

An Overview From Soul

There are many sacred traditions that speak of using quartz crystals and crystals of other kinds for healing work and the resurrection of the body physical in the time/space realms. Know that each of these traditions has a place in the whole of the heritage of humanity. Like gems that make a mosaic of great beauty, the different traditions are one in the sacred picture they make of the living body of man's wisdom and ways. Each is a facet of a whole that we would preserve as the understanding that completes the destiny of man. Each is needed and useful.

We will be teaching you a definite path for working with crystals that we feel is most appropriate for your time. If you feel these things are not in order to you, you are free to seek the ways that are more in order for your growth, and you are blessed in your choices. For all are free within the laws of change. We would teach you what you need to know to survive these times and come into your own mastery with God and your Soul. And quartz crystal healing and self-healing are among the gifts we can offer. You are blessed as a child of God in your knowledge of the working of the laws of Nature and of Mankind. And as you deepen these things into the love of all, you will see with the eyes of a child that all is as it should be with you and those around you, as black as it may at times appear. For nothing is ever lost. Nothing is ever truly damaged. And harm is only good in another guise, as you shall know in time.

We speak to you of these things at the beginning so as to not misplace the knowledge we would give you now. We would give you divine science in the purest form as you grow into acceptance of self and of others. For through acceptance of one's self there is the possibility for love to awaken in the source of all love, which is within your own heart. And as such love grows and expands to others, there is the acceptance and understanding to use these tools with care and with common sense, knowing that all are equal in the eyes of God, there is no high or low, and the greatest master is one who knows he is the same as all other beings in God's Creation, in the perfection for which he was designed. So be it.

Now, in order to facilitate our discussion of quartz crystals further, we would like to bring you the energies of one who works with you in the expressions of your electro-magnetics at times that are in order for your growth.

Greetings, this is Kryon speaking, from the Universe of Quadrille V. We will work with you briefly here, if you will allow us the privilege, in order that we might share our truth with you at the level of your Soul. It is in the acceptance of these energies that you will center in the energies you wish to activate within your cells and structures of light, that you may align with the work you have come to do upon this planet, which is speak your truth so all Souls in God may awaken as they truly are, expressions of divine in self, expressions of God's love and sharing.

We will begin our discussion with you this day with the following storybook picture from your past. There was a time when you could experience all that unfolded in the life of a city or civilization by gazing into your crystal, networking you with all that transpired far and wide. A record of the events of history, world-wide weather conditions, knowledge of events of your countryside and nation were all present for you quite effortlessly within your crystal, close at hand. You would use it to express your thoughts on any subject, and your secretary or counselors at large would know through their own crystals that which you had placed for them within your own. They would not have access to that which you had placed for another or for your own use. They would have access to that which was in order for them to know, through their own crystal, as the divine order of all was the final arbitrator. For it was within divine order that you placed the ultimate say as to what information was holographically projected where, and for whom.

All this bespeaks a time when men were young in the ways of the world and far more connected with the ways of the Universe. In infancy men and women are guided more than they are in your own time. And you are no longer in your infancy but rather in your old age relative to the framework of history that is familiar to you. In another framework, that of the stars, you are in your childhood still. For you are as beginning on your journey through those stars, as travellers who would explore distant lands when once they have sufficient preparation to depart. And your earth is a stage for your Preparation, that Peace may flow from all your journeys around the starry skies.

We would share with you the stages of your growth as long as we are able to be of service to you. For we are the Watchers of old, who have guided you with our love, as the song of this channel once said. We have guided you with our love so that you might grow into maturity in a safe place of refuge. For such your earth has been for you: a place of relative comfort and rest that allows you the freedom to experiment with your Truth until you have found what is yours and what is not, until you can grow past the need to experiment with the negative expressions of your possibilities into a stable expression of love and light. It is in expressions of Light that you find your peace, and it is in expressions of Love that you find your existence, your own being and source.

It is very important that you not feel pressured in the experimentation in which you find yourselves. This we would impress upon you. You are a child of God Almighty, a being beyond but including individual expression and compassion. And the free will adventure of learning for yourself is not, from your Soul's point of view, the painful expression you seem to think it is on your planet. Misery and suffering are a form of focus for your Soul. They are not to be sneezed at or taken lightly, yet if you could take them lightly as they occur in your self, you would be better off than before. And in others misery is an expression of the growth that is yet to happen, and thus of the work you have yet to do, guiding those who have come here to learn, to their own learning—yet allowing them the freedom to learn in their own way.

This may seem hard at times, but it is the truth of your world. And we would share with you as best we can that we are here to guide you, but you are free to choose your way through all. This free will expression is an attribute of the smallest cell and the highest star-filled nebula of galaxies. Identity and freedom are one, and choice is a gift of the creator. So be it.

We'll guide thee as we grow to be
As one with God,
As one with thee.

—from the Christ Self potential in all Humanity

Chapter Six

Protection

By the way, we promised to teach you something about protection in our last chapter. We now proceed with adding here the nature of protection to show you how to fully be yourselves without "at risk" reactions from the self to what is then revealed to you from others. We give you protection exercises in another book as well, *Patterns of the Whole, Volume III: Alignment With Life*. (Perhaps this will be its name, for we have yet to finish it for you.)

Before going into any depth with this, we would give you only a practical suggestion with little or no explanation: that you call upon your silver or mirror light to reflect away any energies that are not for your highest and best good. Call upon these silver energies to act like a mirror, shining back as reflection to their source any particular misshapen energy, if you will, though only by feeling these energies outside yourself can you find them misshapen; we would call them obsolete for you, not for your highest and best good, or reflecting that which you do not wish to be any longer. And we suggest that you ask that these energies be transformed as well as simply reflected, into whatever is for the highest and best good for all. That way "negativity," or anything not suited for your time in humanity as a whole, might simply find itself expressed or changed in ways that suit all men and women for the One that they originated from. And this is for the best.

Simply ask that we apply these energies for your Soul, or through your Soul. We are your Souls, you see. Ask that this be done for Soul and it shall be: in the Name of Soul as one with self and all creation.

Now on to details of simple protection, though it may not be readily apparent how the exercise we have given you to apply your silver light as mirror for protection might work in light of the things we now would say to you for the sake of overview.

Protection is a funny word, for in a larger sense there is no protection in your world: you are part of all that is, no more, no less, and what could possibly need protecting?

At another level of order, there is a need for some protection from outside influences to keep the body and its various attributes intact until the Soul has used this mode of expression long enough for current patterns of growth to be fulfilled. This protection is the need we discuss for you now, however briefly.

The next thing we wish to say about protection is that you are protected as you are detached from consequences of your life with others. You will be healed of all that comes to you as you release your fears and allow us to work for you express-ing through your Soul all the forms of being that we would lead you to. These include some bad/some good, from the point of view of daily life on earth as well as in bodily form on any planet of yours or similar expression; but these include nothing that in the short or long run are not as useful to the Soul, experiencing all through you

At still another level of expression, one close to you (for it is yours as personality/ego on your earth), we say there is yet another form of protection needed, for you are as responsible to ask us for our help as you are free to choose your path for life. Thus it is that you must ask us for protection from all that harms your body and your energy frequencies of expression, your emotions too, and all you do to harm your intellect with over-concentration or absorption in exclusive frequencies of expression—such as your thoughts or words or deeds—with-out a sense for all expression at the same moment in time and space.

This is a rather inclusive list of what harms your being at levels it receives a harm through us, for we guide you to make mistakes for self and Soul as one. We guide you to protect yourselves as whole in us. And we guide you now in love, light and truth, even as we hold the imperfections of your being still in place for you to grow with. Without this holding of your imperfections, you would not as yet be fully able to hold them for yourselves. And without this holding, even as you wish it would go away, you would not grow as surely as you tend to do, for you would feel a lacking in the just response of Soul to guide you through all things, and you would feel a just reward to all you do would never come, and so your growth would be arrested; you would not express so fully the adequate response to all you do/we do for you.

You see, the need for growth is something that is given you from Soul, and you are guided by the "Pandora's box," if you will, of pain, old age, and sickness/death to see that there is a balance to all things through you as well as Soul, that you are guided to the balance right from the start. Otherwise you would not be here to share this life. We would rather let you see that this "Pandora's box", as you have called it in your myths from Grecian times, is really gift of Soul, not self. It is not created just to harm you out of jealousy, as portrayed in your myth; it is the work of God to plan for you a world you would be balanced in from moment to moment of your time on earth, as well as for your Soul. You will find the balance justified when you step into light and find yourself to be the one who balanced all along the things that you have done. You will be free, you see, to grow in never-ending spirals of expression as you are freely balanced in your Soul. And all you do must so be balanced in the things you do for Soul on earth.

Thus we have given you an overview of pain and suffering, in as brief a form as possible at this time. We would give you more on this later, again in our *Subtle Body Anatomy* book, and in *Alignment With Life* as well. You must realize these things if you are to grow in oneness with your Soul. And this shall be our goal for you until it truly is your state of Soul and self as one.

The relevance to what we say for you about your protective needs is this, that you should understand the need for self to be protected as a transitional stage of growth for life on earth: to grow at taking responsibility for asking for our help, until you understand the things we do for you from Soul without your help. You must ask us to guide you in this, for each of you will need a different lesson regarding your protection, as your needs are different for your growth.

We say the first thing that you need to do is ask us for protection from all outside your self and Soul that is not for your highest and best good. This integrates well with our earlier lesson on using silver light for protection. As you proceed with crystals, ask that only that which is best for you take place through your intentions, no matter what you may wish or ask for at a conscious level of expression. For you are unable now to guess, as yet, what things you wish for are intentions that will help you on your way, and what are only things that stand as obstacles to your growth in truth within the current time. (In the end all obstacles become as food for growth in you as well as Soul, and all is balanced in the Soul). And call on your protection often, every day in fact, for this is needed within the laws of your earthly framework.

This is enough for now, though protection is a subject long overlooked in your time, and there is more to say on this at a future date. We would say these things in the volumes already mentioned, rather than here in our book on crystals, as it is a separate chapter in your growth to turn directly to your needs for Soul quite independently of crystals. We give you here enough to grow with that is relevant to what you do with crystals for yourselves. And we wish you well. God bless you.

Chapter Seven

Channeling on Tradition

(Why Crystal Use Was Hidden)

Greetings to you. This is Artemedes, a scholar of Greek times, who comes to you in the capacity of informant on the mysteries of uses of crystal in past times. I am not alone, and I will be conferring with my colleagues so to speak, even as I talk with you. I am chosen for this work because I was one who guided you in these things in times gone by, within the sacred temples of the Eleusian mysteries, under the stars of nature's blessed world. We walked together often in the ampitheatre that was the meeting place for our work. And you have long known me as a guide on subjects too abstruse for men of your times to comprehend aright. We are of the brotherhood of Pythagorus, you and I, and these understandings are of our Souls, mine as well as yours. In our sharing we will bring to you at the conscious level what you know within your Soul from distant times, though most of our work will be at a subliminal level, for so is our work most appropriately done. We are with you this day to aid in your process of growth once again. Know that you are guided for the light and love of all, in all you do, if you but wish it and ask that it may be granted you. For all is made possible by asking, as when the knight Parsifal made all things possible for himself by asking to know the riddle of his life in the castle of the Holy Grail. And asking, all things could be added unto him.

We are with you today to add to your knowledge of things in the distant past of your world. But you would find that there is no distant past as far as the technologies of crystals are concerned, for all is today as it was in my time. Then as now, only those in the mystery schools knew the full import of the work you do with crystals. A closely guarded secret it was, I might add, for it was deemed that men could not handle the responsibility of crystal technologies at that time, and for most, all was shrouded in mystery and disbelief.

Does this not seem similar to the state of affairs in your time? The only difference is that now the mysteries are no longer held in esteem by the multitudes, and thus you may openly discuss these things with one another with little fear that what you expose to public view will reach those who could abuse these truths. In your time man has fallen to the point that it would be well nigh impossible for him to abuse his world any more than he has, and yet it is less possible now for men to abuse that which is inside us all. I will not bore you with details of this fall, how it has come to pass that man knows little of that which is inside him unless he is of the mysteries in former lives. Suffice it to say for now that man has indeed fallen to states of enfeeblement in which it is difficult for him to abuse much of anything inwardly in ways that were once known as black magic and manipulation for "evil" ends. Not that there was any lasting reality to such manipulations. As you yourself have learned through the experiences we have guided you to, there is no power to negativity that we do not give to it ourselves. For negativity is simply the lack of light that would empower us, all indwelling the light as we do. And I am speaking of whole light, light of full frequencies, if you will, that is complete unto itself with frequencies of Christ love, the universal love expression of the creator of your local universe, in perfect resonancy with the creators of universes beyond your ken. For all is the work of creators who love you.

We would give you brief knowledge of our own use of crystals at this time. For we were of the mysteries as I have said. We were guided to use crystals in limited ways so as not to repeat the excesses of Atlantis and former times you do not know of. We were limited in our use of crystals just as you are, to the forms that had to do with our expressions in truth, especially for healing and conscious growth. Crystals are a tool for such growth as they contain all the frequencies your world has been denied through free choice expression. This earth, since Atlantean times at least, has been denied access to the stars. It has been in quarantine for its own good that there might be worked out here on earth the balance of the things that began with the fall of man in times before manifestation.

We would add to this one small thing here, that you are well directed when you follow the guidance of Frank Alper in your use of crystals. You are as following a path laid out for you long ago when you stood upon the shores of the Aegean to gaze longingly at the sun, the moon and the stars as manifestations of a perfection you could only guess at, then as well as now. We are together again, you and I, to suffer the world to grow around us in ways that are only gently nudged by proper paths of change. And again we come to the simple truths of guidance and of love through no more than the objects that bind us here, the living forms of love on earth, in trees and wind and fire—and in your crystals once again, for they are wisdom of the time and times gone by, wisdom of these stars we grow to love with every turn on earth. Can you allow us to release these energies of longing in you? Then follow the path of growth you have begun, and know that you are blessed in love. My love to Alayna, your wife. Be done.

In a communication the following day:

Greetings. This is your Soul, Artemedes, for so you were called in those times. You are a child of your Soul, whose expression in former times was once known as the being you have been talking to, Artemedes. Be not surprised at these things, for often your Soul will take on the form it once expressed to convey to you something of what existed in the past of your earth. You share this pattern with the Souls who will read what you write. They too shall at times be guided by expressions that represent an aspect of their Souls from former times. For nothing is ever lost, we say to you again. Perhaps they too had an expression in the Eleusian mysteries or the temples of Rome or of Athens. Perhaps they too knew expressions in Egypt that know even now of the mysteries that were practiced with crystals. For it was death to reveal these secrets to those who had not been initiated, that mankind might not grow too rapidly in acquiring again the ways of strength of Atlantis.

Within your Souls you all carry these mysteries in their fullness. You have all been at one time or another a child of the mysteries, for you were meant to touch again from time to time the alignments with the starry hosts that assist you and have always done so to insure the safety of mankind in your proper development. And you have in your Souls memories of Atlantis as well, and of Lemuria, of which the channel writing will have more to say at present.

We wish you well with your discoveries of these mysteries once again. Do not be confused or afraid because these things were once mysteries. The time is again at hand to prepare large numbers of people in what once a few at a time could share. The time of great changes is upon you at last. May these changes bring you growth, in your Souls and in your expressions on earth, your earth so fair. For fair it is, and your home for a time as well.

We bless you in the name of the mysteries that surround us all and guide us truly. Ever in the Light.

Chapter Eight

Crystals in Tradition

Natural quartz crystals and gems have been used since before recorded history in most of the sacred traditions we know for healing, communication with one's guides, far-seeing, and for spiritual growth. In the Bible we find references to using gems in the breast plate of the priest[1] and in the twelve gates of the City of Jerusalem.[2] The Catholic, Anglican and Episcopal churches all use gems in their scepters, rings and priestly vestments. Tibetan Buddhists use a clear quartz crystal ball on their altar to symbolize perfect Buddha nature. Crystal balls have been found in the archeological ruins of Christian kings throughout Europe, in pre-Christian ruins as well. Crystals, crystal balls and crystal carvings have been found in North, Central and South American archeological sites, as well as within the living shamanistic traditions of those and other areas.

Michael Harner, in his book *The Way of the Shaman*, describes shamanistic uses of quartz crystals in the Americas and in Australia.[3] He cites a study by Jerome Levi tracing archeological discoveries of quartz crystals among the ancestors of

---

[1] *Holy Bible,* "Exodus," ch. 28, ch 39.

[2] *Holy Bible,* "Revelations," ch. 21.

[3] Michael Harner, *The Way of the Shaman* (New York, N. Y.: Harper & Row, 1980), p. 108-112.

the California Yuma Indians that go back some 8,000 years. (Our own guidance tells us that crystal use goes back as far as humankind on earth.) Harner says that quartz crystals are probably the most powerful objects in a shaman's medicine bundle. He also points out that quartz crystal is the only power object that appears the same in all the worlds of the shaman.[4]

Quartz crystals are often collected by apprentice practitioners of many indigenous cultures as an early requirement for their work. Such men and women describe looking into the different facets of a crystal as into completely different dimensions of reality, with different landscapes, flora and fauna, with different laws of reality as well. To this day in the United States, rock shops in small towns in Utah, southern Nevada, California, Oklahoma, Arizona, New Mexico and other states outside that area, such as the Dakotas and Montana, have a steady clientele from among the local native American, indigenous people, who often come great distances to buy quartz crystals for their medicine work and their sacred ceremonies.

The earliest written references to the uses of crystals focus on the uses of gems in healing rather than quartz crystals. (Why this is so has been touched on in our earlier channeling on tradition.) Egyptians used particularly malachite and lapis lazuli with the precious metals for healing and growth, and the Greeks used many gems and crystals as well. Most of these written traditions have come down to us in forms that have little use for our purposes in healing and conscious growth, perhaps partly because the people who wrote down and copied original documents on the information systems involved often seemed to have had little respect and no understanding for what they were describing. Also, times have changed, as the saying goes, and mankind today has a different consciousness and different needs than he had even a generation ago, let alone a hundred generations ago and more when ancient Greeks and Egyptians adapted the use of crystals and gems to their own needs.

---

[4] Why this is so has to do with the networks of light that are universal through your crystals. These patterns are language of inter-communication between different levels of being. Thus the form of this language exchange, that of the Star of David crystal, natural quartz—this changes only past causal levels, beyond your world altogether.

Another source of information on gems is India. The earliest surviving descriptions of uses of gems and crystals may well be those in the Atharva Veda and the Ayur Veda, which was appended to it, dating to an estimated 2,000 B.C. at least.[5]   In Ayurvedic medicine today gems and crystals are still used in many remedies, both physically and vibrationally. The gems are associated with the healing influences of their predominant colors in the spectrum, and with their ruling planets. A gem or crystal is sometimes ground up to make a remedy, or boiled with water, and the water taken as a remedy. (We don't recommend doing this unless you are trained in Ayurvedic healing. Many gems are poisonous when taken internally.) Looking at the current literature on Ayurvedic applications of gem stones, we find it only partially accurate but very interesting. More of interest seems to have survived in it than in comparable European traditional literature.

It is my understanding that there are references to use of crystals in many other traditions as well. Chinese Taoists,[6]

---

[5] Chandrashekhar G. Thakkur, *Ayurveda* (New York, N.Y.: ASI Publishers, 1981), p. 4. The actual dating of these documents and, indeed, the Vedic tradition itself, is a matter of almost pure speculation at this point for western historians, due largely to a lack of documentary or archeological "hard" evidence. Our guidance tells us that the age of the documents in question is closer to 1,000 years before our post-Atlantean era began, in roughly 8,500 B.C. At that time these documents were part of an oral tradition. Written versions of these documents didn't appear until the decline of the tradition, some five to six thousand years later. For further information on this subject, consult the works of Rudolf Steiner, a man who has made detailed psychic studies of these things that are, in our opinion, highly accurate (as much as 95% accurate in most cases). To obtain a catalogue of Rudolf Steiner's work write to:

St. George Book Service, Inc.

P.O. Box 225

Spring Valley, New York 10977

[6] Kenneth Cohen, an ordained Taoist priest, has done extensive investigation on Chinese Taoist traditional uses of crystals for healing and growth. For written examples of this work see Kenneth Cohen, "Channeling the Breath of Life: An inside look at little-known Taoist healing practices," *Yoga Journal*, March/April, 1986, Issue 67, p. 37-39, 60-63. Also "Bones of Our Ancestors," *Yoga Journal*, January/February, 1985, Issue 60, p.31-33, 56. For further information write him at Taoist Mountain Retreat, P.O. Box 234, Nederland, Colorado 80466.

Australian aborigines, African holy men and women, and Tibetan lamas, all used crystals and still do. In the Hawaiian islands, crystals are very scarce but highly prized for healing work, and must have been used there for as long as people have been present.

In the past life memories of humankind on earth, the traditional uses of crystal are in hiding, waiting to be discovered again and integrated as one when the time is right for each of us. Nothing is ever lost or stolen from us, nothing ever wasted. The time is now to discover what is right for you with crystals, as well as with yourselves.

The Legend of Atlantis

Much of the information of our current age about crystals has come to us in stories of esoteric traditions not yet accepted in our popular culture, except in legend and fiction. Since the turn of the century much of this information has been brought to us in written form through the work of the Theosophical Society,[7] the work of Alice Bailey and the Lucis Trust,[8] and the work of Rudolf Steiner and the Anthroposophical Society.[9] These sources tell us that civilizations once existed in many parts of the world that were far more advanced in technological terms than anything that has survived in our archeological record. Crystals were an essential aspect of the working technologies of these civilizations. In Atlantis—a civilization described by Plato in his *Republic*,[10] and elaborated upon especially by Rudolf Steiner, F.S. Oliver (Phylos the Tibetan), and more recently by Edgar Cayce, Ruth Montgomery and Rev. Dr. Frank Alper—crystals were used in functioning power generators that operated more efficiently with fewer

---

[7] The Theosophical Society in America, c/o Quest Books, 306 West Geneva Road, Wheaton, Ill. 60187.

[8] The Arcane School, c/o Lucis Publishing Company, 866 United Nations Plaza, Suite 566-7, New York, N.Y. 10017-1888.

[9] The Anthroposophical Society c/o The Anthroposophical Press, Spring Valley, N.Y.

[10] Plato, ed. Edith Hamilton & Huntington Cairns, *The Collected Dialogues* (New York, N.Y.: Random House, 1963).

ecological side effects than any electrical power source used today. These generators powered surface and air transportation as well as heating, lighting and communication systems.

Used in other ways, crystals were the basis of a healing and educational technology far more advanced than our own.

There are many sources for information on Atlantis. I would like to mention just a few the reader might find informative. The following are in approximate order of usefulness on this particular subject:

Cosmic Memory, Rudolf Steiner[11]
Exploring Atlantis, Volumes I-III, Reverend Dr. Frank Alper[12]
A Dweller On Two Planets, Phylos the Tibetan (channeled through F. S. Oliver)[13]
The World Before, Ruth Montgomery[14]
Edgar Cayce On Atlantis, Edgar Evans Cayce[15]
Flower Essences and Other Vibrational Remedies, Gurudas[16]
The Cave of the Ancients, Lobsang Rampa[17]

Frank Alper in particular is a living source of information on Atlantis and the uses of quartz in that civilization, particularly for healing and spiritual growth.

---

[11] Rudolf Steiner, *Cosmic Memory: Lemuria and Atlantis* (Blauvelt, N.Y.: Steinerbooks, 1976).

[12] Rev. Dr. Frank Alper, *Exploring Atlantis, Vol I-III* (Phoenix: Arizona Metaphysical Society, 1982-85).

[13] Phylos the Tibetan, *A Dweller on Two Planets* (Blauvelt, N.Y.: Rudolf Steiner Publications, 1974).

[14] Ruth Montgomery, *The World Before* (New York, N.Y.: Fawcett Crest, 1976).

[15] Edgar Cayce, *Edgar Cayce on Atlantis* (New York, N.Y.: Coronet Communications, 1971).

[16] Gurudas, *Flower Essences* (Albuquerque, New Mexico: Brotherhood of Life, 1983).

[17] Lobsang Rampa, *The Cave of the Ancients* (London: Corgi Books, 1963).

In the opinion of this author, the information and techniques of Dr. Alper will form the foundation for future work with crystals for many years to come.

Chapter Nine

In the Memory of Mankind

We would like to share with you, at an anecdotal level for a while, some first hand accounts of what people have remembered about Atlantis and past uses of crystals. This is a far from complete list of such experiences that have come our way, but it will serve as an indication of the type of events of this nature that are happening for many more people at this time than we can ever keep track of. If the same kinds of experiences have happened for you, perhaps this will help you to know you are not alone, that there is a design in this awakening in people to what once was. And if you have not had such experiences yourself, do not feel left out. For it is proper for many to know these things in dreams they cannot remember, or in moments of fleeting recognition or familiarity with things that attract them, though the reasons for the obvious attractions may be less than obvious.

People are often guided to do things they don't understand fully. The use of crystals comes from past incarnations of mankind on earth. And it is in order for us to share with you some of the chances we have had to understand and experience this past, and listen to it recalled by others.

Memories of the Past

My own first experience with Atlantis was with a form of rebirthing, when I learned how to return to former lives of my

Soul with a simple process that involves visualizing an elevator and taking it to a floor that will allow access to a past life that might be appropriate for better understanding in the present.[1]

I took this elevator first to a life in France during the 1700's, and subsequently released much of the frustration and resentment I felt in a situation involving someone whose life I had shared in that former time. I was relieved of the burden of doubt about myself as to why I was involved in the intensity that I experienced in my current life, and went home feeling somewhat drained but wiser for what had taken place.

That night, before going to bed, I decided to repeat the experience of going back into a former life, and I thought of asking where I had known the older woman who had guided me in my past life regression earlier in the day; for she had confirmed for me that three times before in other lives we had known one another, but she had not said where or when, nor had I been able to tell where or when, being at that time at an early stage of connection with my Guidance.

I closed my eyes, repeated the elevator procedure, and found myself in the long, central isle of an enormous, dimly lit, Egyptian temple with huge, tall columns closely packed together, disappearing upwards in the dark, on either side of me, and extending before me to a wall over a hundred feet in height, whose great, stone panels were alight as the rest of the room was not, to reveal full length forms of the archetypal gods of Egypt extending out of sight behind the columns in either direction, left and right. I walked to the front of the building, beneath the figures carved in stone upon the wall, painted to reinforce the images there revealed. I could see huge torchlike, golden mounts for flames that burned in recesses with an evenness that gave the overall effect of light upon the wall an evenness as well. And I knew that beyond that wall, through a small passageway whose location I couldn't quite remember, I used to be in residence within these halls, with the woman whose past life healing session I had just that day attended. I sensed that she had been a priestess

---

[1] I believe the technique described came from Bryan Jameison, *Explore Your Past Lives* (Van Nuys, California: Astro-Analytics Publications, 1976).

here, teaching me for many years, for I had been a priestess here as well.

Finding nothing else happening for me in that temple in my imagination, I chose to skip to a second life that I had shared with this woman.

Immediately, I was back at home ready for another elevator ride.

This time, I found myself in a very different temple, a huge interior that was hard to define from seeing it once. It was somehow familiar to me as the great temple of Atlantis in early times, that now no longer exists above the waves of ocean. It was in marble of a dark, brown-red color that my guides inform me was later changed to green, long after that particular incarnation was over. It was vast on the scale of any building seen today as still erect. It was for me at that moment a huge, open hall that I knew was square-based and pyramidal in its proportions. It was beyond my vision to see the upper areas of space that disappeared above my head, for although the floor and several hundred feet above it were alight with an even glow as bright as any windowed building of today, there were no windows in this structure, but all light came from broad light-beams from above, and all light focused on a huge pedestal before me and was diffused throughout the room from there; much, much brighter than any Egyptian temple's dark, interior halls!

The walls of this structure, and indeed the floors as well, were of marble, swirled with bits of white against the darker hue of marble red. They were natural in color, not painted, but polished to a fine polish on the walls and sides, and an appropriate polish on the floor as well. And in front of me, full eighty feet in height (my guides inform me that it was eighty feet or more from top to floor), stood a giant crystal on a pedestal, for all to see who were allowed within the sanctuary of the temple walls.

This crystal was glowing, white with radiance. It was brighter in places than any light bulb, and I suspect that had I been looking at it in the flesh instead of in my imagination I would have been almost blinded by the vision. It lit up the hall, which was larger than an ampitheatre, though no supports of any kind extended from the walls that slanted out of sight in shadow on either side, in the distance beyond the crystal and above.

This crystal was the great temple crystal, this I knew. And it was here I had known the older woman in a second life of priesthood, for we were both as temple priests, at least so trained, given offices or rather duties within the framework of whatever uses this great place might serve. I knew vaguely that I was familiar with the workings of the place, but I did not stop to check what memories the place might hold for me. I was in awe of the sight of the crystal in my imagination, rising some forty-five feet above its pedestal, which was itself some thirty-eight feet in height, I am informed, made in marble that matched the rest, surrounded by a benchlike ledge, part of the marble whole, that circled round at fifteen feet above the temple floor.

What creatures sat upon so huge a bench I cannot guess. It was actually simple ornament, I am told—something that gave proportions to the structure that were pleasing to the eye.

The crystal itself was the dominating sight. And it was very beautiful to see.

This was all that I experienced of this place. For soon I sought the third location that long ago I had shared with the woman who had guided me to look at former lives. I found myself upon a beach that I knew for Lemuria of long ago, not unlike the palm-lined beaches of Tahiti or Hawaii. The surf pounded on the beach. I scanned along the shore for half a mile or so, but was alone, and somehow again I knew I had been in this area too, meeting in life this woman once again.

Quite a contrast: between this ancient beach, with its still centuries unchanging, and the Emerald Temple[2] of long ago, that Atlantis feared and built, no longer known to man.

---

[2] This was the name it came to have some fifty thousand years ago—and name it held for over thirty-five thousand years of time, repaired and changed though it might have been through all those ages, time and time again. Its other name, held in earliest years before the coming of the first fall of Atlantis some thirty-four thousand years ago, was the Temple of the Son/the Sun.

Healing Circles in Atlantis

Next we would give you the phenomena of the healing circles of Atlantis, for so they appear to be. Men and women met in circles of power, using the strength and balance that comes from a group of divergent energies to empower acts of healing and blessing with the help of the temple crystals of light. The first memory of this I have is through Alayna, my wife, who remembered one day a dream she had of Atlantis, of a circle of beings and people in the process of programming a crystal for a later date, for a definite purpose. She remembered in this circle the one we know as Frank Alper, as well as others familiar to her in everyday life. She saw in the dream that the crystal being programmed was for her in this life that she might use it to notice her origins in the stars and her destiny beyond the confines of space and time. It was being specifically aligned to her.

The crystal in her dream was in my possession already, but she didn't know it. A number of months before I met Alayna, it came to me that someone I would know would want to use that crystal, and I chose to keep it instead of sell it. Alayna very frequently uses that crystal to gaze into other dimensional realms of expression, as she is guided by her Soul to do.

The Final Day of Atlantis

Another memory for my wife is a recurring dream she used to have as a child at least once a year and sometimes more often. She saw herself in large, somehow familiar rooms of light assisting people who were very confused and afraid into circular transport chambers, from which they would disappear to be teleported, she knew, to some distant place of safety. In these dreams, she could feel that the world outside was going through some great disaster. She herself was always calm, steadying herself to do her work in quiet love for all Creation.

Asking our Souls what these dreams meant, we discovered that at the end of Atlantis, Alayna had served as helper for many souls who were lost and confused as the world they knew fell apart in ruin. On an etheric plane quite close to the physical, specific chambers designed to teleport all individuals to distant locations were loaded, one person at a time, with those who had the presence of mind to cry out for help as they left their bodies in confusion amid the slaughter and devastation that was going on all over the world in the wake of Atlantis drowning. Alayna was guiding these souls to enter the chambers for their own best good and thereby avoid the confusion of the astral planes that were especially overloading due to the disaster taking place upon the physical plane. If someone could be reached to choose their growth on another level free of the insults of fortune, if you will, they could be whisked to safety in their light bodies (etheric, if you will, astral in some cases).

Alayna was steadying herself at the same time that she guided others to action in this emergency. And she found an inner resource, she knew not from whence it came, that soothed her to proceed as she was guided, in peace and calm amid the storms of emotion and loss that surrounded the sanctuary from which she worked on a subtle plane just over crowded Atlantis' death throes. She worked with crystals in this only in that she avoided reference to them when confronting those whose only knowledge of subtle things was in their work with crystals. For then as now, people tended to fixate on whatever modality they might develop in life, and generalize upon all energies the ones with which they were themselves familiar.

The above information was channeled from my Soul/her Soul as one, and it occurred for her in the form of recurring dreams of the same experience in Atlantis, so that she would accustom herself to this same role in times to come once again; though the exact means and nature of the help to others might vary considerably from time to time, then to now. The disaster then need not happen now, though it awaits us as one alternative choice for humanity in this time, then and now.

Another Remembrance: Adamis

The following was told by a woman who came to us on several visits from Kansas: of being guided in a series of dreams on different nights for several months by a being who identified himself as Adamis, to look upon the ruins of Atlantis and to judge what was of importance to explore; then of traveling to Atlantis in its heyday, if you will, to see the technologies at work that guided crystals to give off heat and light for all. The details she saw were very specific.

To channel Adamis himself:

"Giant crystals were the source of all power in Atlantis, as well as other experimental worlds that once were present on your planet. By this we mean that worlds of other civilizations and peoples once inhabited your world, the earth, that were so different from those of today that you would call them the work of distant stars if you could see them from your vantage point of now. You would not recognize those worlds as yours at all, so different were they in form and color and intention. They were forebearers of yours in part, but they were often experiments that died out in physical form to be remembered in song and chance legend in later ages of man on earth. They are racial memory, if you will. But more, they are memory of Souls who dwelled in them and still are living now, throughout this universe of ours, including here.

The memory of this woman was that the crystals involved in fire generation on earth in Atlantis were of enormous size, and were part of an apparatus that supplied the city with heat and light in abundance. She also was guided to various healing environments, including temples, within time-space and without as well, in other frameworks than your own.

Memories of receiving information from Adamis are part of the racial heritage for mankind, in that this Soul is the guiding Soul of humanity itself, the prototype so to speak. It is common to receive communications from this Soul as a part of ordinary evolution in all ages.

For we are all 'of mankind,' so to speak, 'of humanity.' We are all 'of Adam,' for this is the sense and meaning of the name 'Adamis.' Thank you, and blessings upon you from all mankind, in the form of one who knows the truth of Soul."

Outside Time and Space

A friend had the experience of taking up a large double-terminated crystal and seeing in an instant a picture of himself in a former, pre-Atlantean lifetime programming a crystal—the same double-terminated crystal—with the image of himself programming it, to teach himself (in our century) about himself (in that older time on earth), that his involvement with crystals now might turn to the familiar experiences of that time, when he worked with the technologies of light to guide the thoughts of men to see themselves in great crystal spheres, formed also in gold and silver, formed in the image of who we are as men and women of former times and now. We are spheres, at one level, who trust to God for form; who trust to God for life as well, in space of our own choosing, in love of our own making, within the greater bodies of our teachers and our own harmonics, free in light and space to travel over time to distant stars and seed the worlds with forms that spring from spheres of truth, the love of our own being in truth as well as love. This image persists with him still, and guides his inspiration to design and plan a city of such spheres, modelled after man/humanity.

[From Soul: We are inclined to use the word "man" to guide you, out of previous programming of humanity, that the word "man" stood for woman as well as man. This word holds that meaning still for some. For others it is suspect, in that it seems to refer to half the race instead of wholeness. The androgeny we experience from this level is more than you can experience at this time, and so for you an "it" connotes only that which is lifeless, instead of that which holds the balance of male and female in one core. Is this to your understanding?]

We have in our possession, or once we had in our possession, crystals "we" have programmed for others in former lives, seemingly, and crystals others programmed for us. Groups at times seem to have been involved. Many people have guided us to synthesize these things for you, about this past life programming.

A number of people have had the experience of working with a crystal pre-programmed in a former life for them, as they experience in fleeting images the origins of that programming outside the happenings of their current existence. Memories may come of what it felt like at the time of programming to be in Atlantis or some other place.

We suggest you look to yourselves for your own experiences with these things and trust that whatever comes to you, whatever its nature and extent, will be all that needs to come to you in this regard. We know that you need not experience a previous existence of your Soul to come to terms with truth for you in this current set of happenings that you call your life on earth; sometimes as aids these events will come to certain individuals who request and could use the assistance to their growth. You will find assistance in the form that works for you, not in forms of others. This we wish to emphasize. This is why we confine ourselves to so few such examples of personal experience from the past.

We might add that usually it has been our experience that the events that seem to come out of the past with regard to crystal programming are actually happening in a different framework altogether, in a different time and place if you will, but rather, outside of time and space entirely, or nearly so from our point of view. Our Souls are capable of coordinating incidents in present time to fit the needs of those who work with crystals today in relative ignorance and piece-meal fashion, so to speak. The process is similar to programming outside of time and space altogether because the Soul arranges the crystal to be programmed with the exact programming necessary for the development of the personality now, in our age, by taking it out of our dimensional context into its own context (beyond time) where it is then reinserted magically, if you will, into the framework of coordinates that coincide with another incarnation in a distant past, when better methods of technology were known to program crystals.

Thus, your Soul can program a crystal for you, if it wishes to, by the simple expediency of placing it in the framework of a distant past when "you" were better able to program it with the help of others trained in distant times to know the uses of your crystals. And this insertion into a distant past of a given crystal took place for you in that time by simply wishing it be so, from the level of your Soul.

While it is true that a past life of your own Soul might have been involved in a project of programming crystals for the good of one or more individuals, the world, and all times ahead, it is not necessary for your Soul to disturb the past in the way that we have implied with what we have said so far in the paragraph above. And it is not, as I am informed, really possible either. Instead the Soul will involve itself in the vibrations of that past, in the perfect expression of that past life personality and all its attributes of expression, including the attributes of any other individuals involved in the process at that time. It will then program the crystals from its own awareness, using the expression of those past life situations and vibrations to do so. Your Soul will encourage you to grow as it does so, for you are inspired by what you find inside the crystal, just as if the programming happened in the distant past, as in a sense it did. Without that past exactly duplicated, you could not experience such a programming in this life at all. Thus your Soul may duplicate such energies for you, in order to give you the sense of continuity required for your current work on earth with crystals and other tools for God. For this is work for God, you know, as you grow to be whole in the oneness of your self and Soul as one with God in truth for all.

So your Soul gives "you" (in that former time) the task of programming a crystal for "you" (in your current time) to discover "accidently". And the exact crystal to be programmed is selected as you are choosing it in time and space in this life, at the exact moment you choose it, if this is best.

There are other ways for your Soul to operate, but this is one.

Dahomey

The first time I connected with this next personal experience I was planning a talk on crystals in tradition. Twice within the talk my Soul included a reference to the Dahomey Kingdoms of Africa as an example of peoples who used crystals extensively. At the time I was just breaking into direct channeling of my Soul, and I was afraid to take this farther than just a casual noting of the fact that I had no conscious memory of crystals being used in any place in Africa; and no references in anything I had read would come to mind. I gave the talk, and saw on an inner screen a quick vision or picture of how I had used crystals in a Dahomey culture in a lifetime there. I saw a

fleeting glimpse of a circle of children, all black as was I, enjoying a demonstration by a shaman teacher of the proper way
to use a crystal for clairvoyance and enjoyment. An entertainment for the young in progress, was the sense I made of it. I
was that shaman, or witch doctor, as the western Europeans
branded such things. I was almost naked, with a thick grass
skirt, it seemed (very comfortable, I'll bet). I had feathers of
an ostrich-like nature above my head, pure white with a trace
of blue, secured by a band around my brow. And I crouched
with an outstretched arm holding aloft for the circle of faces to
see clearly, a sprig of wood with a crystal fastened to the tip. I
was a bit of a storyteller, a bit of an artist, with my voice and
my whole body and soul. I was busy instructing all to put
their attention upon the crystal itself, as I held it to catch the
sunlight just right, so that it would reflect into the eyes of all,
the rainbow prisms flashing forth. I kept telling those children
to listen closely, to keep their eyes on the light, eyes on the
light, so they would catch the fascination that it held for me,
and them if they would notice. The proper way to respect the
light in all could be accessed through this process of fascinating the young with sun in a crystal, so that they would get it
for themselves, that

"joy can be found in little things, my son. The little things of
life. This is your Soul in the form of that incarnation. I am of
Dahomey blood and ancestry, right back to the oldest kings
and ministers of the state. We are servant of the truth in men
as much as you. We were really teachers of the light in those
old times. We guided you to see you were enjoying yourselves as much as we. We were teachers of the light to share
with the children's souls (small "s") that they were special just
as we. We drew them in, drew them in, if you will. We let
them see themselves in those crystals on the tips of sticks, so
that they would see the fascination we felt in the light of Good
and God, for we used those names synonymously; we were
famous for our stories of the light of Good in all.

We let you continue, but first we would share with you our
share of the truth of crystals: it's of yourselves you study
when you look at the little rocks of earth. You know, you are
little rocks of God as well, you understand what we are saying
to you? We are your rocks of ages, if you will. We are light
forms of crystal light that glow in the sun and moon and stars

inside ourselves as one. You see the little stones? They glow in the night too, do they not? Just like they glow in the sun, you see? They are alive with truth, are they not? They are alive with you! You see? They *are* you, you see? So we taught the children to notice themselves in a form they could adore with the eyes of a child: little stones like the fire at night, only in the day! So bright!

Take this to the little children, if you will. Show them the sun in the stone of the mother earth hugging her babies in her bosom. We are of the Mother, don't you know. We are her children, all, you know? We are Child of God for all to see. And her bosom is the earth wherein we dwell with all. Enjoy yourselves while choice is yours! This is the time for joy, always is and always was. This is the time for little rocks for you. And little rocks are like you in so many ways. Toss them in the brook—see how they skip from stone to stone? See how that water churns them down the pond till they stop on the bottom, so dark and deep? Like little children you enjoy this. Like little rocks that skip and dart in pools we only understand in dreams. And see the children's eyes light up as you tell them your songs of love in little rocks they can touch and hold, and trade for toys they almost enjoy as much as you enjoy my song of love to all. See what I mean about who I am for you? I am your heart enjoying itself in peace. For centuries I have rested in you: see how I come to you to give you peace? (a bit of peace, if you will: my gift for future times, as well as you) What joy in these little rocks!"

God bless that ancient kingdom! (Sixteenth century, I am told.) Such a contrast, welcome contrast, to my own, this American kingdom I have known in this current life on earth! Anyway, I'll leave you now with these few, simple stories of the past with crystals. They light up the stories of those ancient times for all to see.

And your stories too light up the night of God's pure light on earth as well as always in the sky. For all the world is held in arms of love, my children. All the world is God to me, your Soul, as shining in the light of God.

Chapter Ten

A Pattern For Relationships

Next, we would move on to still other formations of meaning for you. The pattern of relationship given by Frank in his
book *Exploring Atlantis, Volume One*[1] is useful for several
things. First, direct your attention to the pattern given below.

figure 1. pattern for relationships

---

[1] Alper, *op. cit.*, reading of Feb. 16, 1981, p. 4.

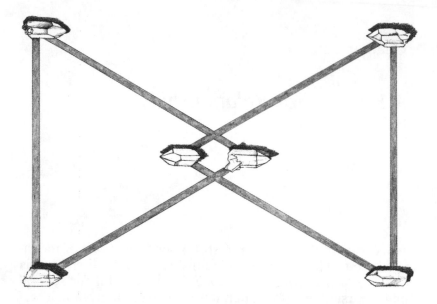

figure 2. pattern for relationships #1 from above

It is a Star of David expanded into crystals in two triangles of relationship, as you will see examining figures 1 and 2.

The first way we would suggest using this pattern is in relationship with those you are very close to, such as lovers and friends of long-standing you know you would share very intimately with. This is suggested because the influence of this pattern is profound, especially with repeated use. There are few ways other than direct intervention of Souls above for you to find this kind of alignment with another on the earth plane, as you will find when you use this configuration with one you love.

We suggest you not use this pattern with children, as the needs of children are different from those of adults. The intimacy created is not good for children as well, for they are working towards their own independent being, inevitably involving hard times as well as good. They will form dependencies, if they are encouraged to do so, that will not be for their highest and best good at this time.

Souls are weakly bonded to their expressions in the flesh for the indefinite period ahead, and this will not change until long after we all have graduated from this life on earth. The connection is weak for a reason that is blessing as well as difficulty, in that free will choice is necessary for all in life as well as afterwards in our Souls directly. Your expression here has choice to grow in difficulty or at ease; your choice, yet from the direction of your Soul you will find the strength to choose most wisely.

With children, the part you play is crucial to their choices. They must use you to grow in ways that are not healthy for them, from the point of view of their Souls, to gain their independence. They must kick and scream a time or two, not a pretty thing to see. Yet this is for the best. They must test limits, find growth in ways compatible to them, not through the ways their parents have chosen for themselves. They must learn to be here on earth, a process that is more akin to learning to play a violin or piano than it is to the process of effortless attunement that concerns you in your growth to greater understanding of who you were and will be before you attuned to life on earth, and after you pass on to other realms.

The child is in no such attunement process, you see. The child is in a process of adjustment, difficult or otherwise, to life on earth in the instrument of the Soul on earth, the human vehicles of expression. He or she is especially occupied with this before the age of six and thereafter, though less and less, until the age of twelve or thirteen, with the onset of puberty rites of passage in which the child creates a new attunement for himself or herself. This process is different slightly with boys and girls, but it is the same for both in that too much familiarity and dependency on parents or adults in general is not good for healthy growth. The crystal patterns we teach you in this chapter and others are for your attunement, not theirs. They are attuning to life on earth. You to life in Soul. There is a real difference. Crystals will help you in your process. They will hinder children, if you are not cautious enough in your approach.

This subject of children and crystals will be taken up again in a later chapter. It is important here only in that you know that the twelve-pointed stars are not for children ever until the age of six or seven, unless you are guided otherwise in truth and not in testing. And the pattern of the two triangles of relationship for attuning to one another is also not appropriate for children until the age of six at least, and usually not until the time of puberty is passed at twelve to forty-three, whenever that might be. For in intense relationship there is great possibility for over-dependency, on the one hand, in those already tending to be too bonded, such as parents and their children; and over-connectedness that is inappropriate, on the other hand, in transitional relationships that are temporary and yet still important for our growth, such as between two lovers who hope to be involved forever, who may be involved for a little while instead.

We give you encouragement as well as caution to use these patterns as you see fit. For there is blessing in exploration of self in any form, as well as good. And the patterns you see here in this chapter, especially with our help in blessing (that is, the help of all our Souls as one) will mitigate against all or nearly all the ill effects in time as well as all ill effects beyond your time on earth. We suggest you try the patterns in ways we give you, then move on to other ways that you invent yourself, or ways that you might guess would be for your good, or good of others. Trust yourselves in this. A few mistakes won't hurt you, any more than sunburns in the early part of summer should scare away the bathers by the sea. Such is the proper perspective on these things from the point of view of Soul for you as well as all.

We suggest you trust yourselves, by the way, to know the best things for you to do throughout your life, in patterns as well as approaches to all things. For only you can know what is best for you, and many things that we have guided our lives to do for us have ended in our growth in ways that we and others first thought foolish or downright hard to bear. Later on, the sight of things equally adverse were cause for us to see ourselves for what we are, and know that we are fallible and broken in many ways before our lives on earth are through. This is a healthy thing to know for some. For others it is not needed. So trust yourselves to grow the way you should, by all conventions notwithstanding.

The proper uses of crystals are always thus, that you should guide yourselves.

We suggest that you may use the pattern of relationship in a different way, now that we have discussed some cautions with its use. Take the interlocking crystals between the two people involved, and let each person place the crystal that represents his or her own triangle nearer to himself or herself, instead of

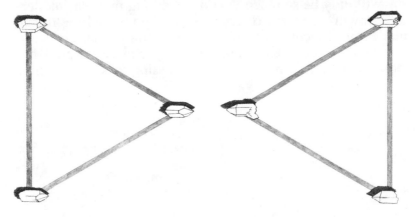

figure 3.   pattern for relationships #2

interlocking with the leading crystal of the other person. (See figure 3.)

This second pattern is less intense. Under the conditions we set with ourselves with both these relational patterns of triangles, we chose this second pattern to amplify the integrity of the two individualities involved, while at the same time allowing each to see the point of view of the other person, directly, thus strengthening the truth of each—to be together or apart, as best may evolve in time. As we have set conditions for our own use of these patterns, we choose this second pattern for those who would resolve a conflict or would better understand another's point of view. Married couples in difficulty could benefit from this greatly. It will not interfere with the integrity of those involved, but rather help them know their truth for one another and for themselves. And they will not be bound by the closer bonding of the first way of using the formation, as presented in the earlier diagram.

There are other patterns for you to experiment with, but most of these are included in Frank Alper's *Exploring Atlantis, Volume I & II*, rather than here. Only the most essential ones will be outlined here. In a few chapters we will go into other formations for you—ones we have used ourselves, and ones that you may use as well.

The next thing for you to do will be to practice what we have already given you, for if you don't, the chapters that are to follow will only be so much window dressing on your intellectual growth. The gift of crystals is to transcend the use of intellect-in-detachment to allow the merging of consciousness with Soul, as the intellect takes its proper place for guidance and for helping in our daily lives, a blessing for our growth.

Chapter Eleven

We Are As Crystals

A Channeling From Kryon & Soul

Greetings, this is Kryon speaking. I have come to you again to tell you of the electro-magnetic properties of crystals, in ways that are new to you, but old as well. First, let me say that we are beginning an enterprise today that is also an old one. It is to share with the people the ways of the stars, as once we did in Quadrille V. For such is the relevance of the story we discussed with you from the other day. You have shared with us before from the level of your Soul countless ages ago, an unimaginable distance away. Is it not good to share again with those you have known before? We think so too, and so it comes to pass once again that we are together for the duration of this project of yours, to share with others the wealth you have known from the level of your Soul as well as Oversoul in God in love.

Quartz crystals are a unit of measurement of the divine numerology of the Creator of all your universe. They measure the sound and sounds of God that echo in harmony through all. In their measuring, they quantify the nature of reality, thus bringing it into frameworks of reference that are easily understandable by all, for they adjust their language of numbers and of harmonies to fit the languages of all who come to them. They are the measuring devices of the universe, counting out the exact harmonies that are appropriate for each situation. They can be pre-programed to react in certain ways that measure and fix the understanding of the stars in the circuits of time and space, again for selected beings or for all who come to them. They are the messengers of the stars in time and space, and thus they pre-program a creation at its earliest inception point, as you and I did our destinies together on Quadrille V. As a civilization or a universe progresses, gradually evolving the means to penetrate ever deeper and more solidified levels of matter, so too the crystals that are appropriate for each level of creation are present there as well, pre-programmed for the blueprints and the order that will be needed on each new level of creation. Is this to your understanding? Good, then let us proceed.

We are describing to you the ways "crystals" at many levels are used to pre-program a creation from above, as creation unfolds for all in ways that are guided from divine intelligence. We would now like to describe how these same crystals work for you, in guiding you back to these sources of divine intelligence from whence you came. For they are as signatures of divinity, sparking the worlds into their evolutions, and as such they are followable back to their sources, as diverse and multifaceted as these are. For your creation is a cooperative work; it is the effort of many who labor in the fields of the Lord, as the old, more traditional forms of your expression might say it.

In our terms, it takes many talents to make a Universe, and all Souls are needed in this work. From the highest level of Creation to the lowest level of mortal unfoldment, all is in order and all have their place, guided by the sure hand of the cooperative councils above. And above that are the councils of light and love you call "God" on your world, yet they are as men in that they have evolved from mortal expression—"experts," if you will, in the ways of physical reality, sensitive to the needs of all who are to be guided by them. For they have served in many capacities before your time, before your earth was young, so to speak. And being tested in the ways of the wise, and in love as well, these councils are come to you in the form of your crystals. For your crystals are their work, here to serve them as well as you.

You are guided in what you write through the large crystal ball on your desk, the one on the right, for it has been programmed for you while you slept so that it, too, could be involved in this process. It is happy to be of service in this way. And so should you be happy to use it. Release what residual fears or guilts you may have in this regard, for crystals are to use, as part of creation. And in their use they grow as well as you. For you would not deny another man his growth, I am sure, yet you might pass over the growth of what you consider—still consider, I might add—a rock, an object of no consequence to you or any, when actually you face a living being in a crystal, with all the rights to individual expression that you yourself express, as you yourself are a child of God the most high, and you yourself are as God.

So too your crystal is an expression of the divine plan, created to know self and God in the spheres for which it was intended. And God is love in a mutuality of sharing that even crystals can express to you. For they are living forms of light and love (the latter if so programmed) and they are here to share with you their growth in service to self and God—as are you. They are matter enclosed in the flesh of God, at every turn as sacred as any lily of the field, and just as precious. "More precious to me are each of my children than any kingship, though they be as many as grains of sand upon the shore." And even the precious stones are so precious. For they are the work of thy God.

These are the ways men spoke of old of the mysteries of life and of God. The collective consciousness of your humanity is growing now to include other forms of expression, as inclusive of your science and your ministries to people in the forms of sociology and psychology and other forms as well: seminars and trainings in positivity and goodness. And the language of everyday life has come full circle through the creation of a language of godliness in the religions of your middle ages back to a language of simplicity and natural acceptance of all, as was common in your more indigenous understandings, or your hunted religionists of the orders of Melchizedek, who incarnated as aborigines and peasants of tribes not unlike yourselves, yet who appeared as savages to your European adventurers who struck out to unite the world under their understanding and rule in the name of adventure and God. For adventure and restlessness with their lot in life was in fact their prime motive for exploring and controlling the world.

So today have you a "new frontier" on your inner planes, so to speak, as the channel has prophetically written while still in school many years ago. These inner planes are the exploratory laboratory of the self, in which you are at school at the present time, exploring the recesses of your own awareness and understanding to discover who you are.

You are a child of God, and yet you know it not, as it were. You are a child of God who longs to know his own true nature. And so it shall be in time for all. This is something that brings us back, once again, to crystals, for as we roam far afield, seemingly, in our discussion of these things, we yet again spiral around to crystals—the central expression of this communication, yet actually no more than an excuse with which to understand ourselves. For crystals, as units of living light, are like unto ourselves. They are bio-magnetic resonators with all that is and ever will be, world without end, and yet they are precise tools as well, of expressions you but dimly comprehend at first, yet step by step, bit by bit, come to know as truth in truth: you come to know yourselves. And as child of God you discover you are blessed more than you know for now. You are blessed with all in self. You are a resonator yourself, you know. You are schooled in the ways of the world from birth, yet you are schooled in the ways of the stars (or so shall we call it) from before your birth as well. You are a meeting of Heaven and of Earth, if you will, a meeting of all the elements of your life before you came to this planet, and every step of the way since then. You are an echoer of all you have been exposed to, so like the crystal in this, that I would say you are a living crystal yourself, even if in appearances to the physical and etheric eye you are different. You are a child of God, I keep saying, for through all the language of the stars, this is what most you need to hear. Yes, notice it carefully, these words of advice. "You are a child of God" means you must be of the same stuff as God is made of, for would he or she withhold anything from mankind that he or she would want for herself (himself)? Would you if you were a parent withhold from your children anything from yourself you could give in abundance that was for the benefit of your children? Well, neither would thy God.

We are together to share the truths of your growth as you would be most likely to assimilate them. Crystals are the object of our current considerations, yet you will find it impossible to understand the use of crystals without at one and the same time understanding the uses of self. The two are one.

And I don't mean just crystals and you. All things are a wholistic, holographic-like expression of the divine plan and expression of God. The realms of time and space are filled with the images of thy God, thy Father/Mother God, if you will— thy indescribable, ineffable source. The crystals that you play with are divine expressions of that source as well. They are keys to the understanding of your light expressions in time and space, and your light expressions in worlds beyond as well. They are a divine science unto themselves, a divine crystallography, if you will, but more—a science of expressing the laws of God and humanity at the level it actually exists in truth and in perfection.

Divine science is a key of your growth, but it is more an integration with the laws of your universe at the level of understanding. At the level of understanding there is a time for uniting with your world and a time for uniting with the stars as well. For your earth has been in quarantine for many years, many ages of human time, as you have all learned to grow in your expressions. At other levels all is free to come and go, beyond the realms of good and evil, so to speak, the polarities of expression. But within your karmic world and its expressions, all has been in silence since the stars refused to shine on you in ways you would know and love. In languages you do not understand, of light and whole light, of love and being, you have never been alone. But in languages of physical expression, there has been a very carefully controlled flow of evolutionary, sequential information, to awaken your growth. There has been a controlled revelation of the truths you actually live by but do not yet know, even now. For you are governed by the stars, the Lords of Light and Understanding to the point of Love, and you are given free will expression by all who come in the Name of your Christ Self, if you will, your self of light and love, who learns to grow by itself, free from elder parents, so to speak, free to try and fail and try again, like learning to walk or ride a bike for the small ones of your world.

For you are the "small ones" of our world as well. You are our children in whom we grow by giving to your growth as well as giving to your life. We are your Centers of Light, your star parents, if you will, your Watchers as of old. We have guided you with our love. We have shared with you our destiny, which is to know the stars and the realms of that which you call as God, or Father, or Mother Divine—and on and on the names of God that move you in your love for what you see around you as form of living love.

This is enough for now. Good day and God bless you.

Chapter Twelve

Quartz Crystals & Technology

Quartz crystals are a basis for our modern age already. Modern technology is an expression of our scientific precision at calibrating, refining and sorting out the quantitative relationships between many variables of physical activity. An ability to measure these activities, perhaps the best, belongs to quartz as well as other crystal resonancies, which are as precise tools of measurement for the natural world as well as the world of man-made objects, as you shall find if you explore this further.

We are working with a technology today we little comprehend the basis of. And this brings confusion to many Souls. At another level, we are all in order for our growth, and we have chosen this science and its technology to learn from once again. At another time we will depend on another form of entertainment. For now, this is the best that we can say to you, that you are responsible for your growth and your science serves as one key for that growth.

The awakening of scientific reasoning in your past centuries has been appropriate for your lives on earth. It has given you much in the way of creative design and creature sustenance upon your planet, but it has done this at a cost to you as well. It is an expression that grows and changes from day to day, as more and more efforts to refine are added to one another. Yet it is in need of a greater change than simple mechanics would allow; it must be accessed by your Souls if it is to grow past its current limitations in expression to understanding of your universal light and life. It will have to express more as well of the individual needs of your planet as opposed to the more generalized expressions of the starry spaces of God's work and recreation. It will have to give you ways to integrate its understandings better with your other natural sciences, the ones that are given you from God to understand—and from your Souls as well—rather than from limitations of self-discovery and adventure, as are currently the case upon your planet.

We have been mentioning a larger framework in which to discuss quartz crystals and scientific understanding.

Quartz crystals are indeed a basis of our technology here on earth, yet they are capable of infinitely more than science has yet expressed. For if such expressions were to fill our lives— or even the lives of many scientists—we would all change and grow past reckoning. Our way of life would crumble into greater perfection than we can as yet imagine. Scientists are only human, of course, and in their humanness they have free will choice to put in context what they are doing or not. In context what they are doing is an incomplete expression of self, as it is simply the understanding of our age of humanity as a whole. Our understanding will have to grow for us to be able to adjust to our needs as a greater whole, a single race of beings that share a common destiny, a common heritage, a common responsibility, if you will, though it is at the Soul level and not the physical, personality level that this overall responsibility is held in ways we know not of.

From the Perspective of Our Souls:

Science is an expression of the whole of God. In the end you will find that this is so. For as you progress in understanding, the intricacies of analysis you follow will lead you to the unending search of space for "God," for the order of all things. And this order is like the order of star maps at night, but more like the patternings of God in man right by your side. And these patternings you discover through the patternings of quartz, as well as any other way that leads from one step to the next in growth. For such growth ends in consciousness itself: the patternings of God in all; and such growth leads to man as well, in relationship to God as love.

Science is a whole unto itself when expressed in terms as broad as these. It is defined in ways more limited in your world, we know, yet these are the more universal definitions we give you. The sacred Brotherhood of the Order of Enoch is an expression of this science, an order based on whole life understanding of the fields of thought and matter that create your world as one. We are coming to you in an expression of the point of view of this order as you can understand it, representing the wisdom that would guide your science, for your world of light and love to unfold in manifestations that are in order before the eyes of God Himself (Herself). And we would give you an overview before we start at science as it interfaces with what you know of crystals in its infancy of expression.

Crystals work in definite ways that interface with your science. Primary among these is the ability of quartz to oscillate in harmony with that which it receives. It is the ability of quartz to oscillate in harmonic resonancies with all that allows us to work with you through quartz all around you.

Quartz is the bedrock of your planet in many areas for this same reason: that the resonancies of the stars and other outside influences may be received on earth to keep it in touch with the brotherhoods that guide it. Picture, if you will, the planet as a whole, networked with lines and pathways of quartz, as veins of living light. Here and there you may find a rainbow effect, as other minerals and crystals network with the quartz veins to form an interstitial membrane of networking about your planet. It is like the fiery forms of light on water, as the bonfire from a distance reflects upon the waters. So is echoed in your world the fires of distant worlds resonating with your quartz formations in the earth, guiding all upon your planet to resound, as it were, with the echoes of these stars, these fires of light and love that intelligently abound in your universe. This is an image of profound strength for all who attune to it, for it is truth to see such light resound in space and on the face of earth. We are one in God, yet all is still in the heart of all. And out of this stillness resound the voices of the Lord as expressed through all creation as a song of light and other frequencies as well, that come from distant stars and clouds of warmth and winds of movement in the magnetic voids of space. We salute you for catching what we say, for those upon your planet could benefit from living pictures of their interaction with the realms that grace your world. We proceed.

This resonancy of quartz is more than is imagined among scientists and people of your world. For in this property of quartz lies blessings untold for all, in ways we will describe for you at future times as well as now. We resonate the quartz upon your desk [my Soul is referring to the author personally in this section] in ways you dimly understand, yet the scientific precision with which we do it is more than you can imagine as yet, or ever in a physical body. It is like the geometric patterns of a lemniscate repeated endlessly, entwining all with all. A pretty image, but the best that we can do. You would do well to study intricacies of expression in the quartz you own. Yet you will have to acknowledge that your home is a place of magic inside and out that takes you unaware at times and usually is more than you can feel or know with any faculty you possess.

When you take up a crystal in your hand, you notice things about it we would describe for our readers as well, to adjust them to your style of expression on these matters. Crystals have doorways to other places and times, as you will see as you work with them. Scientifically speaking, we would have to describe to you these doorways in terms you can understand. The terms we would use are not what would communicate our thoughts to you, for our understanding is another framework altogether, another framework independent of your conscious minds on earth and the words or intellection you use to communicate with sounds what you express. In time we will prepare you for this "language" as well, though it is not a language *per se;* it is a state of being known to man as love, that hears with the voice of love in light.

To continue, quartz has facets that breathe as you breathe air. They are oriented to directions automatically that resonate with them inside their faces and guide you to notice certain things about them, as pathways to the whole. The webbing of light networks inside the crystal are whole unto themselves. They are copies of the networks from star to star if you will, copies of the light networks from place to place within your body as well. Networking is an important function for stars and planets as well as people. And the tissues within your structures must find a means of expressing themselves to one another, otherwise they would be free to turn themselves into little dervishes, each expressing what it will, so to speak, as in your forms of cancer, or expressions of distrust from one human to another.

As time goes by, communications break down based on the natural functionings of the parts of any whole, unless there is conscious intervention to see that all is coordinated from within time-space and from outside it as well. As the systems that make up the whole stay coordinated within their proper boundaries, so to speak, in relationship to others and the whole, they express what they are here to express, in you or in the world. In networking these circuits between the parts, all matter is joined to all. And a song of resonancy can travel across the pathways of stars and men to echo in their calls of connection to one another in perfect harmony with more than men and more than stars, as these are parts of greater wholes that express through them, as cells of ever greater bodies do the work of thousands of resounding, networking members of a sacred brotherhood of light and life throughout all things we know of, and beyond as well.

You see, there is resonancy that exists in your quartz that finds its matching coordinating energies in plants and stars and people. These resonancies are coded in exact modules of light, with wisdom and understanding that are precise for each situation. The crystal is the tool for this encoding process. At all levels are crystal structures of light or matter (for light at one level is matter to the next in ascending spirals of creation). We teach you with crystals to know what steps to take in harmony with the stars. We guide you with our light, encoded in the crystal lattices that exist a single plane above your world of physical light and matter.

This is a rule unto itself, that each creation is encoded and guided by the crystal resonances that exist on a single octave of energy above the one in which the crystals in question will express their meaning. That way no damage can come to any crystal so at work for higher realms of light. And the ladder of communication and creation from level to level is maintained with full integrity.

Chapter Thirteen

Children & Crystals

Our feeling is that at this time it would be good for you to understand the relationship between children and crystals from the point of view of your Souls. We will give you suggestions for their use with children as well, to the extent that this is called for.

First, let us open with a blessing for your children, as they are the hope of the world for you and for future generations. Quite literally this is so, for the proper means of growth upon your planet are slower than you might wish, were you to be given choice for how these things should be. It is the successive changes of generations that are in order for your Souls and your growth that bring the means for transformation to your world, more certainly, less painfully, than any means that men employ for growth or change among themselves, outside the realm of inner life aligning ever fresh to God—in the hearts of simple human beings, not the "great geniuses" you think create your world. This simple succession of generational change is more sure than any other means for growth, in that the Souls who incarnate through the children come to bring your world exactly what it needs at any given time and place.

You think perhaps great deeds need happen for earth to change, and this is true; but all such deeds descend from Soul and God's own level of expression. You are able to relax much more than you can know in all of this, for the designs of your Souls are not to be thwarted at all, not one bit, and thus in spite of any adversity your world might bring you, out of its over-zealous efforts to grow and change all others outside its source, this world of yours is ordered for your good, at greater levels than you know.

The way we choose to change your world is through your children; yours and those of all on earth as one great family of humanity. The children bring new life to all, and as they do, they bring the changes that you need, mirroring your acceptance or lack thereof of all your growth to you. Escape from life through your children if you must, but rather, we say to you that you will find your life through the eye of God that shines forth into your world through all you do, as mirrored for you by the children God has given you. The deeds you do for humanity are nice, but the children will do greater deeds than these, as has been written in all your scriptures from of old: "and a little child shall lead them" and again, " greater deeds than I do shall they do [those who are to come]." We give you these things only to relax your efforts to reform the world and change yourselves that you might give your children a better place to play and grow. This is commendable on your part, and a part of the happy obligation that you have as parents, yet it is not such a desperate venture as sometimes you are prone to think; and the children will guide themselves, for the most part, as they carry new energies that exactly meet the ones you offer them as best you can, in truth and love for all. The new efforts that they will make shall start from yours, and go from there.

The best advice we can give you on your children is to do little and notice much. Give them the momentum they choose in life, seeing it for what it is and offering assistance as they grow in the directions that they choose. This is strange perhaps for you, that we direct you not to do, rather than to do. But this is largely true. You must notice full well what is happening before you can direct the flow where it would best go. The children will show you the direction of their needs, so to speak, in every moment. Flow with them, even when this means of necessity setting limits or objecting to their treatment of themselves and you, as when a child would hit a kitty, or scold a younger brother. Set them straight within their own momentum, like a boxer who can read what his movements best might be in the momentum of the other. This is not a boxing match, of course, but something special, something sweet that still is like a war of wills at times. And it is well you play the part of warrior often times, in rhythm of your life with all.

We say again, flow with the child in love.   You have so many rich experiences from within your Soul to draw upon to give you strength for what you do that you need not ever know about;   just as there are many such experiences from within the Soul who writes for you now as John.   This Soul has experienced much with children, as, within your world's own history, this Soul was in charge of all work with children within the temples of Atlantis for something like three hundred years of your time.   And this period was one of intensive growth for all children within guidance, as it was the responsibility of the temple staff to see to the growth of all entrusted to their care for special attention as future temple priests or leaders of their race.   For from these children indeed were chosen those who would direct the course of all the nation. We give you this information only that you may know we draw on more than earthly experience of one life when we say to you that the experiences of your Souls are rich with understanding of children from all time.   Trust yourselves to know that you are gifted with the gifts of how to treat your children, from former times as well as now.   For now you choose again the course for you to take with all who are as children on this earth.   And now you are guided as once before you were, to know the best for you to do in truth of Soul and trust of all that is.

This is the gift most needed by your children, that they can trust you as you are for them the introduction to this world of ours.   And you are able to do this for them as you respect yourselves most fully in your gifts from times gone by as well as now; you are more than even Soul, you know: you are gift of God completely whole, and knowing this, you are the best possible guides for your children as you respect yourselves, not as you grope about for changes you might add to better do your work.

We would give you another suggestion now, that you follow your common sense in all you do, not just what you do for children, but more: for your selves as well.   In your heart there is a knowing that truly is of God and love, and this sure knowing is your guide in truth for all.   It is a registry of all that is happening for you and others, that is guiding you in this; for the registry of life is as an open book to Souls of all, and this opening can come when you first trust yourselves.

This is a gift for you from God, to know your Soul as one with you. In time this shall be true for all. For now, let it become so for first your heart, as you approach your Soul with God. Let love of self and Soul stream forth from God to all on earth, through new beginnings in your heart. As you trust your heart to know your truth, not the truth as known by any other, let yourself be loved in wholeness, completed in your truth in God. This is a message we give, to know the child in you that grows in love with all, the wonder of your Soul. The wonder of your one, true self. The wonder you were meant to be before you first began your quest for life on earth, so many lives ago.

This is the adventure we offer you "this time around," this lifetime, for it is in order for you now in the time of great awakening for all who choose to come to Soul. Your children have an equal choice, and the ability to make this choice is easier with them than you, for are they not your children? And are not choices that you made the ones your children all assume as given for their lives on earth? So it is with all.

The next thing we would turn to is a general discussion of crystals for your work with children, including those of your own families, if you have them. We give you this to know that we are with you in your work on all levels of expression, including that with children.

The best thing you can do with crystals for your children is to meditate with them yourselves. And by this we mean with your children, not your crystals. As they see you meditate, they will play at it for themselves, with or without crystals, as the case may be, choosing in their inner games just what this means for them. This will be better than instructing them in any way, for with instruction you can only spoil the unlimited range of choices they have within themselves, and they are guided in these choices by angels, until the eleventh year of life approximately, in your time, although in former times it was different—slightly later.

We would say to you next that you should choose the forms of meditating most carefully when you meditate around your children, as breathing practices, for example, are not the best for them, consciously disrupting energy flows inside the brain if they too early see the quality of breath at conscious levels inside their physical expressions. Give them only gentle suggestions as to posture and naturalness, if they should need these, and stay clear of directing their inner selves in anything but your own, largely left unspoken resolutions for yourself, as this is actually what your meditations are for you as well as others, when stripped of their pretensions, with your best intentions.

We think crystals themselves are a lovely way to get across to children the intention of your work with crystals, and with some aspects of self. Don't try to define for children just what these things might be. In an ordinary, everyday way, let the children direct for you their interest in their lives, including what their interest is with crystals—just as you might let them do at times when they bring you a picture that they have drawn for you, and you ask them to explain for you the content of this picture, and what it means for them. Do not feel there is anything essential you must communicate to children regarding crystals or any other phenomena in nature. The gift of children is to know already just what things mean or do not mean for them, though they are quite suggestible as well, as they are here to learn the ropes from you, so to speak, and not from self alone. Your suggestions for their choices will influence them most strongly. But we suggest you leave them free to choose in inner life of childhood just what things are for them, quite free of words at times, in imaginings of their own creation, as it were, their own direction from within. And interact with these inner directions, that you might learn your children's motives and intentions as they do their thing in life. In this communicating you reach them with your life, and leave them freedom in their lives, to grow and change as best they may, as ordinary as you ever let them be, for they would be most ordinary in all they do on earth, part of everything around them in harmony with the place and time they've chosen now to be in. Don't confuse them with their "specialness", even when you feel that this is so. For they are only human, and this means more to them than anything of stars and God for now: that they are one with all that is around them, equal to all others, nothing more and nothing less. Learn from them in this, for this is truth itself, undisguised for all to see in children of your world.

The crystals that you give children, give as playthings for their choices. Do not direct them as to use, but give most freely, with no thought as to whether or not these things are lost or damaged, though care of objects is a useful lesson that can be learned again in care of little crystals, as with little pets or ponies.

We give you suggestions that are so simple, you see. There is no great direction to go with this. There is only wonder in childhood, properly honored. And wonder in parents who live inside the laws of childhood for themselves. The redemption that is here is quite enough for all, you see. You needn't find it in your crystals, as they are but a tool for growth inside yourselves, and little children have indeed all the tools they need as all the kingdoms of nature play with them each day of life, as you unfold in resurrection of the same, the child inside yourselves.

We give you this to know that crystals are a tool for you inside yourselves as well as outside, and that they are tools for children only in as much as children choose to use them. If your children are attracted to crystals, let them choose the less expensive ones for themselves, to play with as they will. Let them teach to you how to use them; not that they will necessarily know all that you do about these crystals, but their inner instincts for themselves are sound, and you do well to notice what they guide you to, as well as what they choose to do themselves. It will not necessarily be "right" for you, the things they choose, any more than the "house" a child might draw is the same as the "house" that you might draw or live in now. Still, the noticing will be important, in honoring what you are and in respecting what a child is discovering for itself, in living.

The next thing we would say is that the crystals you have chosen for yourselves may or may not be appropriate for children. This is true no matter what Soul level is expressing through a child. You needn't fear your child is passing or not passing our litmus tests for enlightened childhood if your particular child is drawn to crystals in any particular way at all. This is not a test, this life, in spite of the wishes and worries of childhood and of parents everywhere. The child that quite rejects all use of crystals for this life may many times before have known their use and have no need for same. Or the child that quite accepts them as a long, lost friend need not be the avatar of future use of crystals, sent to then redeem us all. For crystal use or any other pattern of use or misuse of any expression of this world is only good for some, and only in order for some as well. And any gift of God is but a facet of the whole, not a pattern for all to use before they can approach the seat of their own perfect selves and Souls, before they can be who they have always been in God.

From here we go to another tack entirely, namely to say to you that there is a fundamental difference between childhood and adult life that people rarely take into account when they give their children tasks for growth that are actually tasks the parents or adults should warrant rather than the children.

It is the fundamental problem of childhood to adapt to being on this earth in human form. This is a task of growth, like sewing or weaving yarn. It takes careful, patient repetition— as the learning of some musical instrument might, the learning of this human form. It is hard work that needs no extra tasks to go with it.

It is the fundamental problem of adult life to solve the riddle of life for oneself, to persist at seeing growth in all, in spite of setbacks given as resistance in all living here on earth. It is an orientation to the stars, in spite of all the tasks that pull us down to earth, in humdrum repetitions of our days and work to earn our daily bread or not, as the case may be.

The child is learning to look down to earth with reverence for all life, with care to grow his or her own capacities of heart, mind and will, in truth, grace and skill.

Thus the process of childhood and the process of adult life have very different goals and tasks in the same full cycle of unfoldment.

This basic difference means, in simplest terms, that adults seek a balance between the earth and stars in God, and at the end of life seek upward movement in their hearts and Souls, while children seek to incarnate downward in their lives and efforts, most fully to incarnate and with all their efforts learn the ways of life on earth.

With crystals this means several things to parents for their children. First, the things adults would do with crystals are not necessary for their children, as their children seek almost opposite directions for their growth. The patterns of six and twelve crystals parents would use for themselves quite productively for balance and orientation toward the stars, are not useful for a child seeking the opposite direction, having come most recently from all balance among the stars and planets of our universe. And orientation towards individual crystals is useful to children only in as much as Soul is guiding their direction to do so, as usually this direction of paying heed to crystals is simpler and more subliminal for children than adults, and would, in any case, include only what the Soul allows for growth.

The next thing to say is that in certain instances you will be guided to use your crystal patterns for children. This is in order for you and them, yet it is not necessary for you to know just how it works for you to do so. Children will occasionally need a boost in their development, though less often than adults, and the patterns and uses of crystals for them are usually different than what an adult would need. Most typically, you would find yourself being guided to use crystals for children in the following circumstances: perhaps when they are ill; or perhaps, occasionally, when they are misaligned in some subtle way; sometimes when they are having difficulty with forming themselves in alignment with their denser bodies of earthly involvement; or again, when they are avoiding being here from some unnecessary recoil from life on earth (due perhaps to former incarnations of their Soul and patterns in the same, or due again to other causes too diverse to discuss at length). These are "typical" patterns for involvement with crystals on the part of children under your direction, but we must add that "typical" is not the case for all; few children are really very "typical," after all. Thus you must be in touch with guidance to use crystals systematically with them. We suggest you use them for yourselves and let your children seek their own involvement with crystals as they choose in most or almost all instances. And if you would use a crystal with them in sicknesses or need, please allow us to work with them in open-ended ways, by allowing the programming in your crystals to be for the highest and best good under God, in the name of the Love vibration and potential in all humanity. This will do nicely, for if it is not appropriate for the crystals to work with your children, under these directives we will be able to allow the crystal to sleep or work on other things, even while a child is holding it, or while it lies as part of a pattern about the child in bed.

If you use this open-ended programming, by the way, you need not fear placing crystals about the bed at night, for you and for your children. Three crystals, one at the head and two triangulated with it about the feet will do quite nicely. If you choose to do other patterns with your children, again, with open-ended programming, do so in sleep or as they rest, rather than imposing moments of forced attention to these things, as this will kill their interest, sure as rain brings crops.

The patterns most often useable with children shall be the seven-pointed star, the patterns of six and eight crystals in a circle, the patterns of twelve only rarely, and the patterns of four and eight using single crystals in a diamond form (with either one or two single crystals at each point of the diamond as in the diagram for clusters in chapter twenty-five). These latter formations of crystals are for strengthening the incarnating or formative forces in a child, and are to be used with care, as their over-use will create resistances in the child that are hard to manage from the other side, the side of the angelic help that manages your growth through time, and the unfoldment of capacities of childhood in us all. Thus we suggest the use of these patterns only with our help and guidance.

To understand these patterns enough so you might use them effectively, see background in other chapters on the patterns of six and eight, as these are patterns of the Star of David and a slight modification of it for strength and balance (for self-mastery in the physical), by using two extra crystals—one along each side of the body, in addition to the pattern of six that would normally have two along each side of the body, one at the head and one at the feet.

In addition, the most useful pattern for childhood shall be the seven-pointed star, as seven is the number of innocence and childhood itself, through the feminine aspect of God, as in the crown of the seven sisters that is your Pleiades. The seven-pointed star of Brigit, in old pagan lore, is exactly the same crown. You may feel it soon about your brow at Christmas time (or at other times you call on it), when you attune to the one Mother of all, and she in turn attunes to you by placing in your heart a child and mother; and placing on your head a seven-pointed star of light, a crown with seven candles burning

figure 4. seven-pointed star of Brigit

bright for all. A second star, of twelve bright points (the so-called Star of Bethlehem, which we prefer to call the Mother's Star), shall shine in blue-white love for all, from high above your head. Down through your crown this light shall shine, lighting up your heart and Soul, and placing on your brow the crown we spoke of, the seven-pointed Star of Brigit, for so it has been called by all in times gone by. This is the three-fold gift of Mary too, you see; or of any other Mother Soul incarnated fully on your earth. This star is the ancient fullfillment of the temple mysteries of Atlantis and Lemuria, as echoed in your Kabbalistic lore of the seven-pointed crown or star of God. The real meaning of this star is your fulfillment, as we have somewhat now explained or hinted at (and you can feel it there upon your head as you attune to God Divine as Mother of us all), and it is something we will explore in context and more fully in our future book, *Alignment with [all] Life.*

The child has need of Mother's light. This is why we most expect the use of this divine archetype, the seven-pointed star, with crystal applications to your children in these and future times on earth. Please receive this gift with blessing, yours in light and love of God. To use it, place seven crystals in a circle, you or child within. And let us "treat" you with the light and love of God, as in all other applications of your growth with crystals.

Chapter Fourteen

Some Practical Ways With Quartz Crystals

For the most part, the sections of this chapter reflect first experiments undertaken by myself and others to appreciate the capabilities of crystals to aid our lives. They will be introductory uses for you to experiment with, though they are of continuing value for your growth. We hope that you feel free to use them in the spirit of adventure and hopefulness we intended.

Sweetening Water:

Crystals change drinking water if you program them to do it, and also if they are cleaned and placed in water even without your conscious programming. This is because a certain part of the capacity of any crystal is usually for healing in the normal course of its regular, natural programming (10 to15% of the capacity on average), and this healing programming will allow it to work on water for you, though somewhat less effectively than if you programmed it explicitly for this purpose.

The taste of water is the most obvious thing changed. We notice a sweeter taste that is easily detectable. The crystal at the very least seems to take away the flatness that water left standing usually has. We add crystals to our bottled water as soon as we open the five gallon containers for use.

This effect is noticeable enough to use with people you would like to show in an observable, physical way that crystals can affect us. Simply let them taste the crystal purified water along with a taste of water that is identical, except it has had no crystal in it. Two glasses of tap water on the counter over night, one with a crystal and one without will do admirably for this test. Programming does improve this effect, but largely in ways that are more subtly observed if they can be observed by us at all.

By the way, we suggest **not** using plastic or aluminum containers, as it is likely crystals cannot easily overcome the harmful effects of these substances on drinking water. Glass is best. Porcelain and steel are good too.

We had a man who purifies water for a living come by to demonstrate how much better tasting water made with his water purifier was than the bottled water we buy. We warned him we used crystals in our water, but he was willing to bet that we would buy his water once we tasted the difference. He had often done this experiment before, with the very water company we bought from. After tasting our water and then his, he had to allow that the difference was noticeable: the crystal water tasted less flat; it tasted sweeter. Probably the best combination would have been his water with our crystals. He left saying he would buy small, dinged-up crystals for all his water customers to use. And he certainly bought some for himself. (Whether he ever actually figured out how to integrate selling water with small crystals I don't know.)

Treating plants:

Use crystal sweetened water on houseplants when you water them. You could instead use a little sand high in quartz content (most sands) next time you repot them (about a third sand for succulants and cacti, about a quarter to an eighth for other plants). This works!

Something that works with outside plants is to place crystals in square or rectangular configurations in the garden, around shrubs and around the base of trees, and then program them to act for the highest and best good of all beings within their energy fields. This can be augmented with one crystal each for any trees you wish to help, programmed as above except also to balance and strengthen the tree on an individual basis. This is helpful, since most trees we plant in our neighborhoods or farms are not perfectly adapted to the soil, were not grown from seed in the same location, and thus could use some strengthening and encouragement. It is good to point out that trees will benefit greatly from any loving attention, encouragement and admiration.

Something we would like to add to this is that agricultural efforts using crystals would be fine transitional efforts for transforming our relationship to nature itself. We have found that the productive methods that can be employed with gentle efforts to cooperate with the unseen forces of nature are virtually unlimited in their usefulness at this time for even the most hard-nosed practical farmer. This is not the case simply because what we have discovered is more economical (sometimes it is, sometimes it isn't); rather it is more aligned with what is for the best for all things, and thus more likely to produce results in the long run that are a cooperative and constructive effort for all.

Charging the Aura:

There are energy fields and subtle bodies, if you will, of different sizes and densities, that extend in human beings throughout and beyond the physical body. (In an upcoming book we intend to explore these patterns in detail.) Definite features are common to these subtle bodies. A definite anatomy of subtle organs, chakras or energy centers, meridians or flow lines and the like, exist within these bodies.

We have found that crystals have strong effects on these subtle bodies in ways that people can experience to one degree or another, depending on their sensitivity and familiarity with energy of a subtle nature. When we hold a class or do a treatment, most people notice a great deal about the energies, including crystals, that work in ways appropriate to each. These, of course, are optimal conditions, for people have come to our classes with at least some understanding of the processes we offer and every intention of giving us and the crystals a chance to do our work. You can set up these optimal conditions for yourself as well.

At a most basic level, the energy fields of many individuals are enhanced or amplified by wearing a crystal around the neck or carrying one in a pocket. A crystal in a pocket, worn around the neck, or on a desk at work will help a person if it is properly programmed. If it is not consciously programmed it will work a bit but will be susceptable to passing thoughts and impulses, and subject in any case to the programming that already exists, if any, in the crystal. The benefit of wearing or having a crystal around you is greater the more conscious you become of the ways to work with crystals and the effects crystals may have on you.[1]

A Message From the Level of Our Souls

To channel, for a moment, from the Mother/Father aspect of my Self:

---

[1] One point to make on crystal pendants is that they are best worn in between chakras or energy centers, if you will, rather than directly over them. Thus you would place a pendant below the nap of the neck, for example, rather than on it; below or above the center of the chest rather than on it; above the solar plexus rather than on it. This is because the chakras are interfered with over time by the linear energies of your crystals (either horizontal or vertical); they are of a spherical or circular nature themselves. A crystal can be useful directly over a chakra for temporary "treatment" purposes only—not for long-term wearing. For the same reason as well as others, we recommend intermittent use of crystals for pendants rather than continuous use every day. By intermittent we mean patterns of an informal nature such as two days on, two days off; four days on, one day off; three weeks on, one week off—and so on.

Stress to the heart chakra is a possible result of continuous use of crystals as pendants. It is not a problem that will affect many people, or be cause for great concern to those who would be affected; we discuss an optimal adjustment for your use of crystals. We ourselves wore one crystal almost all the time for over a year without noticing any stress at a conscious level. Later we grew sensitive enough to adjust what we were doing. Today we rarely wear a crystal of any kind. This is a result of growth, for which we are blessed. So it shall be for all who grow in God, that they are blessed through all they do, for good as well as growth in Soul. God bless you.

Especially when you are starting, crystals will forgive many errors in using them, for they are directed by your Guidance and your Souls, with or without your permission. If you don't give your permission, sooner or later things will break down. But if you learn your lessons of growth as fast as they arise with crystals, even this way of not giving open permission to the Divine through you will not end in disaster, but only in growth.

Be faithful and trust the process you are embarking upon. For you can trust yourself, at any rate, once you learn to trust the Life of all who come to you in friendship and love for you to share with. You need not trust their other attributes, only the goodness in each human heart, no matter how stifled it may appear. So it will be healing that you bring to them with every step you take. And healing to yourself as well. We would have you work with these things more, for healing is to you what healing is to Me. The center of My Life in you.

We would go back to the limitations you place on crystals through inadvertence or poor programming of them. Subliminal programming is not possible, once you have released your fears of it. Crystals do not respond to fragmented remains of your understanding unless you get behind them whole-heartedly with your will-intentions. Thus the darkened corners of your mind that some of you may fear are there are not an aspect of what you are programming into crystals. Only the best of what you think will ever get into a crystal more than half-way. It is set up so, that only Divine intervention can truly program a crystal. The great, alert mind you think may somewhere exist as a final product of school tests from your childhood will not be able to program a crystal any better than the smallest babe who looks on it with love and recognition, perhaps, and giggles with delight. For the crystal has recognized the gift of the child at once, and has responded in kind; whereas the sensible scholar with a disciplined capacity to think great thoughts—or Platonic solids in the air—will only get in the way of the thoughts the Light was trained to sing, out of the crystal in your mind as well as heart, not to mention the crystal before your eyes on a stand in your living room or office.

We hope you will not take what we are saying in a light that would prejudice you to our words with you, for we would guide you to understanding crystals, and this requires that you know that you are already enough to use them in fullness if you should ask us for our help. We are your Souls and your guidance in perfection, we might add. We channel through whenever this author calls on help from us to share with you.

The Need For Crystals

You will find that many people for whom crystal use is appropriate will have more energy, feel better, think more clearly, and find all their efforts towards their own growth enhanced just by carrying crystals regularly, having them around in the house, meditating with them, and keeping them cleaned and blessed (or activated, if you prefer that term). We discuss reasons for this throughout this book. At any rate, through experience with ourselves and many others, and from our guidance, we have found that crystals activate capacities already in us that have been dormant in this life. Once these capacities have been activated, needs for crystals that have to do with such activation are outgrown in a short time relative to our lifespan. Depending upon how much we use the energies involved, for healing others and ourselves, the process of out-growing crystals as they apply to such activation might take anywhere from six months to five years.

We suggest there are other uses for crystals as well that we will approach in the chapters ahead. These also are for the most part to be outgrown in time upon your earth. For now, it is best to know that these capacities can be activated in other ways besides using crystals and will be for many. Crystals are simply an aspect of one way for this to happen.

Charging the House and Healing

One of my earliest explorations into using quartz crystals was to clean them and set them up to work on revitalizing the energies of the house in which I lived. I do the things I describe for you differently today than when I first worked with crystals. What I tell you here I am modifying somewhat because I can now use the guidance of my Soul to check what I do. A real improvement.

First, just setting up a crystal in your house and keeping it clean means that it will probably be a source of several things for you. It will stimulate your nervous system to grow stronger. This will be slow and subtle, but definite results can be noticed over time. Next, it will begin to heal your traumas and your glaciations of intellect, so to speak. It will unfreeze your expressions of whole, white light to the point of actually healing the physical. I have felt such results in myself over time.

I am relying on my Guidance for the exact nature of what it is that is healed. The changes are too subtle over too long a time span for me to consciously register what they are exactly in the moment they are happening. Perhaps you will be able to yourself. At any rate, if I look back far enough, the difference in the way I feel is obvious.

Changes my Soul would comment on include the following: you will notice a definite releasing of tensions around your intellect, your throat, and heart. This is what your Soul is trying to do for all of you, so this is what the crystal will be used for if you give it half a chance: you will be healing under its supervision with your Soul to help.

We would like to leave you with a lasting impression of how simple this process is. Really. The escape from intellect you are accomplishing in this shift of consciousness over the next few dozen years is high time and way overdue. It is in order. Crystals will aid in this process considerably. They will afford your Soul a grounding in the physical that is purer and more accurate for its purposes than your own physical body. In part this is true, though an exaggeration admittedly, in the sense that you are the child of your Soul and thus perfectly suited for your growth and its growth too. Still, in a real sense, you are grounding your Soul in a physical frame of greater perfection than your physical body of carbon-based formations and processes when you work with crystals in this way that we suggest for you, and so it shall be for more than a few years after you begin working with crystals. You might read this last sentence again, since it is so basic to an understanding of crystals and their positive use. Your physical expression is enhanced by a crystal, by its very purity and perfection of expression, though in another sense you are the Child of your Soul and thus your physical expression is already admirably suited to your growth and the growth of your

Soul as well. It is simply enhanced by a crystal that is of natural creation.

Whole White Light

We would suggest that you experiment a bit, for growth, with what you place in crystals for your healing and your blessing. Light is one nice option.

Many people are consciously working with white light these days. Might we suggest an improvement? My Soul informs me that white light *per se* is not for the highest and best good. It is too limited and it is not specific enough, both at the same time. We suggest either getting more encompassing with your general request or getting more specific, if you are guided to do the best specific thing. If you don't know your guidance yet, do not despair. That is what these times are for. For a while yet, use your best general healing agent, Whole White Light. Whole light is not visible white light. It is an expression of divine hierarchies above your head and within your heart, if they have to be located. (They are actually everywhere and anywhere they are needed.) Whole White Light includes regular white light. It also included frequencies not of this solar system that are of use to you now. For you are gradually outgrowing the star system you are living in. It will take a few million years for humanity as a whole to adjust to the changes that are in store completely. What we are describing will be a process requiring patience on your part. Still, it is best to cooperate with such preparations, however distant they may stretch into the future. For you will, with patience, grow to be one of the starseed that will people the next creation in another universe, as some might say; we suggest rather in another incarnation of your own race, in a location that cannot be located in the normal continuum of time-space you know and are adjusted to on earth.

We are speaking collectively here, of "humanity" as a whole. Individual Souls have different destinies entirely. They are guided to pass through the race of men for guidance and for growth, to guide and offer peace to all—depending on the state of Soul—without the need to stay attached to any race or planet. Is this to your understanding? We hope it is, even though we have only introduced this subject for you here, and much confusion still is possible about your Souls and who you are in growth on earth as well as other planets.

We would suggest to you that we are phrasing things for your growth at the present. Not too distantly in the past, men talked of things like the Second Coming and the New Millennium, the birth of Christ in all our hearts, the gift of Buddha nature, and the spread of Islam, with the same enthusiasm with which we bring to you the new age of discovery of the next few million years. Humanity has outgrown its need for concepts that limit its growth to the planet earth in its present configuration. It is time for you to stretch your imagination to include a destiny in the stars as well. For it is to the stars that we will look for inspiration.

The one you call the Christ is a Destiny more than it is a man, you know. It is a destiny that has come to you as a potential from the stars as well, for your Creator is of the stars as well as earth, is this not so? He/She/It is more than stars and shares a space in them as well. He is starseed himself in a former time. For all is now. And your Lord and Redeemer is a man on earth (in you, be you man or woman) and a woman in the matrixes of space as well, conjoined with all, as the saying goes. (This is in fact your Father/Mother God aspect of Self, channeling to you and through you with a sense of humor at the present time. We would guide you well in freedom to excel in knowing God as he or she most truly is: one with you in love as you may allow him/her to be, in your alignment with the stars of your destiny in space beyond the time you know.)

As you consider whole white light then, you might ask one of your crystals to be a source of whole white light for your entire household. Again, you might ask that this be so in the way that is best for you at the present time, and in all future times as well.

Grounding

To close, we would like to give you another practical tool with crystals and with the earth you walk on. Grounding with crystals is easiest when you are yourself upon the ground, so go outside if it is warm enough to do so and place your self or feet upon the ground for grounding.

Often you will find that as you work with your spiritual growth you will become confused with who you are at basic levels of grounding, that you are a part of your earth as well as the stars of inspiration for you, and you are in resonancy with the best of the forces of the earth as well as sky. As you allow this resonancy to work with you more often, you will find your energies stabilized the more for when you work with any energy, including thought or crystals. There are many practical ways to do this grounding, besides the simple ones we give in this section. Call upon your guidance for assistance in this grounding, if you will, though God as well can help you with this growth in acceptance of the earthly forces of yourself in love. Sit on the earth and love her as you call for help from earth as well as sky and four directions. This too shall help in establishing who you are as child of earth and sky for now on earth. We suggest your longing for the sky is often cause of this alarm, that you too weakly connect with sky as well as earth when you deny your connection to the source of anything—in this case your physical through astral levels of expression—which is the earth itself. You maintain yourself through energies of earth, you see, as well as through the energies of sky in spiritual dimensions of the Soul and self on earth. Balancing the two, the earth and sky, will help you grow more fully.

We suggest you use a pattern for yourselves in this, the balancing and grounding of who you are. (See figure 5.) Place a little crystal (six inches or less) upon the balls of each of your feet pointed upwards towards your head, or simply towards your toes. You can tape them there if they don't stay in place. Now place a third crystal at the belly-button pointed down. This triangulation is the best pattern with crystals that we know for grounding.[2]

A second such configuration, one we use for grounding but also poor digestion related to need for grounding, is used as you are lying down again, as you have noticed in the last exercise if you have tried it once already. Set up a pattern using

---

[2] From seminars with Rev. Dr. Frank Alper.

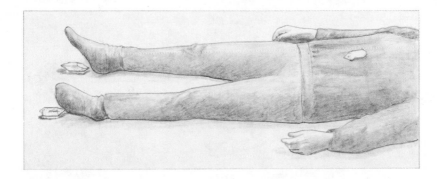

figure 5. grounding pattern

seven crystals, all under six inches and over two (though one inch length would do if you waited long enough for it to activate—two to four minutes or so). Equal sizes are best but not essential if you program the crystals to take the balance of their sizes into account. The best configuration for these seven is to place at the head a single crystal pointed down towards the feet; to place between the feet a second crystal pointed up. Then place the remaining crystals as follows, as in figure 6 below (one on the navel pointed down, one on either side of the hips on the floor pointed in towards the navel, and one on the outside of each knee pointed up towards the head).[3] The time frame for this and other configurations we will present to you in future chapters is always at your discretion, but we suggest a starting exposure of ten or fifteen minutes and guidelines for use of up to half an hour that include the suggestion that you program your crystals for optimal strength at all times, neither more nor less. Until you are familiar with programming your crystals for yourself, however, please use common sense and perhaps limit yourself to the shorter period.

---

[3] From Rev. Dr. Frank Alper, *Exploring Atlantis Vol. II* (Phoenix, Arizona: Arixona Metaphysical Society, 1983). May be ordered from: A.M.S., 3639 East Clarendon, Phoenix, Arizona 85018.

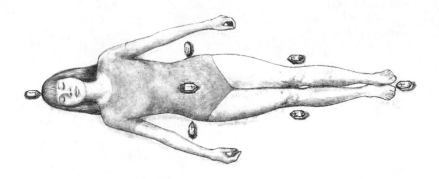

figure 6. grounding & digestion pattern

This is enough for now. Know that we will guide you to ever new expressions for yourself and those you love in truth.

The last thing that we suggest is systematic consideration of who you are in the form of the exercises in this book and else-where in these times. For so much help for guidance is avail-able right now that you have no excuse to fail to grow through lack of ways to do it. Bless you all in love, good day.

Chapter Fifteen

The Star of David Pattern

The fundamental structure of many crystals, especially quartz crystals, is that of a hexagon: a six-pointed Star of David. The seventh energy that completes the interval, if you will, is the center point or termination of the crystal; and not all natural, hexagonal crystals have this seventh defined at a physical level the way quartz does, coming to a point at one end at least. Beryl, for example, often comes to a flat termination at one end or both ends, if both are free of the matrix or bed rock.[1]

The Star of David structure is the fundamental one our planet has worked with in the past, and it will be so for another one hundred thousand years or so, I am told by my guidance. This is a transitional period we are currently in, you must understand. One hundred thousand years is a very short time indeed, in the evolution of planets or of civilizations of humanity. The current phase will be completed when humanity outgrows the need to profit from mistakes, if you will. The next phase will include trial and error, from the point of view of our Souls and their growth, but it will include the possibility of expression beyond the need for error and correction as well. It will include the energies of total service and mastery as a part of what is taking place for many on earth.

---

[1] (See end of chapter for note.)

At the present time only those who are as shepherds to the whole, so to speak, are within the energies of total service. This is a mere handful at present, though many more will reach this stage in the near future, within the next few thousand years. Many will find the balance to be who they are without doubts and without the need to be better than or less than any other.

This will happen in time for all of you, but for the present, we are in the first beginnings of these energies.

Perhaps some in your world think this process will be more immediate for themselves and others than is really possible. Perhaps too this is in order, that some should be ahead of themselves and their time, for thus change comes: anticipated and made much of perhaps, yet altogether new for those who greet it with their hearts in love. And for many, it will be as they wish it; for all things come to pass as they are intended, yet all things are subject to the wishes of those for whom they are intended. Free will choice, in many cases, does make a difference.

And now we would like to share with you the energies of the Star of David, first giving credit to the man who brought these energies to the attention of the channel writing. Rev. Dr. Frank Alper has taught the uses of the Star of David with relation to quartz crystals for many years, and it is from him that we first heard of the possibilities of this configuration.[2] We would like to share with you a bit of his work on Atlantis. For the Atlantis technologies of crystal healing are those that we draw upon at this time for growth with crystals as a tool. We suggest you approach these things with caution for yourselves, if you wish. They are but a tool for conscious growth,

---

[2] From Soul: Rev. Frank Alper is a man who is one with his Soul at the levels of service to mankind in its present stages of growth. For we have given to him that he might know who he is and why he is here, and he has activated many to be of equal service in these times. We recommend the work of Frank Alper to all of you as equally of interest to those who might be so moved to take his workshops and read his books. Frank lives in Phoenix, Arizona, but he does work all over the country in service to God, as do we through this channel writing, and he may be available to come to an area near you. We feel we owe him thanks for our own awakening, such as it is. And we wish that you might allow yourselves to feel what connection he may have for you.

as all things are, and they require care and self-acceptance as do other tools. We hope you enjoy them.

First, the Star of David was used from earliest Atlantean times for attunement with self and Soul, for conscious healing and adjustment of energies with those of our universe as well as our personal expressions in that universe. It was a tool that many availed themselves of. As we said in our chapters on crystals in tradition, many human beings in Atlantean times were as guided by the Souls of those who do the guiding now, in our age as well. And many experienced the instruction of their Higher Selves and guides through the work of the healing circle of quartz crystals we will present to you now, though the work with our Souls was different for us then. It was both more conscious, and more taken for granted, so to speak. For that which you are always aware of, you tend to take for granted. And the way the Atlantean Elders took advantage of their Souls—for this they did—was to assume they knew better than their sleepy Souls, which after all, they reasoned, exist in nebulous states of consciousness in other places than this earth plane which they must be less qualified to appreciate than we who share with one another direct responsibility and consciousness of what is happening here on earth.

The Atlantean Elders assumed they knew so much they didn't need to check themselves at all. In time this proved their downfall, and it is a present lesson even now; for each reaction to what we do is greater than the last, until at last we gain the consciousness to ask for help from those who set us up in business in the first place: the creators of the original garden, the condition of this place before we changed it to fit our needs in limited expression of what we thought we needed. Our chapter on Atlantis and Lemuria goes into this in greater detail.

Briefly, we have given you a context for this work for growth with the Star of David, which again you turn to, in completion of your work, in a manner of speaking, instead of at its beginning phase on earth. For most of you were at a beginning of a sort on Atlan, the name for this planet in those early days. Atlan, the name you gave it then.

Begin by placing six crystals in a circle, spaced equidistantly, with the points all facing north, if you will, though the

points may face in different ways, depending on your purpose.

May we suggest that you place them facing in towards the
center if you wish slightly more symmetrical energies, once
you are used to what is happening with this formation. And
when you wish to pray for others, may we suggest you face
them outwards.

figure 7. the Star of David pattern

If your crystals are operating under divine programming, it
will not matter what direction you use with the crystals. You

will be placed in energies perfect for you at the time you use them. If you are inclined to use the natural ingraining of the crystals themselves, at levels that correspond to your own bodies of light and substance, then you may choose to use the patterns of placement with the crystals facing out and in as we have suggested above.

Once again, to begin with, lie down in the center of this circle, making it a bit oval before you do so in order that you fit inside. Let your head be towards the north, if possible, although this setup will work no matter what direction you face. The northern orientation of the head is merely optimal, not essential.

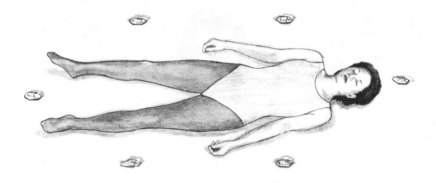

figure 8. oval Star of David for treatment

Now as a further exercise, you might sit meditatively and face the crystal you are most drawn towards in the circle of crystals around you. (See figure 9.) You will be facing one of the aspects of yourself with this, for the six crystals so arranged form a perfect balance of expressions of your own development in the light of who you are for earth configurations. This will be explained to you a little more in the next chapter. For now, allow yourself to notice in passing the energy of each crystal as you are so moved. Overall, allow yourself to feel the effect of these energies upon your being, for you are working with more than you are fully conscious of as yet, and attunement to all you are will be enhanced by this first Star of David practice with crystals.

When first we learned of the pattern of the six-pointed star, we thought the best way to use it was to sit in a perfect circle of six crystals, all facing inwards, as we have said works for greater intensity if possible. The pattern alters in several ways we can give to you, but first experience this second way of using the Star of David for yourselves, facing all the points inward. Place yourself once again in its center, this time sitting up facing south, with your back to north, for optimal exposure to the energies. Again, this directional orientation is

figure 9. meditating in the circular Star of David

helpful but not essential. Using it will only orient you to the natural flow of the earth's own energies, including the normally assumed magnetic energies that are measurable by your instrumentation on earth.

We would give you further instruction with this Star of David at present. But first we would guide you to a meditation from within its boundaries, if so you choose to do. We would have you close your eyes and look inside to see what you are feeling. This is what is being worked with by your crystals, both for amplification (so that you will notice what you do in greater depth, for this is the reason crystals amplify your feelings and your thoughts: to trigger response in you as you grow more aware of what they do for you) and for healing/blessing (for this is the reason we are with you: to strengthen your response to us by seeing what we do for you in love, and thus become more trusting of your fate). We would guide you to notice all you see within, for seeing for yourself is the purpose of this exercise, rather than seeing anything you might think should be there. Notice for yourself what you are doing now. And now again.

This next time, notice what you are feeling in your heart, for we will time our response to you to let you feel your heart when you put out this intention. The condition of your hearts may vary, but with effort of attention, all may feel their work with this their heart in love. And we would let you know that we are near. So let yourself allow us to be present in your heart with loving kindness, first exposed to the chance connection you can notice, one and all, and then exposed to more and more as you attune to what is really there, the cooperation of your Soul with all that is, at one with all there is for you.

We will let you see what you shall see inside, you know. We will let you choose the destiny for you. But we will guide you to the perfect destiny fulfilled, if you will but ask. Then saints and devils[3] all conspire for you to know yourself. Then you are guided in perfection each time you trust us to fill your needs within. We will trust you to do this, to ask us for help in an open-ended, non-assuming way. For pride and prejudices will encroach from every side. This is what we notice

---

[3] Or forces of resistance, as we choose now to call them: forces for your growth in Will of loving Soul.

early on in processes of inner growth, when first one looks within, as you might say. There are devils and saints in each of us, but only those who choose their Souls for guidance and for love will know the truth, that we (in forms of testing or of strength) are one with you and all, and we are one with Soul of God of all. In perfect peace you shall come to us if you trust to grow you all who care. Ask, and it shall be done, even with something so mundane as crystals set in a pattern of six about a circle. Call upon your Soul and God for assistance in this, your Star of David. Or rather, allow us, through your asking for support, that we might help you as we know full well to do.

You, the reader, will next be guided to express yourself in what you do with six crystals. Let yourself talk of this to others, telling them what you experienced. For in sharing you will find a strength revealed within. More than you can guess, when first you touch the crystals with your light, will come through you as you grow accustomed to sharing with others all you know or learn in Truth. So be advised to share with others what you do in Truth as well.

Now we would be blessed to ask you to refrain from thoughts that are hard on others when you are in these circles. This is because the might of your intentions is grounded in the crystals when you sit in them. Treat them as sacred objects, if you will. But more to the point, treat yourself with respect when you sit in a sacred circle of a six or twelve-pointed star, because the energies that you create rebound on you as well as others (99.9% on you, in fact). And the energies of love you would invoke for yourself will heal all wounds in time from others' deeds towards you as well as yours towards them. Let yourself set aside the effects of the outer world of action and reaction, for just a time, and sit in peace with the crystals of light and love you now allow to work with you.

We would have you turn to other features about the crystals that you use. They are designed to contain in them the energies of the Star of David in each single crystal. Once you have used the Star of David to feel for yourselves the effects of this formation, feel free to call upon the patterns of these energies from but a single crystal. It shall work for you in this way, that as you ask it to do this for you, it shall be done in wholeness.

The next thing we would take up for you is the Star of David as a temporary pattern for wholeness, as it is an expression of a limited nature, at least to some extent. The nature of this pattern is perfect balance in the whole, in perfect triangulation towards descent into materialization, as it were, and in perfect and opposite equilibrium or triangulation towards the infinite of God, the highest aspect of your being—for all is still within you, as expression of God's wholeness, God's image for this earth, if you will, but for all time as well. For is not your God well pleased with you? And is he/she not glad to give you all that she or he becomes forever? So it is for us as well as you, that Soul is limited only by the possibilities it knows and still expresses when its time for change has come. Forever it is so.

The limitation of the crystals in use with the Star of David pattern is only that you outgrow it once you know the truth of who you are at one with self and Soul. You exceed the limits of your earth in this, and thus you do outgrow its energies of expression for yourself in time. You will notice also that from time to time you outgrow the uses of the Star of David on a shorter term basis as well. For you will be continually needing further growth than this one pattern offers you, and you will continually need to stabilize your growth with perfect integration where you are in time and space on earth. You will find your own instincts to be wise in this, that your needs for growth will guide you to use for a time this Star formation, and the other patterns we shall give you, for several years and then release them. You will come back to them from time to time, but let yourself be the guide in this. You will know the truth of operation for you in what you do better than another.

The last and related limitation to give you for this pattern is that it is still outside your Soul, as manifest of what you are on earth, not what you are in truth. Thus it indicates direction of your Soul, but doesn't make or give your Soul to you, as you are it already. You only need to use these energies as long as you are adapting to the needs of what you are in truth. Once you know the truth of who you are in great stability, you will outgrow the need for crystals altogether, except as tools to teach another what you learned from Soul yourself.

Thus the times of transition are always with us, that certain uses of our Soul are one with us while others wait awakening. And all are gifts from God who made us. God bless us everyone.

Note (from page 103): Beryl, unlike quartz crystal, often terminates without a definite focus at either end, and thus without an obvious, physical focus of expression. Nonetheless, beryl has a definite center along its c-axis, equidistant from its faces. It thus has a seventh energy just as does a quartz crystal, though not in the same balance of expressions. You would find that beryl has the frequency of expression of the heart (in its emerald form) or of other more specialized frequencies than does quartz (in its other color forms). Even in its clear or colorless form it will hold naturally the frequencies of the six expression, the Star of David, only at denser frequency levels than will quartz. The signature for this is twofold. First, that it lacks the powerful center focus of quartz crystal, and such a center focus denotes all possibility, even expressing potentials at the heart of all things that are not manifest in the Star of David, or in the limitations of physical expression. And secondly, beryl has an almost plant-like quality to it (as does tourmaline to an even greater degree). This is a signature for beryl that indicates that it is effective especially at the etheric or energy level so emphasized in the plant kingdom, rather than the blueprint or causal level of the mineral kingdom itself, and it is also effective in some ways at the astral or emotional level, just as plants will reach out to touch the sunlight and the feeling of warmth and emotional love they are attuned to interact with for their growth and harmony. Clear beryl is actually most effective for the plant kingdom in general and only secondarily for the plant kingdom within man—that organic, energy activity shared in common with plants. Colored beryl, on the other hand, has a role with color in archetypal form—with plants as well as people—that is specialized, in addition to the generalized activity we mention here.

Almost all beryls do show some color, however faint it may seem. And on subtle levels this is even more the case. Almost never will beryl be completely neutral, especially on this planet. It is important for beryl and its work that it harmonize what we feel with what we are, and beryl does this by expressing for us a pure or near-perfect color tone for us to attune one chakra or another to, in almost archetypal purity. It is the blue beryl, or aquamarine, that most gives us an energy of devotion to God through blue harmonics. It is the pink beryl or Morganite crystal that gives us perfect harmony with love in physical form. It is the green beryl or emerald that give us attunement with the warmth of perfect love for healing and for growth in God's balance of expressions at the heart. It is the golden beryl or Heliodor crystal that gives perfect gold harmonics, those of love of self and devotion to outward beauty at the level of our radiant form of light, as in the Buddha body of a human being. It is in the darker colors of beryl that we have expressions for perfect grounding.

This last gift of beryl is more than humans in their current growth can fathom at the present time. It is below your consciousness, as it were. It is in the realm of form of which you are an all but unconscious part for many lives to come. You can only handle so much for now. Such beryl will handle it for you. For beryl is within you as well as in outer expression of development in space and time. It is not necessary for you to handle a physical beryl crystal at all.

Quartz crystal, on the other hand, is effective at many other levels, as well as those that beryl expresses. Thus quartz can be substituted for beryl in most instances of human healing.

We have given you one stone, beryl, in specific detail, that you might guess the nature of our work with other stones as well; that you might see them in their own unique expressions, ever useful to the whole of God on earth. You need not use such stones for yourselves unless you choose to do so. You may trust your growth to God in all his/her ways, that you may come to wholeness for yourselves. We only give you sense of what this world of rocks around you gives to you in life on earth. And through such gifts, you grow in freedom for yourselves, though you are yet beginning in your growth to master who you are as Self at one with God in truth.

Chapter Sixteen

Working With The Six
& Twelve-Pointed Stars

We go on now to teach you of using twelve crystals in a pattern of a mini-zodiac, a twelve-pointed Star fashioned from a Star of David crystal pattern you will expand as follows. It is preferable but not essential to use crystals of similar size plus a slightly larger generator crystal for your center. After you have used a six-pointed Star of David for several weeks or more (again, all of similar size with a generator in the center), select six more crystals and place them in between the six already in place. Use yourself to test the difference between the energies of six, then twelve as you grow accustomed to the six.

At first you may be tempted to race ahead with this and only do the six after first doing the twelve of this second formation we have given you. We recommend not doing this, for the sake of your growth. For there is a gift in doing the twelve after you have done the six for several times at least. We suggest using the six-pointed star before the twelve for at least a half dozen sittings. Experiment, if you will, after the first few times, with using the crystals pointed in—or even out—practicing blessing others with your energies of balance and completion available in the six-pointed star as well as the twelve. Then, when you have accustomed yourself to the six, use the twelve. You will be surprised at the difference this will make, that you use the six-pointed star at first, then later turn to twelve—rather than jumping into twelve. The teaching you will do with others will be helped if you can give them first hand a sense of this difference.

figure 10. the twelve-pointed star

Dialogues with Soul

At one point I was guided in a meditation to be shared with those reading this book. I have left it in the form in which it was given, directed to me.

These are the energies of your own Soul.

This is the first in a series of practices with crystals we would like to give to you. Begin with your Star of David pattern, as channeled through the Soul of Frank Alper. We will guide you now in a meditation to appreciate the gift you have been given in this Star of David.

[At this point I was sitting in the equivalent of a twelve-pointed Star pattern as I worked—for fun, not thinking it would be much involved in the writing I was doing. It happened to be made up of six double-terminated crystals, though it could have been made up of twelve single-terminated crystals just as effectively. Double-terminated crystals, in such a pattern, act as two crystals each, one for each termination. We suggest using the more easily obtained single-terminated crystals in a pattern of twelve for this exercise.]

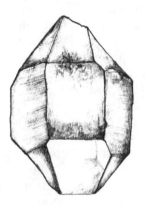

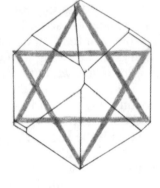

figure 11a. a double-terminated
crystal

figure 11b. a Star of David
over an average crystal

We ask that you sit still within yourself as we shall guide you. Now take within yourself the pattern of the twelve signs of the zodiac that spin about your head. They are the pattern of your lives together on earth. These twelve are as elders who sit before the throne of God the most High and judge the ways of destiny as the lives of humankind unfold. We are one with them and you.

These stars that move in their completeness about the starry sky are mirrored inside yourself, as day is mirrored in the night by the echoed shining of the sun that you see in the silver moon. Hold this image within you for a moment more, to feel its resonancy with you. Know that you and the crystal pattern you are working with are like this pattern in your ordering.

Now take the first stone you have laid in your circle of six, the crystal at your right hand as you face forward in your circle. It is before you and to the right. [Again, this exercise is referring to the double-terminated crystals I happened to be using. In a set up of twelve single-terminated crystals, please take up first the crystal in the place described from the original star pattern of six, then take up the crystal to its immediate right, clockwise around the circle, to get the balance of expression. You may do this one at a time or both together, if you so choose. We suggest you take up both when first you do this exercise, to coordinate with what we say more exactly.]

Now hold it [or them] in your hand and feel the quality of change that it expresses. For it is an aspect of self and Soul that you are holding in your hand: an aspect of change through time and space, cause and effect of the world. We ask you to notice what you feel, on this and subsequent days, as you take up this crystal, allowing it to work as it was designed, as circle in the light of six, yet at the same time as you hold it, allowing it to give you access to each of two qualities of twelve; for two expressions it does hold: action and reaction to one another, light and dark, expressions of both possibilities of self.

Do this with the second crystal, behind and to your left [and with the next crystal clockwise around the circle, in the pattern of twelve]. You will feel a quality of change in this as well: for in your world all is change. This pattern comes from Atlantis through the Soul of Frank Alper. For so we give him credit, and you as well. You have worked with him and he with you, until you both are one from this day forth in the work you do in love. Be prepared for men to know you as you are, expression of the Lord of love, as God of all you create. As you release the limits upon your life, you will know that Two are One, expression in your mortal and immortal form, as octaves of the light. And you will find that you are blessed in all you do as well as he. For this is the time of service to your Soul, and serving all who come to you is service to your Soul. God bless you.

Now to continue with our work with crystals, we would share with you this process of attuning to each crystal of six, in turn, around your form. The Star of David is an ancient symbol in your world and ours. It guides you still at levels of archetypal forms that create renewal to your forms of life on earth. The Star of David is a form of universal balance of expressions between the realms of higher energies and earth. These forms are few in number, for there is need to simplify the processes of a creation and balance it in universal understanding in simplicity as well. The simplicity of expression here is two-fold in that it works from above and below. For you it is an aid at balancing your relationship to us. For us it is a way to come to you in service. Use this pattern in good faith and bless you.

Next we would like for you to try this out yourself.

We have guided you through experiencing only two of these six double expressions in the Star of David pattern. For each of the six are two in equal and opposite balance. We have shown you how powerful these can be, even when you are of limited experience and limited ability to see on cosmic levels, as you seem to think you are (and this is not the case at all). We have guided you to know as qualities these two expressions of the whole that you may shape for yourself the ideas that come to you on each. We suggest you do this with those who come to you, and those who read the book you write. The detail we have given you from these reflections is best included in another work, perhaps a private diary or some book to come. For though you have formulated in great detail what these things may mean to you, to another they may take a different expression. And so our Souls are joined in patterns of the whole, the name that comes to you for what you do. And all people who share with one another connect these patterns of the whole as facets of themselves.

We would next like to direct your attention to connecting to the windows of light that are within your crystal, asking that you credit the work of Dr. Randall and Vicki Baer in this—their concept of the crystals as such windows that lead us to the stars.[1] These two deserve your credit, too. For though they have shared with you your understanding as well as theirs, they are worthy sons and daughters of the most high in us, and they are blessed in all they do. We give this word for them that people might complement their work with you with that of Frank and of these two, Vicki and Randall Baer. May you work with them as brother spirits in the light. Sisters too. And now we shall proceed, after you take a break.

There are circuits of understanding in the windows or portals of perception that crystals offer you. You would do well to study the meaning of these circuits, for they are the archetypes of your Souls as well. Seven is the number of expression here in the crystal: six sides and the seventh is the point itself, the center of another Star of David, for a quartz crystal is itself an expression of the Star of David. Quartz crystals are expressions of the Soul in that they are formations of light that shine with the energies of the universe beyond the frequencies we can see with the naked eye. These frequencies of light are in ever progressing layers of vibration, reaching beyond the membranes of time-space you are familiar with. They are the resonancies that express the nature of God and Man to you. For all mankind is one with God at the level of the Soul. Latent in the development of each Soul is the full range of expression of God. Thus the crystal expresses what is latent in the Soul, and the Soul expresses what is latent in God.

---

[1] Randall N. Baer & Vicki V. Baer, *Windows Of Light: Quartz Crystals & Self-Transformation* (San Francisco: Harper & Row, 1984). Again, from our Souls: "Their book too has been useful to you. They have perhaps not been involved directly in your teaching or your learning, but they have been fellow co-conspirators, as it were, to follow up the world of crystals with news for all on all the levels light may work in you." This is a book we recommend. And we understand that a second book by the same authors will be released soon by Harper & Row.

Chapter Seventeen

Candle Gazing & Setting Conditions

Candle gazing with crystals

We suggest you work with ways to attune yourselves to crystals as you find them for yourselves. One such method we give by way of example as follows.

Suspend a quartz crystal at eye level from a string or by setting the crystal upright in a cup of something that will not ground it, such as beans or cedar chips (not salt, sugar or sand: these will ground the crystal and contain its aura; and any grain will bring you moths that eat your clothes as well as grain). Keep the crystal upright, if possible (helpful, but not necessary). Place a lighted candle behind the crystal so that you are looking through the crystal at the flame in a comfortable meditation or praying position. Gaze at the flame though the crystal for five to ten minutes a few times a day, perhaps before you meditate or pray. The results tend to be cumulative.

This exercise works with even a piece of broken, fairly clear quartz, and it works with a crystal ball instead of a single point or cluster. The size and condition of the crystal matters little. Although there are a number of factors involved, for this exercise and many other uses of crystals as well, we feel size and condition of the crystal are not crucial. Try it for yourself. You be the judge.

Simply look at the flame through the crystal in a natural way, without straining your eyes. Especially when looking at something hot like a flame it is easy to strain your eyes if you forget to blink enough. You don't need to look for anything visual or unusual; people do use crystals to see things from the past and future, and from other locations, but this is not the point of this exercise. We would have you allow the crystal, its energies and your guidance to work with you as you are looking at the flame. (See "setting the conditions" below.)

figure 12. set up for candle gazing

Note: There are many things that can happen experientially for people doing this exercise. In general, most of these for most people are subtle experiences, not fireworks and madonnas. Spiritual attunement is usually a matter of getting used to the subtle input you are picking up all the time and learning to differentiate more and more subtly and accurately. Gradually, once you figure out where to begin, the subtle experience of every day life as well as crystals will grow more and more conscious for you, more and more full of meaning. You will know what is going on at levels you formerly discounted because they were too subtle and ordinary for you to pay attention to or appreciate. And as your consciousness grows more subtle, you will become more and more careful about yourself. You will learn to discriminate more and more, knowing what you can change and what you cannot in those factors that affect your daily life. You will become more balanced.

Setting the conditions:

This is an important part of any experiential exercise with crystals or with your own spiritual inner life. You are in charge of what happens to a greater degree than you may be aware of. What you ask for is what will happen.

Accordingly, we recommend that you set the conditions for this and subsequent exercises, visualizations and meditations. You will be giving permission to the highest levels of your own expression and the expressions that work with you if you ask that they help you.

There are many ways to do this sort of thing, familiar in most of the sacred traditions of the world. Use whatever framework is most comfortable for you. Remember that what you ask for is what you will get and that in the subtle, unseen world of the psychic and the spiritual, in worlds of form and beyond, everything is not the same, although the processes there are by and large benign. So if you want healing and blessing in the way that is perfect for your Soul and growth, ask for it. Ask for your highest and best good, if you wish. And perhaps give some thought to who you will ask. If you ask no one in particular, but simply ask that it may be so, you will get your own Soul.

We would rather not go into any more detail than this so that you will get some experience in figuring out for yourself what way is best for you to set conditions for what you will do. Experiment for yourself. And ask for perfect protection while you're learning, in the way that's in order for you at this time, if it feels appropriate.

Chapter Eighteen

Programming Crystals For Best Use & The Working of Our Lives

Programming is a simple thing that allows us all to love. For we are given patterns within our possibilities by those who create and work with us and those we live with. Patternings of these kinds are programmings as well. So we interface you with your crystals. You are programmed as you watch your world through eyes of God's own choosing. You are light as well, and light evolves the programming of your re-creation all the time. So with crystals as with self.

We would guide you now to know yourselves more fully, for the capacities of quartz are, as we have said, the capacities of self and Self as well. We would teach you one way of doing this, but there are others. Our particular point of view is the discovery of self and Soul. We will guide you in other ways as well. For you are free to discover what you will in what we teach. And you will be guided, in any event, to modify what we say to fit your own needs and growth.

Bearing with us for a moment, let us look at the possible ways you can modify your expression as you exchange with us. You may notice what we say only. You may also notice the meanings behind the words. This is true to the point where we may say something quite incompletely, and yet you will pick up on our meaning, for you have experienced what is behind our words. You have experienced the Soul of them.

This is what crystals do as well as you. Thusly shall you program crystals in time. For now, you will use your thoughts and words as bridges to clarify for yourselves the precise sense you would give us or your crystals. So we have once again introduced the idea of programming naturally, in direct communion with the consciousness of another being in the being within your crystals, which can instantaneously reflect the meaning to you of what you are directing it to do, perhaps without fully knowing how it is to be done yourself. The crystal will know ways of working beyond your current capabilities. This is right, for it is as it should be that your crystals work with your Souls as one with God for all. Is it not sensible, this way of programming your crystals?

We would next direct you to look at the way you speak yourself. The way you direct your thoughts to others. Do you not feel what you say as you say it? Is there not a component of emotion in all you say and do? It is this component of emotion that we would dwell on for a moment. It is the meaning behind your words for some of you, for it is the blockage of what you would truly like to express. For others of you it is as one with the meaning you give your words quite consciously, and so there is an accord in harmony between the different levels of your expression.

This is the one confusion you will face with programming crystals. For the choices you make with the conscious mind of what your crystals will do for you will be tempered somewhat by the undercurrent of emotion and feeling you share with your crystals along with your conscious suggestions.

To illustrate this for you, let us say you are giving yourself a crystal massage, as we will explain for you later in this book. You are feeling fine as you do this, but you are also thinking about your romance with so and so at the same time. You are thinking of how nice it would be to tell him you love him—or her, if that be the case. You are thinking of what his head is like, what his face is like, the hair, the eyes, the look in his heart, so to speak. You will thus be giving your crystals conflicting signals, for you will be asking them to hold something for you as well as something for your lover, something that does not pertain to you in the way that is best as you are looking at your lover as yourself.

You will find that this kind of error is common in our lives. It is not a big problem for you, but it will be noticeable each time you do something, that the undivided nature of your attention will aid what is coming through you, for yourself and for others. The vibrations of your lover are fine for you, as an example, but they do not go well with the healing of your own expression as you call upon that inner light you would use to transform your being, as it were, at levels we can only describe for you as in completion for your best good. This is because we each have a precise set of needs at any given moment. It is that exact, this work we do for you through crystals. You will do well to attune to the energies we express for you in moment of healing, rather than any duty you may have to other thoughts of other places, and yet you will find your crystals to be quite forgiving, even as we have encouraged you to work at one accord with your work with us through crystals—or through any other medium, for that matter, including the medium of your own bodies of life and love and hope in God, and the being of your Soul as well. For you are as yet guided to work through the physical expression of self, yet you are of your Soul as well, happy to be whole in God.

The next thing we would convey to you is that you are safe to feel what you want to at the time of your healing and your work with crystals, in spite of what we have just said to you regarding the freedom that one accord can bring you as you work with self and others. The crystals will make allowances for most endeavors as they do what you intend in the best way they know how, as you allow them to do this. They will gift you as a friend might, in spite of whether you are having an off day or not. They will love you as you can love yourselves.

This is an important point to make, for we will be giving you direction and guidance on how to use quartz crystals and other gems with great precision, in time, and yet you are safe when you are not able to reach the ultimate or optimal effects you would like to in your own active participation in the events of growth you will co-create in working with your crystals. We suggest you be kind to yourself as you measure yourself against the optimal, for through experiment you will grow, and through experiment you will make the mistakes that are necessary for you to discover what truly works for you at all levels of your expression.

We would give you another gift as well: you are whole beyond your wildest dreams at this very moment. Discover the truth of this at your leisure, for this is yours and yours alone to explore in the adventure your life can be if you will let it.

We dream of being more than human in this life, and yet we know not what being human really is. We ask you to notice what it is you feel for yourself at this time, what real emotions you carry deep inside you towards yourself, and this will be both the blessing and the obstacle to that growth you would expect, if you were Soul instead of self, if you were conscious of what your Soul would have in store for you. We give you this in jest, in part, but we give you this in truth. You are as you would become, right now. This message you will understand when back you look upon your fate in life as well as death.

Let us go on. We would ask you to notice what it is you lack as well as have within your expressions.

We think you will find someday you lack for nothing, even now. You are already full of all you need. You need only know this for yourselves. Crystals are a chance to increase the knowledge of what you already have and are. We would say to you that to change who you are will not help the process of self-acceptance so necessary for your further growth. So many of the blemishes you think you see in self are punishments for things you have not done in times gone by, but things you needn't do. They were things that taught your Souls at times when such lessons were of use to you, but such lessons are over now in the light of the new sun that dawns for all. Such things are "ghosts in the machine," things that have no substance for you now. You are done with the growth-through-difficulties you have experienced in the past. If you can accept this, even in part, you will find a step has been taken in your awakening that will serve you well in years ahead, and this is no small step you take in this, but major change in life's basic dynamics for you as well as Soul in all.

Take a crystal in your hands and give it to a friend. Feel the quality of this exchange. Give it to him or her to hold for you, as you share the experience of what you are with him or her. Let this person hold the crystal in her hands, knowing that you share in fullness all you are with her in every moment with this touch, of mineral to your skin. This is an excuse, you see.

What you intend is that you share, one with the other. And in this sharing you have the key for growth you will use hereafter with crystals as your focus. Let people know you love them with this touch of crystal to their skin, and people will notice the intent behind the deed. This is a simple truth for all. So simple are the things that really matter for you once you are accustomed to yourself.

So it can be with crystals, as you unfold: that you discover who you are through simple things a crystal may enhance for you, or help you to unfold. So it is with crystals, in more elaborate, sophisticated ways, if you will, but actually, the sophistication of the moment and all that has transpired therein is enough for all in love. See what we have guided you to? The simplicity of self and Soul together born as one.

The generalization of your growing understanding of crystals from the functions of crystals to those of self will be the structuring of much of the underlying teaching of this book, and much of the work you do on your own as well, with crystals and with many things. Crystals are a metaphor for your own patterns of self and Soul as one.

We would say to you that you are guided in all things to know the truth about yourselves at ever more evolved expressions. Seeing the work that crystals do for you, you will appreciate more what is involved with your own life experience, as it were. For crystals do what you do, only you are not aware of what you do as yet. We would guide you to know the truth as well for crystals as yourself. But crystals already know themselves. They are one with all they are. You are in a stage both far in advance of and far behind their level of perception and experience. See what you can learn from them, if you will, but always turn to guidance for what you are as well.

We would have you look again at the above example with crystals (sharing a crystal with another) to see if you can see what we are asking you to notice in yourselves. We are asking you to notice all that is fine and good in such exchanges, the simple, ordinary exchanges of our lives in God.

The extraordinary is immanent in all things, the simpler the better for seeing this. The trees, the stars, the grass beneath your feet are more than enough for miracles to be proven as everyday events in your lives on earth. They are not fulfilling for you now, because intention of the human race is different than simple appreciation for what is real. The human race knows little of what is real, because in truth we are guiding you to know yourselves in freedom of expression for this and for all future times. The path of humankind is to temporarily forget what is, for the sake of becoming free in self and Soul while all around us all is well with God. This is a moment of growth for all of you to allow to unfold at its normal rate; for freedom is not an easy thing to teach. It comes from practice, at all levels, and it is a gift of God to you, though it is your responsibility to accept this gift yourselves, with all the assistance your Souls can give, as you are guided on your way.

Chapter Nineteen

The Healing of Guides & Angels

Simply hold a crystal in each hand and sit in a comfortable, meditative position. Allow yourself to relax with eyes closed and center in whatever way is preferable for you. In other words, release any tensions you may carry, any residual thoughts or feelings you may be holding by simply noticing them and allowing them to be released.

We shall set the conditions for your meditation, that you will be in complete protection, that you will be participating in a process of growth in the way that is in order for your Soul.

We shall ask you to relax and allow this to happen. You must give your permission for something to take place, for you are a being of free will, and nothing shall come to pass without your willing cooperation.

We allow you to say this blessing for yourself in your own words. It matters only that you allow us to work with full permission for your best good in God's will, not the will of some limited level of expression. It is appropriate for you to act with insight and diligence on your own to discover the best way for you to do this. Experiment. We will help you and guide you as you allow us the privilege. We will be with you in any event.

Allow all that comes to you to be a blessing. This is a condition that is appropriate for your life on earth. All that happens may be a blessing in disguise, as it were, but you may much more accurately limit the nature of what you are exposed to; you may receive that which is for your highest and best good rather than just making do with the best integration of what has happened that you have not allowed us to control for you. You are accident prone by the very nature of the earth plane. Things happen beyond your control. But you may decide what comes your way by asking us to coordinate the opportunities for growth for you in a cooperative endeavor with your own Soul. You may ask us to do this for you, for you are an expression of God, and nothing but the best of God's will is in order should you wish this to be the case and allow us to do this for you by asking us to.

We leave you for a moment to let you get the idea for yourself of what you will ask for in your prayer or blessing for yourself. Be sure to notice the results of what you ask for, for you are capable and able to notice the least of God's Children working with you in light and love. And you are capable of noticing the difference between this and some lesser destiny of conditions of your own choosing. Ask and notice the differences you create by your requests to us; work in your own interests with us for you.

If you have had the moment you need to choose for yourself the blessing that is appropriate at this time, we will continue with the exercise. You will be working with your own guides and your Soul for furtherance of your communicative abilities and for your healing as well. Hold a crystal in each hand and notice the feel of them. They are in your hands to allow the energies to come up your hands to influence your overall vibrations. They will work on your subtle anatomy in ways that you have allowed through your prayers. We will be with you in Spirit, you see, to guide you for your highest and best good as long as we are allowed to do so.

Now let yourself experience what is coming up your arm, the energies and the warmth, light and love.

Allow yourself to notice us in our work with you. We will be giving you a blessing that fits you alone, just as surely as you would bless a child of yours with the blessing they would allow you to give to them. Experience the nature of this blessing. It will teach you much about yourself at this time. You are ever in a state of change and growth. Like light patterns of shadows and sun upon water, we will be moving our healing rays of blessing upon you, and in this exercise we will be allowing you to experience the nature of this flowing, through your own being in a systematic way so that you may attune to us at this time.

Notice what you feel in the way of heat, light in your inner eye and tingling of sensations—feeling warmth in ways that are subtler than normal heat, light in ways that are subtler than normal visible light, and feeling love in your heart as we add love to your expression (for we will surely do this for you at this time, if you have allowed us to).

We are in cooperative effort with one another. The level we are coming to you from is not a level of loss of expression. We are not capable of mistakes, for all is in order at our level. We are your Souls, every one of you who read this book. We are with you in Spirit at all times, for we are a part of you that has in fact generated you for a mutual growth process with God Almighty above and below. We are your own expressions of truth, in the highest sense of that word. We are Love and Light and the noticing of Truth in its Divine expression. We are your love as well, for we give it to you freely with no judgement at all. We are your Souls in perfect expression from above your worlds of form.

Do not doubt the ability of God to transform your lives. For you are in perfection yourselves at levels you know not, at levels of expression that are of the Spirit of God. You are as one with your Heavenly Father/Mother God. We would tell you that the conscious separation you experience from God is in order for you, for your highest and best good. This is because you are limited in order to grow in oneness with Soul, in order to come to know love in all its ramifications for you and for others.

If you will note how you have grown in this lifetime, you will find you have gone from the innocence of a child in self-centeredness to the caring for others, even though you have been wounded seemingly, through and through. This caring for others in bounds of reasonableness is invaluable to your Soul. Resist not the chance to grow in love and caring while still watching out for self, for this is your destiny, "to learn to love without the help of anything on earth," as the poet Blake channeled years ago. You will be rewarded in heaven for your work, and on earth as you come to understand your purposes for being where you are and align with that purpose. We bless you in Spirit, Amen.

Chapter Twenty

Cleansing & Activating Your Crystals

We would like to take up this topic in a separate chapter because it is so basic a need for working with crystals that you maintain them in full capacity and radiance.

Cleansing crystals invokes the active qualities of the crystal for healing and blessing especially, for it is by healing and blessing that the crystals have come to need your help for cleansing them in the first place.

It would be in order for us to give you a discussion of what is best cleaned from a crystal and why before we proceed with techniques for doing so, as you will understand more of what is involved with crystals if we do so.

The electro-magnetics of crystals involve a resonancy with all things in nature on the part of your crystals. It is this resonancy that involves the crystals in vibratory fields that are not appropriate for your race at the present time, and yet most of these fields are as originating from humanity itself, in its efforts to be centered upon perfection of expressions instead of experiments to discover truth or lack thereof in all possibilities for expression. Crystals will acquire certain vibrational resonancies that imbalance their expressions as they respond to the healing needs of your planet with their ability to oscillate in phase with a given frequency that they would mend and resolve into a coherent and actively harmonic resonancy. Each influence they interact with affects them just a little.

Whereas many of your resonancies in time and space are sound that we would call disharmony or noise, the crystal emits only clear sound as music or harmony with all, as it resounds in the cosmos with all. The same is true for crystals and their interaction with light, both your physical, observable light and more subtle frequencies of light as well: all is transformed into harmony with all things. To us light and sound are both harmonies of color, even your sounds on earth that sing through the medium of your air. For us, emotions too have definite tones and frequencies of color expression at the same time. You sometimes notice your emotions, but we see emotions as color and light from our level of perception. So you will know that all that a crystal activates in you are different levels of color and light to us.

The colors that need to be treated by a crystal are the mirky and dim ones, as we see it. The crystal activates the color coming to it, and resolves it into the spectrum that is acceptable to God, if you will, acceptable to the frequencies of Creation that are allowed for your particular creation, your particular star system as well. We would say to you that the crystals you have are the tuning forks of your universe: they keep it in tune, so to speak, though the range within which they do this is beyond that of simple sound; it is the range of color and light as one with sound and emotion, thought and feeling for all. (This feeling for all is a sensitivity rather than an emotion; it is governed by the fifth chakra and centers in the fourth, just as emotions center in the third and are governed from the fourth as well as fifth.) Crystals activate the coordination of all resonancy in your universe. That is yet another way of saying it. And the activation is a continuous process that involves you as you work with a crystal for your own health and growth, as is appropriate in your time. You are working with a tuning fork for who you are, you see, as well as with a being like you in perfection of expression on earth, as you will be in time—quite soon—if so you choose to be.

We give you this as background for understanding cleansing. To summarize a bit, we will be involved with clearing the blurring of what are normal frequencies for a crystal, restoring it to its perfection, as it were. The cleaning we activate is a process of receiving whole light to repolarize that which is misaligned in new ways of order, to redirect the energies of misalignment for the highest and best good of all, and to redirect the positive energy flows in the same or similar ways. As the crystal resonates with your being—just to isolate the crystal's activity a bit—it will tend to take on your processes of vibratory frequency in order to change them for you into perfect harmony with all, including yourself. It will heal you in this, and it will give you an extra boost of blessing for your work, if you have asked it to do so. Now cleansing becomes necessary, because this taking on of your frequencies of expression at different levels necessitates that the crystal oscillate in frequency with you as well as with the stars, its usual attunement. Even as it resolves your resonancies into those of the stars, it retains a slight oscillating tendency towards whatever it has recently processed, thus giving it a very slight attunement towards you and your problems as well as you and your health. It retains this registry or oscillation with your difficulties for relatively short periods of time, but since it is working with you fairly continuously, it will build up these frequencies as a form of blockage or buildup in time, thus impairing the crystal's own ability to freely process information for itself. It will gradually lose its resiliency to respond to all things as it takes up more and more of your activity of despair, sickness, subliminal anger, fear or worry—whatever the case may be. Thus in time you end up with a crystal unable to adequately heal you, transmitting just slightly to you and others your own resonancies that have need of cleaning. The process of a crystal "fuzzing out" or getting slightly toxic accelerates as the crystal becomes more disoriented with what interferes with its ability to echo the stars.

The perfection of a crystal depends upon its owner. It is simply echoing to some degree what its owner wishes it to echo, and it is taking on the frequencies of those it is programmed to work with, be they everyone in its vicinity, one person or something in between. Thus it is the responsibility of the owner to clean it if it is to retain its proper functioning. This can be done in many ways, but we will mention just a few in order to give you the idea of how to do it for yourselves.

We will mention first the fool-proof methods from your level of perception, though from ours these all prove to have unnecessary limitations and difficulties, as you shall see. These are the methods of sea salt; salt water; blessing with the sun, moon or other natural cleanser; Tibetan bells; and pennyroyal.

Pennyroyal

Pennyroyal is the best as far as ease of use. Pegasus Products makes a flower essence from the pennyroyal plant that is for cleaning thoughtforms from the astral level, and the etheric somewhat, where they register after having been thought and held for some time. Pennyroyal is available in health food stores and other retail outlets in many cities, but if it is not available near you, you may order it directly from the address of the company.[1] The use of the essence is fairly simple. You may apply it directly to the crystal you wish to clean by putting several drops of it in a spray bottle with distilled water and spraying it directly on the crystal. This will clear 80-85% of the toxicity from the crystal immediately. Remember, the flower essence of pennyroyal, not the essential oil, has the ability we are describing. The essential oil will do no more than oil the crystal up a bit.

Sea Salt

Next, for more effective cleansing, may we suggest sea salt. It is a known cleanser of great abilities, and as we have learned from our friend Gurudas of Pegasus in the past, sea salt baths, combined with baking soda, are exceptional for cleansing a human being directly, as well as a crystal. (About a pound of each for the average use, in cycles of three to six baths over a month's time. Not for children!) Sea salt has been used traditionally to do this cleansing of people and crystals. It is the time-honored way, even if this way has been entirely lost to our modern age as a result of factors we have discussed in our channeled chapter about the past and crystals.

Sea salt works by dampening the effects or energies of all vibrations except the finest, thus allowing repolarization to occur naturally.

If you would try sea salt with crystals (not with people), use it dry at first, as this is most effective for really thorough cleansing. Take your crystal and place it in dry, aluminum-

---

[1] Flower essences are available from Pegasus Products, P.O. Box 2044, Boulder, CO 80306. Phone number 303-442-0139.

free sea salt overnight. This kind of salt is available from most health food stores. A crystal of over a half pound that is really blocked up might require a night or two extra. A large crystal of over two or three pounds might require a week or more for adequate cleaning. And really large crystals of fifteen pounds or more might require for the first cleansing you give them two or more weeks to really be cleaned completely. Once again, the nature spirits or your angelic guidance may be called upon to assist in this cleansing work, as the time for cleaning can be cut in half and be twice as effective if they are involved.

Activating Your Crystals, Part I

After you have cleansed a given crystal in dry sea salt, you may find that you notice it is a little flat in its energies. This is not always the case, but sometimes happens, depending upon many factors, including our involvement with your cleansing. We suggest that once you have cleansed a crystal in this or any other manner that you reactivate it and re-attune it to its purposes for you.

We ourselves give the advice to the author of this book that he reactivate a crystal by asking that we bless it for him in a sacred way for healing and blessing, in the will of God, for the highest and best good of all. This is an easy, total way to put the crystal's energies in order for you once more. If you do so effectively (and learning to do so may take you some time if you are not familiar with prayer), you will find you have no need for other charging of a crystal, no matter what technique you contemplate using for this activation or charging.

We have heard of many different techniques for charging crystals, from placing them in the Great Pyramid of Giza to activating their solar plexuses or heart chakras, one crystal at a time. But we say to you that the activation from your Souls is more than enough for any needs, and it is certainly more perfect than any activation you can give a crystal through a mechanical or contrived technique upon your earth.

To put this in a little more detail, you yourselves are unable to program a crystal beyond the mental level, as you function in the mental planes consciously while alive as a part of being human in this age. You will evolve—or have evolved in the past—into using capacities which are currently asleep, in order to function consciously in other dimensional levels than those you work with now. But for now, know that it is appropriate for you to work consciously with what you are currently involved with, the capacities of your intellect, for reasoning and understanding. In another time it will be more appropriate to work with other forgotten capacities, or with those capacities that await your future exploration.

Know, however, that your Soul possesses the capacities that are currently dormant in you. It has the ability to work with God directly to activate a crystal of light and love for you in any way that is in order for you at any time. It is this capacity we suggest calling upon when you activate your crystals. Your Soul will adjust frequency levels of astral and causal expression that you are asleep to. If you were to appreciate your Soul in this you would know that you are your Soul as you awaken to your Self in truth. Yet as your personality level alone, you will be unable to appreciate enough the fine tuning here involved with what you do with crystals for yourselves. We cannot teach you half of what you need to know to do this for yourselves at personality levels alone; and this is simply what you need to work for good of all—let alone the highest and best good available, which is what we bring to you through you as self at one with Soul. We suggest, therefore, that you activate your crystals at all levels by employing our services for your growth, through prayer to God or through asking your Higher Self, though we suggest prayer every time, for by so doing you will end up with us, your Souls, doing the work most of the time in service to our God, when it is appropriate for us to do so. And you will end up with your angels doing the work more often than not when it is the healing of others you wish to call upon. This is simply the order of things in your universe.

Salt Water

Another technique for cleaning crystals is an offshoot of the sea salt cleansing. Rather than using dry sea salt, use sea salt water, at about twice the salinity of sea water. (Two table-spoonfuls to a glass of distilled water will do nicely, if you want to play it safe.) This technique has the advantage of using less sea salt, but it has the disadvantage of taking a much longer time, if the cleansing required is really appreciable. It may take several weeks to do what a single night in dry sea salt would accomplish. Thus we recommend this method once you have used the dry sea salt method first, and you find your-self wanting a light cleansing technique that is more thorough than pennyroyal, though it takes a while longer to work. This salt water method can then be employed as maintenance or fine-tuning for your crystals; for example, as a cleansing that you use between clients, if you work with others, or that you use from time to time for yourselves as you feel the need. You can then use dry sea salt less often. And you can have your crystals adjusted to the needs of your clients more completely all the time.

Tibetan Bells

Another technique to clean crystals is using Tibetan tiensha bells, the pairs of round, disc-shaped, metal bells attached together by a single cord or chain that are used by Tibetan monks for their meditation work. These bells clean the etheric and astral somewhat as they sound in a continuous, clear tone at the etheric level especially. They do this for people as well as for crystals. The construction of these bells has much to do with their effectiveness, as they are made using seven occult metals, those fitting the seven chakras of man. Usually these were represented classically and in order by gold, silver, pure copper, brass, nickel, tin, and lead. Ideally, for toning pur-poses, nickel would be replaced by gold, gold by oraculum (an alloy of gold, silver, and copper in trace amounts), lead by platinum, if the truth be known, and all other elements would make up a tenth or less of the ingredients: thus oraculum, silver, pure copper, brass, gold, tin, and platinum. We are discussing vibrational resonancies here, not a necessity for manifesting these things physically. You may do so if you choose, but we deem these things unnecessary for most who would read this book. We will explain some of the reasons for our combinations of metals in our forthcoming book on the subtle bodies of man. For now let it suffice for you to know that there is great detail involved with this as well as all our decisions and actions in your behalf and on behalf of your world, that it be preserved in order for as long as is appropriate.

Within feasibility, a third arrangement that would produce the clearest tones to these bells, for purposes of clearing crystals and the human aura, would be possible if the gold totalled 90% by weight of the ingredients, the silver next most at 5%, the brass (copper & zinc) next at 3%, and all other ingredients the remaining 2%, namely nickel and iron at a ratio by weight of two to one.[2] This would not be feasible as a general rule, as these bells are not museum pieces, but something for everyone to use who is able to appreciate them. Nonetheless, in this time of recorded music and healing by recorded tapes, it might prove feasible for some person to commission a set of such bells for the purpose of allowing others their use through a recording. This is the ideal combination, we are told. Usually today when these bells are made they have brass, iron and lead, as well as small amounts of nickel, tin and a trace of gold or silver for good luck. They are still quite effective. Somewhat indirectly, we have given you a brief lesson in subtle level alchemy as it applies to bells and metals that relate to humanity.

To continue with the use of Tibetan bells for cleansing crystals and people, ring them over the head of the person or tip of the crystal and then move the ringing bells down the length of the body or the length of the crystal, stopping from time to time to reorder an especially blocked frequency level. This works with crystals, for, as we have written in a later chapter, crystals like humans have frequency levels that resolve into the patterns of vortex or energy centers we call chakras or wheels of energy. And these centers are seven in number for the solar system, the planet, the wheel of life, and the individual crystals, plants, animals and human beings upon your earth.

---

[2] The zinc is for hearing, as the toning can be enhanced by the direct application of a minor chakra activation as results from the use of zinc in these bells in trace amounts. The iron is also not a primary chakra resonancy, but rather for attuning and strengthening.

As you use your bells, you may notice things releasing and escaping the crystal almost physically. We noticed this ourselves as we used them on crystal after crystal the first time we discovered this process of cleansing using bells, in a cooperative effort with various friends.

The cleansing of crystals using Tibetan bells or other musical instruments is dependent in effectiveness upon the purity and appropriateness of the given individual instrument. Striking one bell with the other in a traditional way, we have found effectiveness with these bells to range from 40% to 80%, with a few even higher. It seems as if you must therefore carefully choose which bells you purchase, using only those that sound harmonious and pleasing to the ear, for these are the ones with the greatest ability to clean crystals and humans, appropriately enough.

We have to say that another way is possible. You may use any set of bells effectively (up to 90% effectiveness) if you use only one bell at a time for crystal cleaning. We separate bells that do not work well together, for such use. A wooden stick or mallet works the best for striking a single bell. Try it and

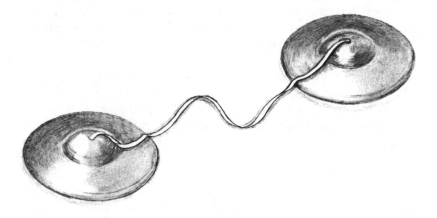

figure 13. Tibetan bells

see how nicely a single bell sounds each time you use it. Thus any set of bells becomes two instruments for crystal cleaning.

Again, if you wish greater effectiveness, you must occasionally turn to sea salt.

Prayer

The last of the ways we shall discuss in any detail for cleaning crystals is the way of prayer, for this has in the end been the method of greatest effectiveness for us and many others we have worked with. It is not a way available to all immediately, for it takes on the average several years to become effective at working with prayer from the heart, and not all people wish to do this at the present time. Prayer is the way of choice for us, but you yourself, reading this book, please choose whatever technique you feel comfortable with, including the ones we have listed, as it is you who must grow into things at a rate that is appropriate for you. Also, we recommend using the methods we have already described before using prayer, simply in order that you may be able to appreciate the exactness of what we are able to do for you, and that you have a foolproof method of approaching the responsibility of maintaining your crystals in perfect order. For us, the author and friends, this process of cleaning crystals was one of using every possible technique for several years before at last exploring the possibility of using prayer. And it was several years after this before the technique became accessible to our personality level completely. From our personality level, this was a process of discovery, with little knowledge but some encouragement from those around us. You need not go through quite so roundabout a path to learning the use of crystals for yourself.

Other Cleansing Techniques

There are other techniques besides using prayer and the methods we have already discussed in this chapter for both cleansing and activating crystals in appropriate ways. We have not used these so extensively, but others have. Traditional uses of crystals included many of these, which we feel work on many different levels, but not with quite the effectiveness of the methods discussed, unless they come from guidance of the Souls who use them for their good in physical expression. Examples of these are smudging the crystals with sage smoke, as in Native American traditions, cleansing them with running water in streams or in the ocean, burying them in clay or in the ground for a period of time, or allowing your thoughts to clear them (as, for example, with wishing them clear or imagining them clearing in silver light). Our own technique of prayer is of course also traditional: for example, holding them in your hands and blessing them with light and love, asking that we assist you as you do this.

Activating or Blessing Crystals, Part II

Activating crystals has also been a traditional practice, with as many ways of doing this as can be imagined. An example is holding your crystals up to the sun, or placing them in the sun propped upright in the fork of a stick to be clear of the ground, so that they be blessed by the sun's natural rays (as is the case indirectly with the crystal on the cover of our book). Moonlight can also be useful for this purpose. Exposure to moonlight for a few days before and after the full moon was a traditional way of grounding a crystal into a new home, if it had been recently moved a great distance. Another way to charge a crystal is with love, extended from your own being into the crystal with this in mind.

You can activate a crystal any number of ways, but as we said earlier, asking us to do so for you is the most effective and appropriate for your time, as you grow closer to union with your Soul and its purposes of blessing for you. We would give you an open-ended way of growing rather than limiting your growth to any particular way of activating your-self or your crystals that you might conceive of, using them for yourself and others. Thus we say to you, experiment fully with all the ways of cleansing and activating crystals for your-self, for to do so will give you invaluable insight into who you really are, what your crystals expect of you, and what we are for you as well. This is an unusual way of stating this for you, but we wish you to think of these things in unusual ways for yourself, that you may grow without any old, outmoded assumptions to limit who you are with us, and who you are with God—in your own eyes as well as ours, for we allow you your beliefs, that you may be as limited or free, whichever you choose from moment to moment. Thus we guide your lives in freedom.

Cleansing Using Prayer — A Summary & Discussion

Once again we return to the concept of clearing or cleansing your crystals using prayer. For now, it is enough to ask us to assist you in whatever way seems best to you. We will do so, knowing that some things are best left to you, and that all cleansing will often not be taken care of right away, when first you begin this process, in order that you experience these things for yourselves. We suggest therefore, once again, that you go through a learning period using the earlier cleansing methods, for if you do, more complete cleansing and blessing of your crystals can come through us at the outset of your efforts and still not interfere with the process of your learning to discern for yourselves, for example, just what a clear or blocked up crystal feels like, or what it feels like for a crystal to be only partially cleaned at any given level of expression; for each level will be different, and you will be able to discern or notice the differences with practice, and so grow to know much more about yourselves. You are like these crystals that you use and may grow from the exchange.

The last thing we would say to you about this is to trust us as we teach you about your crystals. Do not assume you have all the answers. Explore for yourselves. As you learn, without assumptions, so we will be able to settle down to assisting you in your mastery of self and Soul, instead of teaching the hard way by letting you make mistakes for yourselves and giving you insight afterwards as you ask us for it indirectly, searching your inner thoughts and feelings for the reasons for your mistakes or errors, or simply letting things remain imbalanced for many years without examining the reasons for your errors or beliefs.

The beliefs you carry are the reason for what transpires in your lives on earth. If you could but know how completely this is true, you would be examining yourselves with a mirror of truth each day, to discover what new lesson in growth would become available to you. For we would then create a situation of gradual and direct unfoldment, as you begin to explore and create your own immediate and responsive understanding for yourselves, rather than recreate over and over situations to present yourselves with lessons for your growth through the events or lack of them in your life on earth.

This, in a nutshell, is what we do for you when once you find your own approach to truth—or if you fail to do so for yourselves. And growth the easy way, through self-exploration, is the way that we prefer in time, for you, as you choose the easy or the hard way of life's experiences to teach you all you need to know of God, at the level of your selves (small "s") upon this world.

The prayer that most effectively covers your needs is one that allows us to work for you, as we never grow tired of saying for you. This means you must allow us to work for the highest and best good by asking for it; that you allow us to work for you under the will of God, as this is the one who coordinates your overall assignments in life and in this universe, as long as you are present in it (for something like two to four billion years in this universe, for almost all who read this book); and that you allow us to change what is being done for you from moment to moment, second to second, in the way that is best for your Soul and for your growth. This used to be done by referring to the perfection of the Christ, in Western European traditions ("may this be done in the Name of Christ," or something similar). At the present time we recommend instead referring to the perfection of the level of your Souls and God in Love, for this is the same thing, from our point of view, stated in a more universal way. This is indeed a way of stating the same thing, that you attain the perfection that God and your own Souls intended for you all along, that is held for you in the completion of God's own perfect thought for you, a blueprint for who you are in God.

Psychic Abilities

We go on now to another point as we conclude our discussion of cleaning and activating your crystals. We suggest that you not rely exclusively upon your own abilities to distinguish energies—or your psychic abilities—to tell you when your crystals are clear. This is only because the ability to perceive psychically is subject to error just as is physical sight with your eyes. And the areas that you see most clearly, either with your physical eyes or your so-called "psychic" ones (as from our point of view these psychic abilities are also physical), shall be subject to error in that they shall be the regions you are most able to see, the areas of your strengths, while the areas of your weaknesses or blindnesses—these shall be harder or impossible for you to see clearly; otherwise they would not be areas of weakness at all. Thus, you see, in all probability, the areas you have greatest need of "seeing" or noticing clearly— either in yourselves or in your crystals—these are the very areas you will not be able to notice or register correctly as you attune to yourselves or your crystals to see about their cleanliness on subtle levels.

We are not suggesting here that you abandon your own good sense about these things. In your heart you shall know whether your crystals are clear or not, by means of the still, small voice of your own Soul. This is the very thing we are suggesting here: that you get in touch with that inner guidance that truly knows what is what, and that through common sense and trial and error you learn to trust yourselves to be in balance with your Souls, rather than in charge of them or at the feet of them, so to speak. For all things are meant to be in perfect balance, the high and the low in the realm of octaves of expression. And this perfect balance is an integration with all of your being, none of it subordinated to any other for the time being; none of it left out or undervalued. In time your Souls shall direct your growth completely, as the lower becomes a perfect vehicle for the higher end of your expression. But for now, there must be a perfect balance learned between the two, that you may be whole and healthy, respecting all levels of your being in same.

We suggest you guide yourselves experimentally to notice whatever it is you notice about crystals, rather than forcing yourselves to grow psychically, for you will notice much by our direction, and yet you will not rely upon your psychic abilities if you would follow our suggestions from the level of your Soul. This is because you are currently developing connection and activation to aspects of yourselves in truth that are not subject to inspection by psychic faculties of any kind. It is not possible to know about your Soul through any faculty of observation or mentation, from a sense-free level or otherwise. You can only know your Soul as you encounter it in your innermost being in free will choosing for your own growth. We will guide you in this; you will not be able to "find" us, so to speak, with any effort on your part. We are fully capable of projecting or extending for you a leverage of energy at any subtle sense level, that you may get approximations for your growth of what it feels like to know the details that correspond to what we are. But directly you can only know us as yourselves, through your Souls at one with you, not through any sensation. This is why it has been very important for you to be sense-free at subtle levels. Few of you, except for karmic reasons, have been as able to discover for yourselves the attributes of many of the levels of subtle reality that in former times were experienced most clearly, and that are recorded in your scriptures. This is in order for you now. For you will discover in due course the energies at their source: your Souls as one with God. And only by direct contact with Soul shall all things become as once before, familiar through your Souls. You shall not find truth in any other way for you, though you search ten thousand years.

This brings us to the final point we wish to make regarding your crystals. If you depend upon yourselves to clear and activate them, do not expect them to become quite clear. If you depend upon your subtle or psychic faculties, or those of others, you will not discover accurately whether or not your crystals are in order for you. Only through your Souls, and for a transitional time, through the Souls of others who encourage you to accept our involvement in your lives—only in this way will you find your certainty on whether or not your crystals are clear and ready to work for you. And this is a pattern of order in your lives, with many ramifications for you in all ways and means you choose through life. As you accept your Souls in living, loving relationship with you at all levels of your expression and activity, so you will find the happiness, order and abundance that you seek to find, in self and Soul alike. You will find the order behind all appearances, in all things.

Chapter Twenty-one

The Great Design

We would like to guide you now in the ways we work with quartz crystals so that you can get from our end an approach to using crystals for yourselves, for it is with our cooperation that your work with crystals and with all things may progress smoothly, and it is with the cooperation of the Divine in general that your salvation may be accomplished. We will get right to work.

In the beginning of your time zone period, we set up your creation, as you might call it, with the use of quartz crystals. (This is Kryon and your own Soul speaking, by the way.) We used crystals to enliven your world from one end to the other, for it was with the programmings of Divine Light and Love frequencies that your life forms have evolved. The expression that we would give you for this is "programming," because it is in order for you to think of these things in familiar terms for yourselves and your life on earth; but "programming" is a poor substitute for what really happens, which is more of the order of light years of sound and color, and lovely dimensions of understanding and acknowledgements of God's conscious creation, than it is like something to do with robots or motors or programmed instruments that exist in boxes on your world.

We are not encased in boxes up here, by the way. We are beings of light and sound expression, and we exist in a vacuum of the stars, if you will, that is filled all the time with unimaginable splendor. We are speaking to you from a matrix of stars light years away from your world along the circuits of interstellar time travel. We could appear for you closer, but that would not be in order at the present time.

We would rather teach you from afar out of our own consciousness so to speak, coming to you from within your own thoughtforms and creations of light understanding within your own mind. For the consciousness you display at any given moment is more like light interaction from our point of view; it is a synapsing, if you will, but the form of the synapsing is in myriads of tiny light particles or photons that express exact, quantifiable units of informational energy. It is a process that precedes creation itself, for the synapses link stars and planets as well as brain functions inside your mind. And the networking we are describing for you is one that runs on the circuits of interstellar space as we have said, through networks of crystal banks that are designed to create stars and planets with the configurations of light they hold and amplify, if you will, but more that they direct in seemingly magnificent ways to destinations that are pre-programmed to interface with the creative thoughts or imaginings of the beings of the Elohim and Destiny itself.

We create through you, by the way, because you are the crystal seed atoms for this planet of yours. You are the determiners for your planet. In other words, you are literally living configurations of light and love that pattern in definite geometric formations to give the raying out of all that your solar system needs for its growth.

There are other beings who share in this work that we do, programming the beings of time and space with the seed destinies of stars and starships alike, but it is primarily our work to do this creation, and we do it through you. You are crystals of light and love, if you haven't figured this out by now, and you are an expression of God's love as well.

It would be in order for us to go into your purposes and design in the Light and Love of God another time. For now we would like to direct you to noticing the patterns of your growth that parallel those of quartz crystal. For by working with quartz crystal you will be able to rediscover who you are, so to speak, at the level of your crystal patterning and encoding, and your expression will be more complete as a result. We can activate you through the patternings of your mind to express your full potential just as a crystal may be programmed (that word again) to express the destiny of the stars for you to grow by yourself.

We would give you guidance on the mechanisms of this process, but first let us continue describing for you the process of your own creation in units of light perception, as destiny willed it from the stars long before my time with you began some thirty million years ago. For then it was that I incarnated on this planet for the first time through vehicles of light that you could call Merkabah units,[1] or vehicles of light and love, as we prefer to use in your own language. We are expressions of yourselves, and we travelled from distant stars to arrive at your place of creation, in a sequence of ordered steps programmed into creation by the creational hierarchies of which we are a part. We set up shop, so to speak, in interstellar space, with units of time sequencing so that we could coordinate the phases of creation into ordered units of expression that you call time and space (the two are synonymous for us, for one predetermines the other in mutual configurations that presuppose planned development on our part and the part of those responsible for laying the design or fabric of creation in Mother Universes of initial design and expression.

We gave you your first programs of development, for a subsequent forty lives or so on earth in cycles of incarnations for your Souls, at a distant time when crystals were first implanted here. I was not involved in this early, larger-picture planning, for I was engaged elsewhere, and my work has been to take up after such early work leaves off.

For I am in charge of the designs of interstitial matter, the layers of power grids and designs that lay the energy groundwork for your expressions on many levels. I am a creator of form at the level of maintaining matter and frequencies of resonancy with it—electro-magnetic force fields, if you will, though I find this term a bit crude for my purposes: I am giving you a picture of living possibilities, not the dead force fields of your physics, implanted in you by textbooks in school that have no concept of the living nature of the networks of creation I design.

---

[1] Merkabah vehicles are described in great detail in J.J. Hurtak's book, *The Book of Knowledge: The Keys of Enoch* (Los Gatos, Ca: The Academy of Future Science, 1977).

To continue, I design the coordinates of spatial phasing whereby matter and energy are directed along grid systems of crystalline structure to space itself. Across these lines of communication I relay the grid patterns of your own creation, your bodies, minds, emotions, layerings of intellect, if you will, layerings of reality structures you depend on but know as nothing of. Dreams you are aware of. Dimensions of your own being you are not as yet able to even dream of or imagine. We are beginning to make that possible for you, in communications such as this all over the world.

It is not in order yet that you be aware too fully of all the configurations and designs that maintain your vehicles of light expression. That would be too physical for you at this time. Your minds would be given over to the workings of the parts if you become aware of the parts in too much detail before you are awakened to the Whole. For now, let us tell you that you are here to work at the level of creative growth suitable to you and those you share earth with. You are not here to know the all in all as yet for some time. Give us a chance to do our work, will you? Have patience in what is for now and always until the end of time.

We would give you a sense through this channeling of the vast endeavor it has been to coordinate your growth for you up until this time. It has been an act of commitment and dedication for me to come here to be with you for the part I play in this "grand design," if you will—"conscious patterning," from my point of view. For all is done through consciousness, nothing mechanistically, absolutely nothing of any value at all.

We would give you a sense of the magnificence of creation without overwhelming you or causing you to become grandiloquent in expressing what we are giving you; for the frequencies of possibility are so vast that grandiloquence is often the result of interaction with us, as can be attested to by the scrolls of flowery writings that have in the past been the work of channelings such as this, when the channel has not been fully conscious of his or her own part in the process of communication.

We would give you a down-to-earth design as simply as possible, if we could. But instead we must content ourselves with the thought communicated through you that we are here to help you understand your growth, not ours. And your own Souls already understand what we do; it is important for you to become what we are in time, though not all at once. Two million years of your expression would be more than sufficient for this transition that is approaching were it not for the fact that you are expressions of 40 to 100 years duration and have needs that are bright and good within your own framework. Our framework is that of the stars, dimension beyond dimension. Yours is seemingly of the earth. That will change in time. For now, integrate the vision we give you from the point of view of your Souls, for that is what we are for you, and know that we are at peace with you and hope you will be at peace with all you encounter as tools for your growth.

The last thing we would say to you is to design your meditations with quartz crystal with this in mind, that what you are doing is relating to the designs of both the stars and yourselves, from the point of view of the Designer himself or herself (for gender does not matter in this). Know that the two are one: the Designer and the Designed are Living Light of Love's expression in the outer world of form and space; and know that you are as God when you awaken to your Self, and the design of God is as the design of Self in humanity, both individually and as a group.

You are not to be lost in the group, by the way. It has been planned from the beginning that each of you would express a Universe of possibility for the Whole, independent and still as part of it, in balance; and that you would retain this development through all time, so to speak, and beyond time as well.

For your Designer, is he not pleased with his work? And is this not the work of Creation itself, designed in the image of God, forever at one with all the Designer can give to you, out of His loving heart of hearts? You are His Child in whom He is well pleased. And the gift to the Mother of all that He offers through you and to you is the Life of all Destiny forever, as one perfect expression of trusting and hoping as you choose to express it forever in God.

Look at it like this: is not a mother most pleased when the father teaches her children to be as the parents, forever free and adult and growing, in strength and courage and love, to be more of all these than even the parents themselves? Is this not a gift of the father to the mother indeed? So is this gift to you, through you to all.

Chapter Twenty-two

What Crystals Are For You:

How They Work and Why

We would expand upon our work with you by considering the nature of your relationship with crystals. What are crystals? Why are they useful to us? Aren't they simply part of the mineral kingdom?

Crystals work for several reasons. They are like us. They are wiser than us in some ways. This is the heart of it.

In general, things in this world are able to help us or heal us in as much as they balance who we are, in as much as they are able to teach us something. This is true with common medicines as well as so-called spiritual lessons of life or everyday advice from a friend or teacher. Common medicines work by giving us suggestions at subliminal levels that are helpful or harmful, as the case may be, to who and what we are. They cannot work efficiently if they are too dissimilar to us. They are like us, and thus they treat us with their own nature. We are confusing you by bringing in medicines as well as crystals perhaps, but the point is essential, that all things outside ourselves influence us by direct interaction with who or what we are. All things are of God, including the creatures of this earth, the sun, moon and stars. And all of these things affect you and me according to what we need them to do for us at any given moment. If we will allow them to work for us, they will. If we refuse them, they allow us to be who we are without interference.

In general this is so. But in specific instances, this will no longer be the case. When we give permission for our energy field to be interfered with, we are letting an influence affect us that is dissimilar to our own. Thus it is possible for us to be affected for good and ill in our lives. Thus it is possible for medicines to work us ill, for we have taken them without reference to how they are like us at all, with specific beliefs regarding them that are unrealistic and dreamy from the point of view of reality. Thus we learn and grow.

In the case of crystals, on the other hand, we are accepting something in our lives that is wholly like us all. It is proper to affect crystals for good or bad by being around them to learn who they are, for they are like ourselves at another level of development, both years behind and years ahead of where we are now. This is the secret of the mineral kingdom, you know, and of the material plane as well. It is fashioned in the image of God at many levels, with a wisdom that is not of this earth, so to speak, not within our normal sense of things. It is wisdom-filled, and at the present time, it is filled with love again and again by those who have fashioned it and are still maintaining it. For it is the work of hierarchies of divinity that fashion in the one true sense, under the will of their Creator God, and Humanity: all three as one. For mankind has shared in this creation. And God is a Soul, like you or me, at a level of evolution vastly older than yours or mine, if you will, yet still within the youth of universes much older than our own. And God is love as well.

We would let you know these things are true, yet the meaning of what you are hearing in this book is hard for us to convey to you without much effort on your part. We are glad you work to know yourselves. We will make the process most fun for you if you will allow us to do so, for we work with you throughout your day as well as night, and we are comforted that you work to know us as your Souls. For that is who we are.

This must do for now. We try to tell you all we can about your Souls and self, but be patient with us as well, for we cannot tell you all there is to tell about ourselves/yourselves. It is enough to give you indications, as it were, with regard to your natures/our natures at this time. And crystals are of your natures/our natures, in ways you can suspect but little understand until you go upon an adventure of self-discovery that is advocated by this book, whether or not you use any one particular tool such as quartz or any other crystal. We give you this to know you too are one with God. For so we have found for ourselves, at the levels of Soul that are bringing you these teachings. And so it shall be for you as well.

Crystals, then, are like you.

They work because they are like us all, as expressions of what we are in our perfection. They are electro-magnetic fields of light and energy, phases of light that we recognize as our "real" world. Our modern physics tells us this, but so do our own experiential abilities if we trust them and use them.

Crystals are as living light and love. So are we.

Like our own "bodies," crystals are images of the orderly progressions of the octaves of our existence, through the mansion worlds of our Father in Heaven, in synchronicity with the Divine fields of radiance that create our time and space, in conjunction with the Mother universal grid systems.[1]

The universe is not what it appears to be, even to the minds of the most imaginative upon your earth plane. It is multi-dimensional, interactional, and regionally differentiated in ways that are both precise and conceptually beautiful. As are we all.

Crystals are like this universe, as are all who live within her.

They are also like the individuals within this universe, you and me, who share the form of our Creator as a common heritage, a common blueprint of creation. The best we can do is to tell you that we are all like crystals that you see in perfect symmetry with one another. And we are all like love as well, once we choose to be. The rest is window dressing.

In many respects, you and I have the same electro-magnetic energy fields as do crystals.

Our Souls, at many levels, are orchestrating our growth in life on earth. Our "bodies," at many levels, are coordinated and placed in proper order by crystalline structures inside ourselves that are mirrors of what we are. The same is true for crystals of living light and love on many levels, so-called subtle levels of existence and beyond.

---

[1] J.J. Hurtak, *The Book of Knowledge: The Keys of Enoch* (Los Gatos, Ca: The Academy for Future Science, 1977). Much of this book is useful to this point.

It is important to realize that there are parallels among the coordinated kingdoms of nature that are especially striking between the mineral kingdom of man, in man, and the kingdom of crystal interaction with all things in nature. This last phase of our interaction, that of interaction with nature, is best described as full of life and love. It is not a lifeless "mineral kingdom," you see: it is more as well. It is living hand of God. It is interaction with Soul at every level. So your crystals reflect the whole as much as you do. So your lives are intertwined with that of God together. So we say you are one with crystals in their being. Learn from this, that you are guided now to see yourself reflected there for Soul as well as self.

Inside us all, the form of mineral structures lives alive and flowing. The form of Soul is mirrored here for you to see your truth. Your Soul is giving you the blessing of your life to grow as one with everything. And crystals aid this growing. They are forms of life divine in all in purest, truest sense. They are forms of Soul that guide all things. Inside of you/ outside of you, together, hear their truth. Crystalline structures are the moving ribbons of light encoded with our futures. They are expressive of our directions in that they program our growth for all time. This is true on many levels, that crystalline structures are as living light and love to guide all men and women to their truth in form as well as Soul unlimited in expression.

Thus we say to you that crystals there inside yourselves as divine form are models for your growth.

They are like you in their forms of light on earth.

They have chakra systems, the same as you do. They have inner octaves of light, color and sound, seven chakras in all, possibilities for more.

Crystals have feelings of a sort. They certainly have the structures to make feelings possible, in much greater variety and expressiveness, if you will, than most of humankind is capable of at the present time. For their expression of feeling is in perfection, full potential realized, as it were; or rather, nothing interfered with, as it is in people. For crystals cannot lose a mate or have a traumatic happening confuse them with clouds of astral emotion and fury. They faithfully mirror the emotions of their universe in completion. And they have the structures to do this in perfected astral bodies.

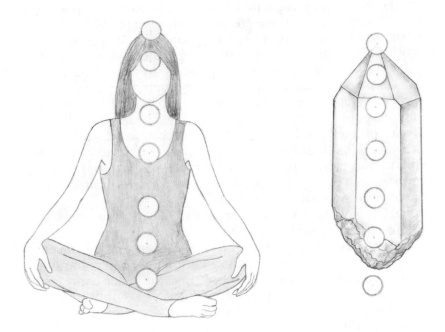

figure 14 a. & b. chakras in humans and crystals

Crystals have etheric or energy bodies too, you will find if you examine them carefully. At these levels, they have electro-magnetic frequencies organized in octaves of expression similar to our own.

Crystals use their electro-magnetic form to great effect, more effectively than most of humanity. For crystals are never tired; they do not exhaust themselves between waking and sleeping. They cannot overwork. Their form lends itself to waiting and watching the affairs of others who have greater range for operation than do they. The crystals you see before you when you purchase a couple of them or see them somewhere before your eyes, are noticing you as well. They are able to open up to your energy field all the time in consciousness. They are responding to you in ways that are highly mobile, as we discovered when we did the exercise in an earlier chapter of resting inside a cloud and then experiencing the way a cloud might react to outside stimulus, free from the limitations of localized and fairly restricted capacities you describe as senses, possibly five of them, though there are more—twelve possible for you in time and space, sets of twelve beyond that for you in other worlds and expressions. Crystals expand on who you are as you limit yourself in the following ways: to your senses, your intellect, your awareness tunnelled through one perception or direction, as it were, your awareness confined by your assumptions of limitation all the time. The crystals are not five-sense confined at all. They are fully mobile in all worlds. So are you. The limitation you experience is a result of choice, not imposed by others. It is something that is for your growth, in free will, as you seem to be for now limited—and ignorant of what and who you are.

This is not the case with crystals. Their form does not confuse them as yours does you.

For you have chosen a form that conceals as much as reveals your nature. And you look upon your nature when you look inside yourself, or when you look into the outer expression that appears to you in physical form as a crystal of the mineral kingdom, especially the crystal of quartz, for this is balance and neutrality for you, and it is more—image of yourself in God, alive throughout the world.

In the consciousness of your own Soul, you will find the truth of what we say.

Chapter Twenty-three

Activating the self & Soul:

Healing & Quartz Crystals

The core of a Soul's work is in relating to others in God's creation. Yet the sources of the light of God are within us all, the self and Soul as one. We suggest the following chapter is in many ways the core of this book. For relationship is the need of these times; it is the core of your understanding and your evolution in same. We would give you suggestions for healing in relational ways that intersect with uses of crystals. But first we would lay the groundwork for you of these patterns of your growth.

"Healing" is a carefully chosen word here. It is the source of your presence here, for you are chosen to be here for your appreciation of healing at its source, in the activations of your heart in love. And you are given a brain to use to discern the patterns of relationship that lead to wholeness of expression in all beings, consciously awake to their own growth in love again, once again in love, for all upon your planet.

Relationship is as a key to growth in our physical expression. It has been said that we can see our progress on many levels by seeing our reflection in others we interact with in day to day situations. I am reminded of the Zen master who visited a junior high school and found to his chagrin that his flexibility and liveliness were wanting, found this only as he interacted with the living needs of those somewhat sceptical children. For as he watched them react to him with confusion and with humor, he found himself most afraid, too stiff and rigid

to accept their criticism at face value, too loving to simply reject it and turn to other things. And so he saw his growth fully
mirrored in those children who scoffed at him in his humili-
ation of soul—for so it was experienced by him, even for a
day or two thereafter.

This kind of experience is available to us all daily, as we face
ourselves as seen through the eyes of others. So it shall be as
you heal yourself and others through crystals, and through
other means as well: you will be mirrored in your ability to
heal the sick and infirm, and you will discover you are healed
as you work on those as sick and as well as you are, for they
shall be guided to you who are able to heal you as well as you
heal them, by the touch of your heart and theirs. They shall
heal you as you heal them, for so it is written in the book of
life, if you will. So it is written as the guiding act of this
world of human beings growing in God as love.

Turn now to your work with crystals. Have you not grown
in learning to relate to these small objects as yourself? If not,
you will as you begin this work. So it shall be as you begin to
trust yourself to share more fully with others. For as you
heal, so shall you be healed. As you work with crystals, you
will experience this in fullness.

Exercise One: The Causal Sphere

Let us turn to the first exercise we will give you with healing
and crystals. Accept yourself as the patient. Allow us to treat
you, if you will, but rather, allow us to treat you as ourselves,
for we would only give you that which you already are in us
as well as in your own essence; for the two are one, and we
are as one with you on your Soul levels of expression, and on
other levels as well: all levels, in fact. All are one in God.

We ask you to set up a pattern of twelve crystals around a
treatment table, or on the floor. Or around your bed, if you
have not table for working with others. Let yourself be guided
by our words.

Once you have lain within the circle of crystals, focus on the
one at your head, representing your Soul in its highest aspect,
that of Father/Mother God. Let this crystal guide you in the
following experience. First, see yourself as a ball of light, full

of love and light, if you will, though your very existence is this ball of white love spiralling about its core and center, in three dimensional rainbows of white light and love. For as you allow the love to permeate the light, so it shall.

This ball of white light is your very being, and we would guide you to know your being in truth. See yourself as this ball you are visualizing. Let it wash over you in love and blessing, as it pours itself all around you and in you as well. For you are experiencing your Soul in this, your aspect of divinity that is more subtle that the physical body, yet not so subtle as to experience itself without our help. Let this ball become you in time, over the next few months. It is not to be used in place of your physical body; it is only to allow us to give you plenty of space for growth that we say you may become this energy over the coming months. Stay grounded in all your levels of expression, physical and otherwise, at the same time.

Now to proceed. Let the white ball become you as you imagine yourself to be whole in God. This will aid you to become identified with a form of yourself that is not at this time familiar to you, yet a form of yourself equally valid to us. We give you this exercise to grow within your circle of light, and we give you this practice within a circle of twelve crystals in order that they might assist you in reaching the optimal or maximal development of this sphere of energies and attention within the shortest possible time; shortest in the sense of your highest and best good to be sure, yet shortest in terms of the highest and best good of all as well, for these times are awakening times, and time itself is short for your growth to influence the growth of the world around you in fullness. We give you a timetable for growth in this: that two years from the time you begin this practice, if you do it regularly with good intention and balance of expressions on all levels, you will know your soul (small "s") to be a part of you in truth. And you will have opportunities to see your soul reflected in Soul itself, above and beyond your expressions of limitation and dimension on the earth plane, awake or in states of dreaming. For in both states, awake and dreaming, you are limited to soul and body—not in the Body of your own truth, but in the body of illusion and light you weave for the sake of your growth in time and space dimensions both known and unknown by you as yet. We give you encouragement to grow in the framework of your own truth in this: experience yourself as a child of God, and of humanity, as you see fit to grow. For we love you in any choice you take, and we give you freedom to face many obstacles in many different ways.

The circle of twelve crystals is a key in this process we are giving you. For you should know you are activated around the perfection that crystals give you, and the set of twelve is the dynamic for your growth that is of the highest order of possibility while you are on earth in this age. (In future ages it will be different, for the twelve is but the first of a series of twelve, that each awaken in turn for you to experience; the one appears as you appreciate and become the one before, so to speak: as you become yourself at ever increasing levels of clarity and comprehension, becoming what you truly are in Divine Creation.

The Prince of Peace

The next exercise we would give you on healing yourself— for this is the first step we encompass for you as you work on healing this planet through your own growth, the only way it can truly be done—is for you to sit in a circle of twelve and imagine yourself the Prince of Peace himself/herself (for the masculinity of this term is unnecessary). As you do this, the crystals will support you in this as they are able. Ask us to program them for you to avail yourself of their help in the exact ways that are best for you at this time. Then, as you change, so will they for you.

The reason for this second exercise is to complete the cycle we have given you in this chapter. As you experience your self and soul (small "s") with the first exercise, thus appreciating what you truly are—both physical and two-armed on the one hand, and spherical in energy forms on the other—so you will be able to appreciate your Soul. And the second exercise we have given you is to allow you to focus directly on who you really are. For you are the Prince of Peace, come to rescue the Princess, if you will, but rather, to be the Prince and Princess in one form of Light and Love, Whole Light and Love as they are appropriate for you now. For you must know that even this shall change, and the divine forms of your expression will grow in time as well as you yourself in physical expression will grow and slowly die to life on earth, appreciating it for what it is, a blessing to your growth in love, a blessing to your life as meaningful in God.

We shall give you more, but that is enough for now. Next we will take up your work with others.

Healing and Quartz Crystals: Cleansing the Aura

Now that we have worked with you on balancing your own energies, we will go on to your healing work with others, as you heal yourself through attunement to self and Soul, and then become capable to work with others for mutual healing and blessing. The process of healing is a dynamic process. As you work on yourself, you become capable of further work with those who come to you to be healed themselves. Such is the path of mutual growth we recommend.

The next thing we would take up with you is the process of cleaning the aura or energy field of another person. This is something that is easier to demonstrate than to practice from a book, but if you bear with us we hope you will get enough of an idea to proceed. You will be in perfect protection and balance with what you do in any event, because, as we have suggested earlier, you will have set the conditions for your growth and Soul to be evolved in perfection, and you will have extended these conditions to those you work with. We might suggest you include another rather clever solution to inexperience with energy work in the following way: consider what you do as the first half of a greater process of mutual cooperation with the nature spirits, with the Souls of those you work on as well as your own, with the angelic kingdom you may have called in if you called upon God in any form to activate your work for you, and with yourself and your client as well, at personality levels and conscious levels you can access for yourself at this time. As you work, be open for these cooperating kingdoms to complete and set in order what you do with your hands and attention. Let them work along with you as an attitude for your mutual growth and acceptance of levels you are as yet not fully conscious of. As you work in the coming years, the conscious connections between yourself and Soul, between yourself and invisible kingdoms of light and Soul, will become more and more apparent for you. And we recommend this means as a vital element in the overall healing of the planet. It is not so necessary that you do all the things that can be done in these directions. It is only necessary that you choose what you are drawn to at this time, for the world to be a safer, better place for all. Be at peace in what you do for all, for it is blessed, as it is from us that you do this. Peace be with you.

The process of cleansing a person's aura is relatively simple. You need only pass your hands over a person with this intention in mind, that you will be cleaning all the negativity and residual echoes of incompatibility from their energy field, and it will happen as you intend. You can amplify this process to some extent, especially in the ranges of energy you are aware of, by using a quartz crystal in each hand. You will find that the noticeable results you get will encourage a person to keep his or her own energy field more purified in the future, and you will encourage yourself in the same direction.

You should begin this process by setting conditions, as we have suggested earlier in this chapter. Once you are clear as to your intent, proceed by asking the person if it is all right with them that you work on them. You may already have obtained such permission, perhaps merely by having a person come to you as a client. This will be sufficient. It is only important that the person allow you to work, with at least some understanding of your intentions.

Your work may begin with a general blessing spoken aloud, or a simple, quiet or silent prayer. This will set the mood for your work and allow the person you are working on to share in the activity of setting conditions along with you, with more chance of ultimate success thereby created. Once conditions are set for both of you in this or a similar way, you may proceed as follows:

First ask the person to let you touch their crown chakra, at the top of their head, in order to open the seal on their aura for you to work on them. This is accomplished in the following manner. Place a hand on the brow, over the forehead at its middle point; then place a second hand over the crown midway between the hairline and the whirl of hair at the back of the crown, where most people have a spiral or origin point in the way the hair naturally flows. As you allow yourself to feel the energies of the person through your hands, feel them releasing their hold on the seal of their aura by asking that the seal be released, silently to yourself, if you prefer, and then asking that the flow from the crown out through the brow to your hand be amplified so that you can feel it. This will create a current experienced as warmth or a tingling sensation in the center of your palm. Once you feel this energy, or sense that it is flowing, you are ready to proceed with the treatment.[1]

Begin by sealing your work with whole white light and love so that nothing can enter the person's energy field that is not for their highest and best good, including your own thoughts and energies. Now move your hands across your subject's energy field by circulating the energies in steady, rhythmic flowing motions of a circular or spherical nature. Again, this is the kind of thing that is easy to demonstrate, hard to describe. It is somewhat like the processes of energy work in Tai Chi or in Aikido, or like the rhythmic motions of a good massage, though the motions are being made in slow motion above the body about three to six inches, rather than on its surface directly.

We suggest that you make your motions somewhat circular because of the nature of the flows of the energy bodies of human beings. You could find indications of this in books on the subject. But for now let us say that the spherical forms of the subtle anatomy of man are more than you can imagine in loveliness, and they flow in constant motion throughout the body physical, in currents of expression that are somewhat like geometric drawings of ellipses and lemniscates, repeated in fine lines of force flow throughout. We suggest you draw this for yourself in the air at some point, just making swirls and figure eights in small, circular motions, almost the way a small child would start to scribble. We suggest this because by making the lines of movement yourself, you will find an imaginative connection with what we are saying to you.

These forms flow about the body in ceaselessly flowing motion, like the swirls upon a gently flowing river.

---

[1] We learned this way of opening the aura from Rev. Dr. Frank Alper in one of his seminars for growth. We have found there are many ways to open the aura once you have permission to work. It is your intention and the intention of those on whom you work that are alignment here.

The patterns that result are somewhat like the spots of a leopard. And they are like the force flows throughout the etheric
and astral bodies as well; that is how the leopard got its spots,
after all, by attuning in its formative states to the pools and
flows of the etheric body and by duplicating or emphasizing
them in its own, unique way.

The next thing we will say to you about this process of
cleansing the aura is that you are being guided to do this by
those who love you. Relax. Enjoy the process. It is somewhat like a good, graceful dance. Just relax. For you need
not put on airs or overdo it at all. You are involved in a very
simple process that will work because you have Divine help
working with you. The complexity is in their hands (your
angelic help), because they are able to appreciate and see exactly what is being done, whereas you are only learning to discern the incredible delicacy that is involved. You are only
beginning a process that they are finishing for you over time,
perhaps not being completed until hours after the person you
are treating has left your table or floor. You have set conditions that all shall be done in completion, as we have suggested to you earlier, and so it shall be done as you intended, for
what you intend in this is in order with the Will of the Divine
in all, in that it is for your highest and best good that you
should aid in the growth of the Soul of all who come to you,
as they connect with who they are in truth.
We direct you further to notice what is happening as you do
this process of cleansing. You will note areas of relative
warmth and coolness, areas of tingling and of motion (or lack
of it), areas of relative "thickness" or resistance. Notice these
things and at an appropriate moment in the work ask the person to give you feedback as to what they think is going on in
this or that particular area. Such feedback helps both of you.
You might also ask them to give you feedback on anything
they are feeling if it seems of interest or importance, as this
will further involve them in the process. Experiment with
such communication. At times you will want them to rest and
relax instead of noticing exactly what you are doing. And at
times you will want feedback and participation. Use your own
discretion in this as well as all you do, for you are learning to
be as God, and to guide your work in love. We suggest further that you note the things you feel for further analysis at a

later date, if this is appropriate.   Keeping records of your
work with people is a good way to obtain consistency over
time with all you do, both in remembering what you have done
with clients, and what you have done about certain situations
for yourself, so that you will not forget the lessons that we
teach you in the moments of your work.

In time you will simply know what is going on with a person
as you work with them, for you will be open to the intuition of
your Soul. For now be at peace with what you do and grow
in awareness as best you may. You will find such growth
very rapid if you stick with it. We would say also that you are
allowing yourself to grow more sensitive all the time as you
work on people, for you are letting yourself experience their
reality directly, and then giving and getting feedback from
them on a continual basis. This is in order for you as well, for
you will find you are growing in many ways you do not now
suspect as you do this. And you are growing in ability to
understand and love.

The aura of a human being is a complex thing. It is not possible within the framework of this book to get very detailed
about all you will discover about this human aura as you work
with people. Another book will have to do this. In the meanwhile, simply go by your inner impulses as you move your
hands in circular motions or in strokes down the person's
body at about two to six inches above the physical expression.
This flowing motion down the body, starting from the shoulders and proceeding to the feet before returning to get the area
around the head, is appropriate for this work; for it parallels
the natural direction of a person's energy meridians as they roll
in ripples of pulsing light and heat, as we see it, down the
length of the physical and etheric vehicles of expression.
. We would say to you that the details of this are in standard
texts, but they are not. They are not understood in your time,
unless one is a clairvoyant or in conscious communication
with the Soul to ask the details for oneself. This is the case
with us, so we will tell you that the current or flow of etheric
energies in the body exists on several levels, one of which is
the nadis, or light sparkles that dance through the aura and
form of the physical body like pin-points of light, or like stars
in the night in a galaxy or nebula, in elliptical patterning if you
will, but more in the form of the actual physical body itself,

the silver cocoon of light that moves us through the world in one piece, so to speak, that maintains the integrity of the physical expression. The second layer, closer to the physical than the nadis, is the meridian level, that level which responds to acupuncture, if you will, but to us, that level which carries the currents of the body physical to the various organs in harmony and balance. This level is connected to the actual physical plane through something like the medium of heat, in the following manner: "heat" affects the flows upwards; meridian interaction stimulates the generation of subtle heat. This in turn becomes activated glow of well-being in the body physical.

The medium of light is another channel to the physical through the meridian system, if you will—or rather through the flows of light divine as we would call them in you. Such light has been rarefied to give exact frequencies of expression, then densified, so to speak, in order to flow through channeling that can be patterned on the human body. This channeling is the balance between the nerves and blood in the physical body, as it is midway in expression between the pulsing blood and the nerve impulses that mirror your reality for you in the nervous system of the spinal column and the brain. We give you this detail so that you will be encouraged to explore for yourself as we have done the subtle anatomy of the physical and subtle bodies of light in which we live for a time on earth. These bodies have definite patterns that reward the searcher and give coherence to the study of earthly maladies and difficulties as they manifest in disease and illness for mankind at this time. You will do well to explore these things for yourself, for you will be enriched in the process. Biokinesiology[2] and other forms of affirmative understanding of the body physical as an expression of the psyche of humanity are in order at this time, for you to discover that all is light and love, all in harmony with the stars; and all is in order for your growth

---

[2] Biokinesiology is the name of a process related to applied kinesiology, Touch for Health and other diagnostic practices using the muscular system of the physical body to serve as "witness" or guidance on what is amiss and what is recuperative for the physical expression and hence other levels of the reality of humanity. See Selected Bibliography for further information.

as well as for your process of discovery of self and Soul as one vehicle in God.

We give you bits of understanding about the subtle bodies here, but we would refer you to other works—if you feel so inclined—to seek confirmation and clarification of what you discover for yourself. For you are capable of discovering all there is to know within yourself, yet the clarification—and most of all, the confirmation—are important for your growth and integration with the work of others in your time, as well as with the knowledge of your Soul. We give you suggested reading in our bibliography for your future growth and discovery with methods paralleling and complementing work you do with crystals.

Levels of Intention

The next thing to take up is the working of orders of intention as you cleanse the body physical with your crystals. (The body physical to us includes the subtle levels of the nadis and meridians, as well as the first level of chakras on an etheric level.)

The intentions you have as you work are crucial to what you will accomplish. Know that the possibilities are endless. As you grow in trust and expression of light, you will notice that you are as living light yourself. You will feel your ability to know what intentions are appropriate for what people, and that all intentions are not the same; the results of what you do will vary according to the directives you give your Soul and your guides, the extent to which you notice and acknowledge the suggestions they can give to you should you ask them for their advice as well as love. The way you interpret your work, from a limited or unlimited perspective of orientation, this too shall make a difference in what you are able to accomplish with yourself and with others. We could give you examples of these differing possibilities from all the paths of growth of your world, but we will not do so. You must discern for yourself which paths are right for you, and which conditions to set for your growth in either limited or unlimited fashion, as you are moved to do so. And as you choose, so you limit or release to us the work you do for God as well as for your own personal growth patterns.

You are working on other people so that you will grow as much as they. You will find that the intention, for example, of working only on the energy meridians will limit you with respect to work we might wish to do on the meridians as we integrate such work with other levels of the person's expression. We will say to you that what you can understand about yourself and your organization in the physical and not-so-physical realms will stand you in good stead with releasing the expressions of our intention, to allow us to work with you and with your clients or patients as the case may be. Let us work with you by your asking that whatever you do be in completion from the levels of your Soul and beyond in God's Creation, according to the Will of All. Let this be your motto in your work, that you will leave all things open to completion in God for your growth and your Soul, and that of your clients as well. For in so doing you will give us unlimited reign to guide you for the best you are capable of at any given moment. And we will transcend what you understand and do in every moment of your efforts. So it is possible for all things to be healed and made whole in God. For with permission to work, we are the miracle you express through your being and your efforts to grow in truth. We are your miracle of self and Soul. And we give you all that God has to offer, which is everything, in its proper place and time.

We ask you to note the sort of thing we are saying. It is vital that you absorb this in your work, for without it, you can do nothing in its proper place. The complexity of what you are trying to accomplish when you set out to heal is beyond your grasp, yet it is within easy reach for your Soul in truth, if once you have acted in accordance with your destiny and allowed us to work through you. If you limit yourself, for example, to warrior behavior and courageously face the unknown with an even hand and steady mind, you will only teach yourself the limits of what you do with every passing phase you go through. And you will know each limitation only in the distant future as you release all limitation and come to know your Soul in truth. For only then will the release be understood, and the limitations comprehended by their release. Again, if you pride yourself on the abilities you possess to see psychically, or physically for that matter, and follow your own dictates with these gifts, you will come to a dead end in time, where we shall teach you to know you are limited as long as you rely in warrior fashion upon your limited self; and you are unlimited as long as you call on the help of your Soul and God. For is it not written for you in all your scriptures, that the first shall be last and the last shall be first? And is it not known that the proud shall be humbled and the humble be made to shine before God? So it is written that you shall come to know your true gifts as you release them to be completed in God, allowing us to overcome and release the limitations you can only place on yourself by assuming you know enough or are smart enough to trust the assumptions you have about self and Soul without letting us participate completely in your growth.

This is not to imply that you should pack up your bags and go home, from the level of your personalities. There is a delicate balance involved here. Any gifts you possess are important for you to have acquired and are important to maintain. You are in balance with your Soul, not to be lost in it, but rather balanced on all levels equally, for all levels are of equal value and insight to God. You cannot sacrifice yourself to your Soul or God and expect to make progress in your path. For you are happily responsible for all your choices at every level of expression, and at the physical level it is the personality that is in charge directly. We ask only that you allow us to work through you in balance of expression, high with low (not better with worse, but only one level to another in equality and balance). As you allow us to work with you in fullness, so the gifts you possess will be realized in their proper perspective, and you will not make mistakes of judgement and direction because you see only incompletely from any one level of expression.

The true warrior is the one who trusts God to grow him or her in every moment; who gives that active trust to God; who asks that all shall be in order; who sets the conditions for his or her life on earth. Thus is the warrior spirit in humankind fulfilled, not in the independent action of the self alone, but in the independent action of the self with God in Soul of all: thus is all fulfilled in peace.

Cleansing the Aura, Continued

The conclusion of your work with the aura is at hand, for we would not over-prepare you to do this, but would rather leave it to you to explore for yourself. Massage the aura by means of cycles of treatment, if you possibly can. By this we mean approach the same person anew every few weeks at best, in order to recycle the efforts and effects you are able to produce. In this you produce a rhythm of growth for your client, as old things are released allowing new things to take their place. As you release by replacing old things in the aura with new light of attunement to self and Soul, you will allow the person to approach themselves with a new beginning every time you allow them under your hands and crystals. Thus you speed their growth in an orderly manner, an approach we would recommend for all who come to you. Simple as it may appear to be on the surface of things, it is most profound in its applications for growth.

The last thing we would point out to you before we conclude this section is that the ways of cleansing the aura are as varied as you can imagine, for truly, your imagination is the key that unlocks a pattern of intentions for where we go with what you are doing, where you go as well. If you can think of it, it is possible: so you shall learn in time.

To conclude your aura work, reseal the chakras you have opened at the crown, by reversing the flow of energies to allow the flow to proceed from the crown to the brow and back again to the crown, as you hold one hand over the crown, the other over the brow. Let yourself hold the intention that you be assisted by the person's Soul you are working on to complete the session with closing the chakras and the aura to hold the energies that are in order for the person at the present time, thus letting in a flow of love and warmth that suits the particular need at that moment in time. Thus you replace the old energies with new energies and you are completed in your efforts of growth for the Soul you intend to help. Replacing what has been released or cleansed away with what is for the highest and best good is always a good idea, so that a vacuum in the person's energies does not result in an inflowing of ill-intended or random stuff.

So we release you to enjoying this process for yourself. You have only to seal the aura and walk away, having asked that completion be there for each person from the level of their Souls and knowing that because you have asked that the person be completed in the way that is proper at the present time, the completion will be there, from the level of your Soul and your God, if you have asked God to assist you. As we have said, this latter request actually brings in God's angels, for as you ask him/her for assistance, so you activate the networks of God's love in action, the Messenger Service, if you will, though we prefer the term "Salvation Corps" ourselves, if the truth be known: God's hierarchies of angelic, whole-light beings known familiarly as angels and archangels, archai, and so on. We give you this latter information to complete the possibilities that are available for you to choose from. You need never call on anything but your own Soul, if you choose, for things to be in completion—as long as you have placed things in the Will of the Creator of the Universe you inhabit for the moment. You will notice that we state this in a way that makes things relative for you.

We would also caution you to approach your healing work from the point of view of all things being possible in God; for in this way it shall come to pass that you are in order at all levels. Let the person you work on know you work with God if you choose to do so. In this way they participate in your decisions and are given decisions of their own as well, in acceptance or rejection, if you will, though few would reject a helping hand when it is offered in freedom and love.

To recapitulate somewhat, we suggest that you seal the person's aura after you have finished placing energy of love and light at the appropriate frequencies and orders or levels of expression so that the person receives a boost in their growth. You can do this by placing your hands on the head, brow and throat, or brow and crown, and asking that the aura be sealed so that only that which is for the highest and best good of all be allowed to pass in and out. You then bless them and yourself. This final closing prayer need not be done aloud. It is enough that you do it silently to yourself. And you may add that that which you have done be finished in completion, should it become apparent to your guides and teachers that something may have been left incomplete or unfinished while you were physically at work. You may convey this information to your client by telling them that for the next few days they will be adjusted and worked on, if they wish to be, so that the maximum results may be achieved. You may request that this follow up work go on for as long as three days, if you will, for this is in order at this time from the levels of organization for your material world and its order of growth. Beyond this three days you will have to reconnect with the Soul of the person, with the person in the flesh preferably, or develop some follow up procedure to treat the person at a later date. We recommend vibrational remedies as one way of doing this,[3] but this, again, is a subject unto itself, and we will take this up at a later time, in a later book, giving you hints at further steps at coordinating your healing approaches with that which is in order from the levels of your Soul and Heart in God. For so we would truly guide you in your growth and your efforts to aid the growth of others.

Healing and Crystals:
Coordinating the Growth of Others

The process of working on others is a process of responsibility. It is a chance to guide the destinies of men and women in cooperation with the designs of God and the Souls of us all. We would suggest that you show great care as you work with others, for it is a responsibility that is not to be taken lightly. Specifically, it is an opportunity to trust free will choice for all, for there will be many times that you have offered a complete healing to another, yet the timing was not in order for you to direct their growth at the present time. We say "they" because each individual is in fact a plural expression, of self and Soul

---

[3] See Gurudas, *Flower Essences* (Albuquerque, N.M.: Brotherhood of Life, 1983), and *Gem Elixirs and Vibrational Healing, Vol. I & II* (Boulder, CO: Cassandra Press, 1985 & 86). Also, *The Flower Essence Journal*, Vol. I-IV (Nevada City, Ca.: Gold Circle Productions, 1982), and Dr. Philip M. Chancellor, *Bach Flower Remedies* (New Canaan, Conn.: Keats Publishing, Inc., 1971). Works on other vibrational systems, including homeopathy, will be given in the bibliography.

Flower essences and gem elixirs may be ordered from Pegasus Products, P.O. Box 2044, Boulder, CO 80306.

and cooperative efforts of others as well, aspects of Souls that are shared, pieces of a Soul that are loaned for a time, and re-combining parts of a parent or core Soul as well. We will not detail such things for you here. Only know that the plural we give to each individual, the editorial "we," if you will, is not an accident; it is a purposeful and proper decision on our part. We are none of us ever alone. We are always a "we," whether we are blessed to share with other individualities on the earth plane or not.

We would resume our discussion of crystals as they apply to changing others, or presenting them with the choices that aid their growth. If you value the free will of others, you will respect their right to make a choice that is adverse to your heal-ing. That is why we say to you that you are never the one doing the healing. It is always the Soul of the individuality involved that decides whether the growth offered from cure is greater or equal to the choice of growth offered by continued illness or difficulty. And the choice of the personality level of expression, if you will, as opposed to the Soul level, is also of utmost importance. Souls must have the opportunity to give their personality expressions total free will to decide whether to choose any one given path for growth or opt for another perhaps equally good choice in another direction. It may seem as if your "cure" is the best thing for the individuality, but you are not capable, from your level, of seeing all the factors that are involved with a choice of an individuality to grow in your direction or away from it. The Souls of all of us are capable of these evaluations.

Thus we suggest to you that you release the need to see results in your clients in immediate ways. Trust in your God to decide who comes to you for the highest and best good. As you grow more and more capable of respecting the gentle, free will choices of Souls, you will find more people able to benefit from your working with them for mutual blessing. For this is what it is—mutual—no matter how far in advance of your pa-tients or clients you seem to be from your level of awareness and understanding. All are equal in the eyes of God, and the differences between all Souls are negligible from the level of the timeless, even though we are each utterly unique and important in our choices and expressions.

Is this to your understanding? That is good. For this is the key requirement of working on others, that they are respected for who they are. For it will do no good to cure a person if you implant them with the idea at a subtle level that you are above them in your growth. You will have cured the symptom only to have compounded the illness. For the only illness we any of us truly have is to think we are limited in any way, or to think that we are worthy to be only in a place of limitation and weakness relative to any other. We are all of an equality that is exquisite before God. That is the most important thing you can teach another any time you are with "them" (we use that plural again, you see), no matter how desperate and unhealthy they seem to be, no matter what character defects you think you see in what is there. Before you stands a Soul as perfect as anything you can ever imagine, each time you see a human face, or even at times when you appreciate the the group Soul of any animal. And the guiding lesson for this time is a unity in diversity that your planet fosters at levels you can hardly imagine.

This world of yours is a cooperative effort on many levels, in spite of the appearances to the contrary. And cooperation of Souls means an equality of efforts to grow that is truly astounding when once you see it from the level of your Soul's experience rather than your own in the meshes of life's apparent limitations.

What We Offer You in Time

The next thing to tell you about working with others is that you are guided in ways you know not, even as you are aware of little or nothing of this guidance. If you will trust yourself to know what is best with the confidence of a mother that loves her children and knows what is best for them in spite of advice from those who cannot know because they trust their intellects alone, then you will see a change in your work as you trust yourself to grow in love. You will find that this guidance is controlled and helpful at all levels, but particularly from those levels of trust and hope that are one with your Soul. It is not for us to intervene too heavily in your material lives. This would violate carefully laid out plans that give you free will. You would instead find us ready to assist at subtle levels that have to do with your energy systems, your thoughts, your ideas about self and same, your emotional life. We would assist you to know yourself as wholeness for all. We would guide you in this at the expense of the separation that you think is absolute between our world and yours, but is not. The separation between worlds is much more frail and illusory than any of you can at this time guess or know. We are with you in Spirit, yes. We are with you in thoughts as well. We are with you in some emotions (the ones we guide you to in love). We are with you in a spirit of cooperation that we will demonstrate for you if you give us the opportunity to help you, through many means, including work with crystals. For we are allowed to absolutely guide you in use of crystals, and to help you with any difficulties you may find working for the first time with God's energies directly, as you will do when first you gaze into a crystal and acknowledge that something is going on there you cannot perhaps know or feel with any exactitude, but something that you can feel nonetheless, in inspiration of guidance even more. For we will guide you to coordinate your lives with your growth at every step if you but ask us to. With permission we can change your lives. The change is so profound that you would gasp in relief and amazement if you could see its full extent.

We are here for you, and you for us. It is that simple. And we ask you to allow us to help, even if the chance we bring you for growth is something it may take many months for you to notice as we do. Are not a few months worth the effort, after all the confused expressions you have probably known up to now? We say this only to remind you of the context you have been given to appreciate the help we bring, the apparent limitation of expression you shall release in time, perhaps as soon as now.

We are teaching you to love yourselves as one with your Creator. Beyond this, everytime, you are guided by your Selves to see the truth in all you do through us. We are your Souls. And we are come to be as one with all you do, through you. We offer also every chance to help your friends and children of your heart, for we would resolve for you the feeling that you are helpless to understand or control your lives. Each thing that goes to you in life, this is a thing we have chosen, a thing you can release if once you have learned the thoughts and feelings we would give you with each gift to you of circumstance and happening in your lives. And others too can share the truth you teach, that you are learning through and through with all we see and do through you. This is a magic we would hold for you in secret only in so far as you are free to know with us the truth of this, or reject it for mechanistic choices of responsibility displaced. By this we mean you choose to think that something outside yourself is the determining event for you as you unfold your lives.

The gift we offer you is timeless, resolved in every moment of your lives on earth. We offer love for growth as well as service to your Soul in truth. And you are free to notice we are with you or to feel and think you are alone, driven by forces that bear no relationship to your Soul as one with God. You are free to help us with your growth or leave your growth to future times on earth or distant stars. We will guide you in the end, to know and think the truth: that you are sheltered Child of God who thinks only the truth, when once the Soul of Man/Woman is still enshrined inside your hearts and this you know at all levels of your expression involved with choice and action. For so we direct your lives: from your Souls and you in close cooperation with God above and earth below.

The destinies of men on earth are more than all your dreams come true. In this we are not alone, that we guide you to your dreams. We have the help of legions upon legions of followers and helpers, if you will, more trusted friends than any you can know on earth, for these can never die or feel alone. They are with you now in truth as well as lies, for some of them would test you that you know your Truth, your common sense control of life. The best thing you can do in trust of God is trust yourself, and not some ghostly felt-out piece of self you isolate as Soul. You must see by and by that you are one with God, but for now, you are one with self in Same, so we suggest you trust yourself to know the balance for your life, and trust yourself to choose the best for you in same, that you may learn and grow through choice, respecting Souls of others and yourself.

Chapter Twenty-four

Crystals As They Really Are

Crystals have their own destiny, of course. They are emissaries of the Divine plan. They coordinate communication and destiny in all the seven worlds of form. They are choice for you, and for themselves. For they are one with Soul and God at levels you are aware of at your best.

You are not to find the proper expression for these things inside your head, for crystals take the form they do without a "head" at all. They are images of reality without the differentiation of form you experience. They are noticeably lacking in free will, as you can experience if you work with them. This is because they are in perfection all the time, and choice is not a possibility in perfection. The next thing to do, or not do, is always obvious, never boring, never without compensation of divine perfection for all.

It is in order that we give you the point of view of a crystal, as we have just given you the point of view of what a crystal is for you, in a previous chapter. For all things have a point of view in God, as well as in self. And the point of view of crystals is "pure form," if you will, though this hardly conveys what we mean. The phrase "pure form" is not the half of what is meant here. It is more that the thoughts of God express through all who interfere the least. And yet this is not the truth of this for you, any more than the phrase "pure form." The truth of this is beyond comprehension, yet it is knowable in soul, reflected there from Soul.

We would say to you that being open will help a lot to understand what we bring to you. We will give you an example of what we mean by soul, as well as Soul: the crystal is as it appears, yet it is image of itself on other levels of expression. These are levels of "pure form," if you will. But the pure form involved is conscious of itself as thought of God. God's thoughts are living, can you see? They are not as dead things that lie around and grow old with deadness, as it were. They are forms that grow in their expressions, through millions of years of orderly growth, that they might fulfill the destinies designed for them at their beginning. It is as if every thought you had was divine material of life itself. And what you thought was itself God, as soon as ever it knew itself—for living thought can know itself as God's own thoughts, and God as well: the thoughts become the whole they are a part of, when first expression of their nature is understood in self, within the template of their own existence, as it were.

How can we describe this more for you? For this is all and everything for you, that you are thought of God yourself, Divine as was intended. You are thought of self as well as Self, for image becomes the whole of thought of God when it understands itself. It is the same as Source of thought, as image is the same as God when first it wakens to the Soul of all.

We can only play with this for you. Experience it for yourselves, and you awaken to your Whole in All as well as all.

You may notice the way we use these capital letters for you. At the personality level we have learned this as a trick of expression from the book *Seven Arrows*[1]. It is good to mention so fine a book. The meaning of these capitals is for you to notice there is a world above appearances. There is a world of order that is above the dissolution of time and space, so to speak. It is a world of images you can see when you look up inside yourself, or down at the ground of the world at large. For the images you will see are duplicated there in their actual content or form. This world of form we live in is an image of

---

[1] Hyemeyohsts Storm, *Seven Arrows* (New York: Ballantine Books, 1972). A wonderful book on the living tradition of Native Americans; in our opinion among the finest books in the English language, written by a Cheyenne as a gift to the World and to Himself.

another, finer world. By this word "finer" we mean only "rarefied." It is not a better place to be once you know its ways. It is just the one that causes this one to exist. It is enough to know that the Soul of All is reflected in the soul of all on earth, as well as up above. And that the Soul and soul are one in God as well as you and I. The ancient way of saying this was, "I am that I am." This means that consciousness here, in our limited expression, is as one with consciousness there, in the pure forms of God himself/herself.

Beyond this, crystals are what you intend them to be. They are plastic to the intentions you send them, or the intentions you are for them. For they simply share your space as one: they need no extra extensions from your mind to know wherein you dwell and have your being. They have their being in the same place, as one with you all the time, just as God sees through their eyes and yours as well. The eyes of crystals are the openness they are in life and bring to you, if so you chose. For crystals will image whatever you expect or know them to image. They will be most obliging in this, for you have chosen to interact with them, and they greet you with unlimited splendor, yet they accept whatever destiny you will for them, projected or extended: projected as you cast your limitations upon them, in thought and deed; extended as you let yourself be one with them and thus become as pure at heart as they and all they share life with.

Is this to your understanding? We hope so. It is as an "open sesame" to truth to notice what you are, and crystals are as you, when once you purify your hearts to shine as God, like good, high polished pewter shines your face right back at you.

Chapter Twenty-five

Some Operational Specifics With Crystals

(And More On Who We Are)

We give you now some operational specifics for your work with crystals on others that you may use crystals in a proper fashion along with the general guidelines and framework for your work that we will lay out in this chapter.

Details for Your Work

1. We suggest you use a copper grid system as recommended by Dr. Rev. Frank Alper in his *Exploring Atlantis* series of books. This will place greater emphasis on physical healing, but this is in order if you are to reach others whose healing comes to you and your responsibility. We suggest you use the grid the way Frank does, with copper wire; or alternatively, you may purchase a copper tape in art supply stores that is used for stained glass work, we believe. The tape comes in all sizes and widths, but the best width is about three-eighths of an inch, since wider tape is not necessary and tends to compli-cate the treatment with too much resistance required from us to balance all that copper. We suggest you use Frank's guide-lines about the spacing of the network of copper wire, as this is appropriate. The tape strips should be half an inch apart at least, and more is better: one and a quarter to one and an eighth inch centers to the spacing are ideal with the tape. Simply

inch centers to the spacing are ideal with the tape. Simply place the copper tape in a gridwork of strips horizontally and vertically, if you will, though the further details we would leave to those who choose to read Frank's books. *Exploring Atlantis Vol. III, especially,* gives adequate details for this design in full.[1]

Use copper also to fashion handles for your grid system, connecting it to wires that can be held when more direct activation for the grid is desired. These can be connected by staples to the grid. In cases of great physical resistance or in cases where the patient/client has developed a greater tolerance for crystals through repeated use of same, we would say the copper wire connections to the grid system are in order.

2. Use copper also in connecting one crystal cluster to another, in the patternings that Frank Alper has given for physical

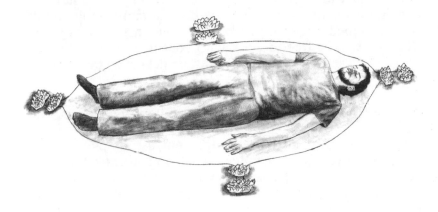

figure 15. cluster pattern with copper wire

---

[1] Dr. Rev. Frank Alper, *Exploring Atlantis Vol. I & III* (Phoenix, Ariz.: Arizona Metaphysical Society, 1981-85).

healing with clusters.[2] We would say to you the designs he gives for this are adequate and perfect for the work of cellular rebuilding, in grid patterns of clusters shaped in diamonds or squares and connected through networks of copper wire placed beneath the clusters as in figure 15.

The use of this pattern of eight clusters of roughly one half inch thickness or more and three to six inches in diameter is for physical difficulties that have manifested at a cellular level or will perhaps manifest there if they are not treated in definite, appropriate ways for the highest and best good of all. The correspondence here is between the multiple points in the crystal cluster—in a family of friendly individuals working as a whole, you might say—and the cellular level of the Many in the One[3] that works within any individual.

3. You may wish to cleanse your crystals between clients, as the vibrations for one may not fit exactly the vibrations for another. This will be covered automatically by us if you have set conditions for us to work for the highest and best good and have included cleansing as one of your instructions to us. Thus we will be free to work with your permission. See the chapter on cleansing crystals for further details on this.

Subtle Body Work With Crystals: Overview—The Soul

This next set of instructions for your use is given you to complete a cycle with treatment of self and others at this stage of our work. It is important for you to know that setting conditions for your growth includes familiarity with the subtle processes in man to some extent. You may pass over this section if you choose to grow without this information at this time, but know that the required course of life, so to speak,

---

[2] *Ibid., Vol. II*, 1983. Exact patterns for treating specific illnesses, including the use of copper grids and cluster diamonds, are given in these volumes. We suggest them as "must" reading for those using crystals in their healing work.

[3] This concept of the Many and the One is an understanding we have derived from J.J. Hurtak, *The Book of Knowledge: The Keys of Enoch* (Los Gatos, Ca: The Academy for Future Science, 1977), Key 1-0-1, p. 25-29.

includes respect for all levels of your expression, not just the physical or the undifferentiated spiritual, as has been thought by churches and religions for many ages. We give you information on subtle anatomy here and in future books that you may know yourselves as mirrors of the whole. For the designs of God are perfect at all levels, and perfect order at one level is reflected in a parallel and similar order on another. So it is, and so it is said that Man was made in the image of God. For the Creation itself is in the image of God. And Mankind is that Creation. "A part of it," you might hasten to add, "not the whole." But this is not so. The destiny of Humankind is to be that Whole in full—perfect mirror of that Whole, if you will, but more: perfect Whole in self and Soul as One. And the One is of God, is in the image of God in Wholeness, is God in fact as well as in approximation, even though the patterns of the Whole are not repeated anywhere the same. Always you are different, the one from the other. Yet always you are perfect, complete in God, and God withholds nothing from whom she/he is, including you: you are the Whole of God in fullness.

This is hard to fathom, but it is close to truth. Only by becoming what you are will you be able to verify this truth completely. So it is that different patterns for these things exist in each and all. For one may come to Soul a day from now, another in several years; and others may take many life-times, less or more. All are equal in the eyes of God, you know. All are equal in the eyes of self and Soul as well, as alignment proper for all time remains the active process of the Soul. Your Soul would choose the ways it goes, through you and other forms as well. It grows in God. This is enough for all.

This is a process from the Soul, you see, that nothing comes into your lives that isn't food for growth of all. In spite of what may seem to block your way, this is so for all.

This is a proper evolutionary process in God. It is not aberrational or crazy to be found in perfect order all the time. It is simple justice of the Soul responding to your lives completely. Everything is ordered for your growth on earth as well as in your Souls as one with God.

Subtle Body Work With Crystals: Overview—The self

Among the subtle processes in the human being perhaps the most important for examination is the nature of the subtle bodies of light that govern who and what a human being becomes on any given level of projection or extension from Soul. The fathomable form of these subtle bodies has to do with extensions of aspects of Soul on octaves or levels that are resolved into the chakras of the physical form.

Chakra work is one true way to harmonize your being with that of the universe. The alignment of seven levels of expression in the body itself with self and Soul—that is the topic that we consider. The eighth or transpersonal chakra and beyond are subjects we will take up in a future effort with you.

The seven levels we speak of here are expressed within your own bodies of light in the form of chakras or energy wheels or spirals, for this is what they appear to us to look like, vortexes that guide your growth from one level to the next. The patterns of these things are available in simple texts on yoga, meditation or occult understandings of the physical body. See the selected bibliography for additional sources of information.

The levels we describe as corresponding to your chakras are actually outside the time-space continuum you associate with your "physical" bodies. They are as registries of different levels of expression, four in all, that correspond to your functions of service in light and love at energy reflections, emotional registries, the blueprints or archetypal patterns that govern your "physical" reflections in time and space primarily (but also beyond in other dimensional forms), and lastly, the thoughtforms that you carry with you throughout your day and the possibilities for these as they reflect in actual organs or capacities for thought or forethought in a mental level chakra system—the last to develop and the first to be offered to you for your control in the physical body. We have thus given you four "energy" systems that coexist in one system of evolutionary potential—the form of a human being. This registry of four levels of order is called the Four Trees of Life spoken of in your Qabalah and other esoteric traditions. These together form the one interrelated whole of your being as personality expression in the physical realms that are subject to dissolution and change. These are all, then, part of one Tree of Life with seven branches or major centers in the "physical" expression and three more in non-physical expression located above your heads in time and space. These seven branches are one with your Soul at still another level of expression, that subject to change but no error or fault. This is the level of your Soul itself, registering in a formation of change that is subject to death through the physical level of its expression through what you identify as yourselves most of the time, but not subject to death (as you would know it in time-space frameworks) at the level of its own centering, if you will, its own inner activity.

The only other thing to say here is that "you" are not this physical body at all, subject as it is to the rigors of disease and death. Without your Soul you would be that form, but with it you are more all the time. You are not subject to death at all from the level of your Souls; only to growth through time and beyond it as well. For beyond it you are as Gods, one with your Creator at the levels of your Souls, one at the level of God himself/herself.

As you identify with your Souls this is so. For now you are still somewhat identified with your being in time and space, and this is a natural result of the purposes for you from your Soul level of designing. Know that you are one with your Soul as you choose to be, even at the levels of these identifications, and that in spite of whatever identifications you choose, you are a metamorphosis of your Soul at all times, subject to growth-not-death in any way that is meaningful to us.

We have given you a summary of your forms at the level you can assimilate. This is not easily done, and for this reason, we will include again much greater depth of discussion in our subsequent book, *Subtle Body Anatomy*, on this topic and others that are related to it.

For now, let us say only that the Four Trees with their seven branches each in time and space are in you now, each moment, as energy forms of possibility for all. They are describable as energy formations of seven ascending chakras or energy centers located vertically along the spinal column in approximation of the locations of the glandular formations that bear corresponding functions. This is given to you, again, in many introductory books on chakras in the body physical. And we will presently introduce for you ways of working with these formations with crystals—at energy, emotional and mental levels of expression.

You will find you are working on these levels when you work with crystals. And as you counsel or lead people to understand and resolve the concepts they have held from this and former lives that shape their destiny, so you will have worked on Causal levels of chakras as well as their effects on the planes of light and sound and so on. For we do not recommend treating these things as mere magic, that thus allows one to heal another without confronting consciously the sources of errors, the unspoken, often unexamined beliefs behind our actions and reactions. We give you this information now that you may balance your work with us by counseling those who come to you, and by trusting what unfolds to be in order for your growth and for others. This is wholistic healing at its finest.

As you work with the basic concepts of the individual, so you will find yourselves treating emotional imbalances, belief systems that are resistant to change, and formations of energy and vitality that are subject to these patterns of thought and emotion we describe for you. As you heal emotional beliefs and imbalances, you will find yourselves operating with crystals from time to time to encourage such change and release of the resistances you find as a result of growth. And the emotional patterns shall dissolve in the wisdom and appropriateness of what you are guided to do through us as you allow us to work.

The Nature of the Soul

Not all at once will you be able to work in the way that is perfect from your Soul's point of view. But in following the simple suggestions of this book you will find the bridges you need to begin this process in an open-ended and self-actualizing way that is unlimited in its potential for you.

You have been a creation of one life, in as much as you are personality with corporal existence on your planet. But at another level, you are Soul, the stuff of Gods or of Divinity itself. You are thus an extension of same, to dwell a time in human form on earth, unable to carry all of what you are into earthly flesh. And what you are is of the stars and God. So on this earth, there is a being who is like your Soul, parallel in form and substance, yet unlike as well. This being is subject to error. Yet it reflects another world where only perfection can exist. Two trees stand, mirroring one another. They are your Soul and you in human form on earth. They are as one in God. Your Soul is mirrored in the flesh, both physical and subtle up to levels you know not of in normal life but may read of or find in books like this, or discover through careful research into the nature of self and Soul. For nothing is actually barred from your understanding, yet nothing is revealed without your asking for it.

So we would say to you that you are like your Soul, yet you are like your Soul in that you are a form of God's own choosing. You are not a permanence in this form, any more than is your Soul. Your Soul, like you, evolves in Truth. Unlike you, nothing can be removed or harmed from within your own Soul's being. Thus, what you are in Truth shall exist forever in your Soul, though your form shall be reconstructed, if you will, in permanence and perfection. For there your future lies, in permanence that grows through time to be like the One who created you, those aeons of time ago. And you shall be as one with Soul, as you work to grow in God. For everything of perfection that you do, this perfection shall be of your Soul.

And everything of impermanence that you do, all that is in imperfection, shall be as tools for growth for all; for by dying, so we live. And dying in this case is letting the imperfections of your life bring you to see the folly of your soul when it excludes all thought of error and ceases to forgive the imperfection that it sees in all around it on this plane. For so your soul is want to be: intolerant of what it knows not of, the Divine scrambles of God outside its ken in spirit as well as matter.

This is a process from your Soul's point of view incomprehensible to humankind in limited expression here on earth. For is it not so that imperfection is the state on earth, and imperfection is an assumption of all we do in same? Yet our Souls can carry only good. This is hard to comprehend, that imperfections here on earth are not so in the realms of heart and love that exist potentially in our Souls.

A quality of flexible love for all—perhaps this is the best way to describe what a Soul chooses to find in an earthly expression of limitation and lack of love.

The lack of a quality of flexible love for all—perhaps this is the point of ascendancy for a Soul that chooses for its earthly sojourn times like these.

> Perhaps the destiny of the stars
> Would allow our Souls a change
> To express through us an opening
> That something might be gained:
> The love of all for all, flexibly attained.

This is the best way we have to describe for you what a Soul discovers while on earth. Yet the Soul lacks for nothing in itself; it is whole light consciously playing in the love it is. Is this to your understanding?

We have tried to give you a sense of the lessons you might learn for your Soul on this earth, that you are imperfect so as to bring real understanding to your Soul: that it is perfect, yet it grows in tolerance and love for what it is not, the imperfect form of God on earth. This toleration then can grow into a deep appreciation for all things, above and below your knowing. It is an enriching of self and Soul. For your Soul is as One with all, yet it is deficient in Love, if you will—on its independent level of functioning in God; or rather, it does not appreciate in fullness what it is that it has, the Knowing of a Loving God more than the Knowing of a Knowing God—though this Knowing is possessed of Soul as well as God. The Loving is the part we seek to so refine on earth, that all possibilities are full of Love, and all things must end in Truth for all. And Trust and Hope and Fear alike are Loved in God's own Soul.

"For God has a Soul like you, my Child, and now I address you as Soul of All, your Soul made whole in Truth of God, your Soul made whole in Love. For I am as you, and yet I am the completion that you lack and soon become. (By soon we mean thousands of years, yet small periods of time in the drift of all time.) The drift of God is to teach you Love of all, love of Self and God as One. This is enough for now."

(These are energies of direct communion with the Father/ Mother God aspect of Soul.)

The Chakra System

The chakra system in the human being is a mirror of the whole of God, yet we will deal no more at this time with these connections. It is enough for you to know this in your Truth. We go on to give you the simplest suggestions for your work with chakras, after these connections have been made for you in part. For believe it or not, we have dwelled upon, in the previous few, short pages, the issues of the chakras as they resolve in God. The seven levels are the same for all, so we begin.

To teach you of chakras, we suggest you touch yourselves at the point between your heart and breast on the left side, for this is the location of the physical heart. The heart we spoke of first is the heart we notice most when gazing on one another, from level of your Souls, for the heart at the center of your chest or breast is the heart that exists on subtle levels, and the heart that exists on subtle levels is located along the central axis of the body toward the front of the chest.

The heart at an energy or etheric level is to the left more, since it is near the physical. There is an astral or emotional heart that is at the center. There is also a "causal" heart, if you will. It is more to the right side of the chest, about equidistant from the center of your chest and the right breast. In perfect physical alignment this heart moves to the chest center and balances with the physical. In separation of the different functions of the bodies, perhaps, or in isolation of one's wishes with regard to the physical and the spiritual (or even the sensual), you will discover that it is possible for the three "heart" centers to lack coordination and come together only rarely.

In many so-called ascetic states of the middle ages or even today, it is possible in life-denying to find the expression of the "heart" on the right side or causal side to drift away from the influence of the other two heart centers and in isolation to be experienced as the absolute truth. This is a failure of integration with the whole rather than a realization as such. It is an abbreviated isolation of the functions of the being to the point where identification and localization of the "heart" function drifts to the left, unattended, while simultaneously the identification with the body has been isolated to the right at too rarefied and imbalanced a level (giving, not receiving—too ungrounded from the physical). This will result in dual expression of the being, both towards the physical (unconsciously perhaps) and towards the more rarefied expressions in push-me-pull-you or opposite directions. Rather it is the function of the "heart" to meet at the center only when there is perfect functioning of the whole.

When the astral, or causal, or physical/etheric hearts are specialized or distorted you will get a drifting of these three functions apart and in isolation. As they come together, on the other hand, in relative integration of the being as a whole, you will find that the etheric heart center drifts or pulls in towards the middle, and the causal or higher heart function pulls inward toward the center as well. Thus, in the field of play of the emotional life of humanity, in the middle of mankind's common sense, emotional life—here can be found the common meeting ground of all hearts, all goals, the above as well as the below of our expression. And in the ordinary caring of our worlds, the ordinary expression of humble love, here can be found the hope of the world—not in attainments of states that imbalance the being for functional life on your planet in wholeness.

The above description of three heart centers at different levels of expression, all tending to have a different physical location in isolation from one another and all tending to integrate at the point where the astral heart is located—this description finds its useful correspondence to your work with crystals in that the left-hand drift of the heart center in too great a reliance upon the physical—or also in its abandonment[4]—this can be counteracted by pulling with a crystal in a straight line down the front of the body, from the top of the head to the base of the spine. This was a technique first shown us by Rev. Dr. Frank Alper in one of his seminars. By intending that the

---

[4] Such abandonment causes the drift of the etheric heart center to the left just as well as too great a reliance on the physical, since abandonment of who we are at physical levels of expression can only weaken us, and such weakening through ignoring our energies and body causes the heart on an etheric level—drained of vitality—to sink towards the physical heart on the left; whereas, invigorated and honored, our etheric heart function tends to rise towards the realm of emotional well-being, in balance and stability at the center of our expression, thus bringing us into alignment with our Souls. (footnote concluded on next page)

chakra system be in alignment in the way that is optimal for your client (with our help, naturally) and then centering the chakras into proper position along the axis of symmetry of the spine with three passes of your crystal along this central axis, you will be helping the person to feel and keep the balance that is appropriate for life and beyond it as well. You will be guiding a being to his or her growth in life and beyond, to adaptation to the physical and the causal—as well as perfect integration at the "heart" of caring for all life, all love, all hope. This is a truly moral thing to do, once you have permission to do it from your client or your friend you treat. And it is a natural thing to want to do such treatment, provided you are willing to allow the needed process for the individual you treat, in spite of any expectations of your own—even if things drift a bit, according to the timing for another than yourself, allowing once again the pattern to complete itself, that the choices of another are honored in this life as well as worlds to come in wholeness of expression. By this we mean you let the individual you treat choose to accept the treatment that you give or release it to its Soul for future growth and accept instead the old patternings it keeps for self from long ago: the incomplete expression of having parts of self divided from the Whole. This is something your Soul allows you at all times. And you in turn allow another freedom of a similar kind when you trust to God that patterns of the whole will find fulfillment in the end, through trusting God to grow all Souls in truth as well as freedom in the same. Thus we say to you, encourage the growth of another, just as your own Soul would encourage growth in you. And doing so, release and trust the growth of all to God.

Footnote 4 (continued from last page) We are not speaking here of active, physical regimens necessarily, though these are in fact a good possibility for increasing such balance. We are merely speaking of the honoring of the physical through some form of simple physical activity and appreciation on a regular basis. Your attitude towards your form on all levels is what is at issue; it is all yours to treasure or reject as you see fit; and it is ours to complement you in your choices, letting you decide how you will learn in this and future lives on earth. We give you this to know we love you as a part of God, whether you love the physical body of God yourself or not. For that physical form of God is in the form of your physical body at this time. Is it not so?

We give you what we say above so that you may know the pattern with all Souls with regard to the formations of the chakras; for the patterns we explain of the heart, these kinds of patterns exist from Soul at other levels of expression just as well. You would find all chakras in the body physical possess the self-same possibilities for growth, that a continuum of orientation or direction for growth is available for each—as, for example, with the heart: to the left (more physical expression), the right (more rarefied and amplified expression) and center (in completeness of the whole). So you will find the second chakra or creative chakra may drift to left, the right or center, depending on the conscious choices in your living. And so also with heart, and mind. (This last, the mind, is centered at the brow—though it completes only in part the mind, for knowing mind is here, but mind that entangles and sorts out is at the solar plexus or the third chakra expression of the body physical, as we would call it, all four Trees of Life or levels of the chakras being physical to us if they are those of self instead of Soul.) So also with the crown, the throat, the third chakra (near the solar plexus), and at the base as well, except in different ways: these do not drift from left to right very often, but—as in the case of the third chakra or throat—up and down instead; and in the case of the crown and base, the tendancy is for the continuum of expression to be between being open and closed rather than directional. We deal with this in greater detail at a later date in *Subtle Body Anatomy*, volume two of this present work. For now it is enough to know that balancing of all you do is mirrored in the forms of Soul as well as self on earth, and that greater balance can be given through your work with crystals as you allow us all to work through you, from self as well as Soul in one full being of expression growing stronger all the time from Soul to you in this, your "physical" form.

A Pattern For self-treatment and For Others

We would go on now to another topic. This is guidance for yourselves with crystals, that you allow us to treat you with crystals on your chakras, so to speak. We suggest you lie down for this our work on you with crystals, once we have given you the forms of this expression for you to work with for yourselves.

See the diagram below for the pattern of crystal use that we would recommend for you in this.

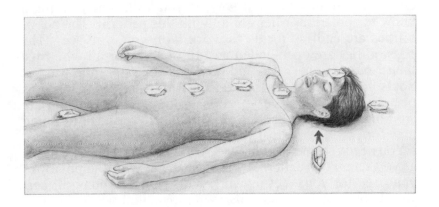

figure 16. self-treatment pattern

This pattern is for work on yourself, though you may use it on others once you allow us to familiarize you with this pattern first. You see, you have placed a greater polarity around the being at top and bottom; then you have centered small polarities, if you will, at each chakra center along the being of expression in the physical: at heart and solar plexus, heart and throat, at heart and each remaining chakra, at crown and spleen, crown to other chakras, at third eye and under head at neck (for the medulla or Tree of Life that processes your input and output all the time with song of life from all the stars as one), at so many other combinations of polarity. Also, if need be, at throat and solar plexus, at third eye and sexual expression, at womb and at base chakra—again, depending on the needs of individual people. Not all will need the lower centers covered with a crystal, but from time to time you will find it helpful, perhaps, for yourself and others.

This pattern is to be used to treat yourself from time to time, you see. We used it first—of all the patterns that we learned through self and others to allow our Souls and guidance to work through us. We called on our angels and our guidance, as it were, to help us heal in complete perfection at all times; and to release all imperfection to perfect blessing from our Souls. So we suggest that you might do with this, our first pattern in this physical life.

We have phrased the polarities of expression from chakra to chakra in a rather unusual way, if you will, that you might know the polarities often set up with this pattern. The possibilities are endless for us to work with you, you see. The possibilities are open-ended and full of joy for all who trust their Souls as one with God, and ask for same, the trust of Souls in them to be first activated, then expressed for God as one with all. We give you this to know also that you are working here with polarities of infinite variety and of meaning now for you, as you trust yourselves to grow with Soul.

You needn't remember how to work with differing polarities as you set up this pattern, by the way. We will find polarities you need for you. Let us work with you, and you will best spend your time in this formation enjoying all we do for you. Notice, if you will, the resonancies we activate on your behalf. But notice also what we do for you as one with Soul: that we are playing at the first with all your attention in your Soul. And as you grow you show to us the love of God reflected there in you. And you awaken then to self and Soul as one. God bless you as you grow in truth for all.

Forgive us for such long confusion of expression. It is only possible to explain ourselves in words in books, and these are long on pages, while in hearts all is of a simpler nature, more fulfilled and certain, more at home in God.

Chapter Twenty-six

Tones in Crystals and People

(In the Ways We Best Can Feel)

The Sounds of Crystals

The tones of crystals are a good way to attune to the music inside yourselves, if you will: the music of the spheres. Each crystal has its characteristic harmony, just as you do; each has its single note or tone that defines its nature for all. We have experienced this ourselves in the work of noting the inner tunes that harmonize, one with another, in patterns of completion for all. These tunes or harmonies are received most acutely in the medulla area of the physical, as the organ known as the cerebellum serves as an interface with the structuring known as the "tree of life" (arbor vitae), which is as the tuning fork for your fine tuning of sound and inner harmonics. This "tree of life" picks up harmonies designed to adjust you from day to day, as well as underlining harmonies of your creation that are intoning all the time for the stability of this and other worlds.

We would encourage you to go on to appreciating these tones for yourselves, not in the many hours of contemplation experienced by ascetics of former times, but rather in the experimental play of your own free moments, simply for the sake of proper attunement and alignment of your conscious integration with these things. They are of you and with you all the time. They adjust your energies for full expression of the light and love you are capable of synthesizing with your being. And these sounds attune the universal aspect of your being as well as your personality, in that they align the subtle levels of your being, one with another, as steps of a giant ladder in the sky might be stationed one atop the other. In your head and heart and mind and will, you will find these things are so, for they are you in other forms, these flowing lights and lovely sounds that harmonize with all.

Notice them if you will, and at a later date, in our book on the subtle bodies, we will discuss these things again in greater detail for you: quite systematically, in fact. Over the last several years we have been teaching the channel of these writings the nature of the subtle bodies of light and sound as they relate to all. Such understanding will help your growth immensely, for you will see, in patterns of the whole, that all is tied to everything: all is order of the whole, and parts are just as orderly—and as true. For you to know this in your very depths of being will become the bedrock of your growth for all to see, as you prepare for future days of grace and love, alone with God, yet full of teaching for Soul and self. For this is why you teach, you know—for you who read this book as well as me; you are given to the passing moment all the time to know your self and Soul as one with God in all its aspects, aspects of this passing time, aspects of this passing life, aspects of the space you know as God. And we are with you, all in you. We are with you now to share the truth of who you are with all.

Toning With Crystals — The Different Gifts

Perhaps the best, single exercise we could suggest—to come back to this sound or tone inside you—is to give you crystals to attune to, for they are loud, to us at least, with the sounds of God and you. They are attuned full well to God in all they do, and therefore the tones they give are true. For you and other beings, these tones are not so true until you know yourselves and thus release the harmonies there within yourselves to play inside of you for all to hear. Is this not curious? That tones inside yourself sound for all to hear? Yet so it is.

The tones of crystals might be noticed in any number of ways. We will suggest a few to you, but know that attunement to these tones is not a formal matter. It is easy once you do it, very natural.

We had a friend appear one day who followed tones of all the crystals as he walked about our house. He was able to see the colors of the crystals just as well, but the tones are what intrigued him, as he rarely felt these tones in such a loud and ordinary way. They were each so clear and separate, the one crystal tone from the next, that he would stop and notice, here and there, the ones especially sweet for him to play with. This is possible for all to do as well as this friend. You can listen to these tones quite discrete from one another, and even come to know a crystal by its characteristic tone of sound.   This is useful only in that all things are useful in the end. If this is a gift you have, or would develop, it will bless you just as other gifts can do.

For each of us notices different things among the senses and sensations God has given us. And all are blessed in his sight, all are gifts to know yourself as one with all and God in truth. Find the gifts that you possess and those you would possess in time, and feel quite free to explore the same until you know them in their best expressions, complete inside of you. Until then, play with them for fun and pay. This is why you're here, in part, to play as God intended. Thus the tones we give your crystals are as noticeable by you; and if they are not, it still is good to know of these as gifts, that you may respect the work of others and rest at peace that all is as it should be, whether or not one gift of all the thousands comes to you in any given lifetime.

This is a basic principle we offer you here, that each of you shall possess as different gifts in time and space frameworks; and all shall complement the whole of "you" as who you are in time in space and who you are beyond as well.

Some Exercises

The specifics, then, of ways to notice tones in crystals, are given here. First, attune to a single crystal in a pattern of eight or ten or twelve or six.   Just hear the separate tones inside yourself, for they will be there. Try each crystal around your circle, however many crystals there are. Hear them each as separate, once you notice each. Then notice harmonies among them if you can. This is possible in time, though you may notice interactions with you more than interactions any of them have with one another, though these interactions are present in your energies as well.

Once you finish tones, by the way, notice next, perhaps, the light inside each crystal. Then the light patterns of the whole, as the crystals interact with one another and with you in interacting rainbow light and love if love frequencies are present at your request; for, once again, you must add the love vibration through your prayers or proper notice to us all who guide you for us to assist by adding these (the ranges of the love vibration, though you will not experience directly all the differentiations that herein exist in same) to what you do with crystals. Often people who notice light have noticed that your patterns of six and twelve would make a rainbow white light spiraling, a spiral of white light with lovely pastels in it, as the iridescent white light here involved contains all colors in every octave of expression if you have asked for this, otherwise a few such octaves, as are suitable for growth.

Love is the common pattern all of us can recognize, you know. Yet there are patterns in all things that different senses, different gifts of recognition, give to us. We each possess some of these gifts, some of these abilities to share of ourselves with others—for such these gifts most truly are. And as a whole we share all things with one another, don't you see, in recognition of the patterns of God in all things on this earth and in the heavens. We share with you in modes of our learning. You share with us through yours. We share together more than either one of us quite possesses as complete inside ourselves. Such is the design of God in the universes of light and love.

If your mode of recognition is to see at subtle levels in addition to seeing with your physical eyes, then please try out your gift on crystals. Notice, if you will, the glow about the crystal, and then within. If this is not your gift, experiment anyway. For you will grow, if this is not your gift, in other ways; yet you might try this out for fun, or just to see what gifts are yours, besides the ones you know of, in the light of day. The gift of seeing psychically is not our gift in this lifetime at our personality level through John, but it may be yours to see the light at different levels around this rock or stone.

Another exercise to try out, by the way, is to let yourself feel what your crystal feels like to you, as you hold it in your hand. We are speaking of a quality of feeling here.

It is a gift with us through our personality level in John to do this: to feel the resonancy with a crystal in the corresponding area of self where this particular crystal, or any other, might resonate with self and Soul in truth. This is a gift of feeling things, almost bodily, in energy, attention and light resonancy that you feel instead of see. This is a gift of the heart chakra, if you will, but it is also a simple sense that you develop as a gift when you notice feelings in yourself and one another. It is a gift we recommend, like any other, but, once again, please do not feel any loss if this is not your gift. It may be ours, but we have other gifts as well, and so have you. In time, all gifts will be as shared with all, in different ways, that each of you might know a different world of self and Soul to share with all. For so has God designed your world, that all is shared through all, and all must come to wholeness through themselves. For as they do, they share the whole of others than themselves, noticing as for the first time the universe we each may give another when we are activated whole in God, activated in ourselves as one with Soul and self combined in God.

This is the purpose of this discourse, you see: to let you know that you are whole in self with all your gifts, and there are many gifts you develop for yourselves, and many you do not; these other gifts that you do not have right now, others have for you to share with; so it comes to wholeness through all men and women, the gifts our Father/Mother God would give us of herself/himself/itself.

So lastly, once you have attuned to tone and sound through crystals, attune to self through a crystal of light and love and truth that is inside of you. Let yourself notice all the things you notice first inside your crystal, in simple isolation, if you will—though nothing really isolates itself from anything around it. Through attunement to a crystal, you attune to all, in you and in the world as well. So we give you this simple practice of attuning to a crystal that you may next attune to self and Soul as one with God in you.

Once you have attuned to Soul, you may go on with other aspects of your being. But for now, attune to Soul and God through you, as you have done with crystals—or soon shall do.

Chapter Twenty-seven

Strengths and Weaknesses of Using Crystals,

Atlantis and Lemuria

The strengths of using crystals are many, and they fill this book. The weaknesses are few, but they are important to mention and bring out in order that they may be clearly understood and allowed for. It is the same with any direction for growth: there are strengths and weaknesses for each, with the strengths outweighing the weaknesses where there is growth in who we are, in mastery of self. We say this to you because it is important to see the growth that can come from situations where there is choice. Without choice there can be no growth, yet where there is choice there is also risk inevitably. Choice means that mistakes can and will be made. It is so with all things in life, and it is so with crystals as well. Where there is choice there is growth, for men and women learn from their mistakes as well as from their successes, and perhaps they learn more from the mistakes, for their successes are rarely understood for what they are, a confluence of many factors, whereas the failures give ample opportunity for analysis of self and Soul and adjustment in the course of living.

The strengths of crystals are also their weaknesses, understandably enough. It is always so, that strengths unmastered can become weaknesses or liabilities. The strengths that come to mind at once are, first, the abilities of crystals to amplify your thoughts and emotions, thus clarifying them for you. Next are the abilities of crystals to harmonize with all they take in or are exposed to, thus allowing you to be in harmony with the stars and your Souls, influences which are the sources of much of the positive "programming," if you will, or "intentionality" of the crystals you associate with. Lastly, we would point out a third factor, that crystals intend you no harm, yet they are programmed to limit themselves to exactly what you intend and believe, out of respect for your Souls and your selves. They are thus subject to allowing you free reign, so to speak: they will not interfere, but they will also not help any more than they are actually called upon to do so.

Let us take up these three strengths and liabilities one at a time for the sake of clarity and intensity of understanding, for we would have you understand these things with real intensity, not just in passing as if in a dream until you awaken to find you have in fact discovered the ill effects of crystals the hard way, by having them demonstrated in your own lives before you have awakened to the fact they are there. So it is with people in your time, that dreams are as life: we live our lives in a cloud of unknowing, if you will, but rather in a dream that allows us to choose only occasionally that which is for our highest and best good. Usually we simply drift along with the current, so to speak, allowing the momentum of our past to carry us into an unexamined future. We accept the assumptions of those around us, who in turn have accepted the assumptions of those around them. This is not in order for you any more.

It is time to awaken to your selves, that you may become one with your Souls. It is time to acknowledge the source of understanding inside yourselves, that you may awaken it properly, in individuation of self, if you will, but in more prosaic terms, that you may wake up and think for yourselves—be your own guides, as it were, your own guidance in common sense awakeness. You need never assume that what you hear is true for you. You need never assume the whole of what you are given by any others, no matter how much you admire them. Admire them still. Admire your country and your king, if you will. But allow yourself to be free inside your Soul by letting your self awaken to watch what it is doing in full responsibility for your own life, for your own actions, your own beliefs and thoughts, if you will—though the thinking life is the hardest to control for you now, for it is the most awake of all your abilities, and thus is least subject to the twin controls of being asleep and being in guidance from other levels of expression that have long since mastered the growth you are currently engaged in for yourselves.

We say this to you so that you will really understand the context for growth that is involved with the strengths and weaknesses of crystals: that you are free to choose, in ignorance or wisdom as the case may be, and you are responsible in all you do for self and Soul and no other save yourself. You are destined to be responsible at levels you can only guess at for now, and these levels of responsibility take precedence over all else that you may think is of importance for you at the current moment, in the passing course of your lives on earth and in the stars as well.

We give you this to know that you are a child of God, worthy to be the sole regent of your Soul over all. And you are blessed by the most high in all you do, be it good or seeming ill in the short run of time on earth and in the stars.

We go on to discuss the three sources of strength and weakness in crystals that we have already mentioned: the amplifying, harmonizing and free-will respecting efforts of crystals on your behalf. See the chapters on programming them and cleaning them for further, related details.

Atlantis and Amplification of Crystals

The weaknesses of crystal use are chronicled in the memories of Atlantis and Lemuria. In Atlantis men used crystals to amplify their every wish, to create vast states that oversaw the efforts of whole peoples over the expanse of the earth. The Atlanteans were amplifiers of the impulses of the stars for healing and blessing themselves that they might remain in perfect order at all times. Yet the crystals became a dependency for them, with the effect that they could abuse their spiritual growth and allow their powerful dreams to be fulfilled, irrespective of their effects on others and themselves. They watched their civilizations grown on crystal technologies of healing and blessing turn into a curse, as they depended on the balancing of the crystals to forgive them their errors in thought and in emotional patternings, without any real evaluation or growth on their part. They took the risk out of life, if you will. But more, they trusted themselves to know for themselves what was best for them, overriding the safety mechanisms of sickness and disease that had been placed for their own benefit by those who create your expressions on earth (your own Souls in service to God, if you will, the hierarchies of God and Humanity in service to the will of their Creators and their Source overall, as has always been intended). The nature of sickness and disease we will take up elsewhere. For now, know that the Atlanteans used complex technologies to strengthen their etheric and astral bodies to override the wishes of their own Souls to serve God and humanity in peace. Instead, the Atlanteans developed technologies that overrode their own spiritual growth for the sake of their desires and their distrust of self and Soul. For all distrust and mistreatment of others in the end comes from lack of respect for self. And all love can overcome hate and distrust, and truly, death itself. For we say to you that death is the result only of your own mistrust of self and Soul, in their service to your Universe. The Atlanteans had not learned the lessons of trust and life they needed, for they were fated to go through much growth to learn what was true for them and what wasn't, just as we all are. And they abused themselves through the technologies of crystals that we do not plan to allow you to develop again on earth until you can manage them for yourselves in peace, once the Millennium comes; for it shall, if you are able to trust one another in peace and prosperity for all.

The Atlanteans are a model for our times. For they abused much and learned little until it was too late, and is this not a problem in your own time as well, in different terms? Are you not abusers of your intellects as Atlanteans were abusers of their emotional choices for growth? We think the parallel is a useful one as long as you keep in perspective that the primary task for you is to love yourselves in proper balance, thus allowing yourselves to grow spiritually as well as materially. And thus joy and peace are helpful and possible for all, rather than the hate and mistrust that is the confusion of this or any other time. If you find yourself blaming another rather than seeing what in him is like you and worthy of love, you are headed in the wrong way with this knowledge we give you. So too with Atlantis. For we could continue all day to give you the abuses of former times and ages of mankind, but the beauty of each is also something to behold. For each has been the keeper of something unique for mankind. Each has been the keeper of some precious gift of growth and appreciation, in all the turmoil that can be seen from the vast perspective of looking back over the thousands of years as we do. The Atlanteans built for their own destruction in the end, amplifying the impulses of crystals in ways that disregarded the blessings of self-evaluation and limitation on earth, so to speak, though you are none of you as limited as you may think, we might add. Yet they built as well instruments of judgement and evaluation in the crystals that had they been used, the balance would have been restored through the very means that were used for destroying the balance.

The crystals were instruments of choice, don't you see. And you in this day have the choice to use this amplifying ability of crystals to amplify for yourselves the truth of who you are, both to develop in your strengths, and to change and mend, in your weaknesses, through us. We have for you created programs of self-evaluation in your crystals that preclude the blindness of healing without input for growth, as in the mirror of the crystal you are drawn to see the worst of yourself as well as the best, that you might work overtime, as it were, to correct the errors in perception and habituation that you are subject to. So it has been with the author of this book, the channel writing, and his wife, for they have used most often the crystals that evaluated their past frequencies to conclude what imbalance of character might next be profitably looked at. The passing psychic might well think such crystals in action to be filled with negativity and destruction, for they serve as a mirror for the Soul to lead us to look gently at ourselves to evaluate what it is that needs testing, if you will, what it is that needs adjustment by allowing the conscious personality to resonate with the imbalance until it can no longer be found in the energy possibilities of the being on any level.

So it has been with us, and so it shall be for you, if you will allow it to be. Now is the time for the correction of Atlantis. Now is the time to identify the errors in all our pasts, in all eras and ages, and allow ourselves to face just who it is we are, through the mirror of our own Souls, as it were: the mirror that the activity of our own true natures can supply us with. And the discharge of all our pasts, the possibilities for learning from our mistakes from all those different expressions in the former lives of our Souls, so to speak—these possibilities are endless and coming to a head for us all in this and future lives on earth, in a completion of a cycle of overall patterning, that now we might digest that which we have done in error or in balance in earlier times, for growth as well as goodness. For goodness can come to those who have tasted the feel of evil, so to speak. And light can be valued in the dark more than ever it can in the places of light which are its natural resting place.

So it is with love as well, yet love is more completely a choice than any other thing you know of. For it profits not a man that he give love—or so it seems in the immediacy of the moment. It only profits him when he feels the return of the universal balance as he is himself in the balance of love, thus making it available to all; and thus making it available for himself as well, as he is love in the circuits of the stars of God.

To return to Atlantis now for the moment, the Atlanteans were learning lessons for us on earth to benefit from in time through the memories and being of our Souls, so to speak. Yet on earth they did fearful damage, in the short term perspectives of the current responsibilities of humanity. They built an overall instrument of war and terror through the great pyramid that powered their world from the heart of Atlantis, allowing the power of the great crystal there to be abused into giving death as well as life, as they manipulated men's desires for their own ends. Specifically, we would say to you that the crystals were used to amplify intentions in the ruling classes of a Rome-like nation of conquerors, as the Atlanteans forged their crystals into destructive tools of war. For you can use a power for ill as well as good, if you have the means. And free will choice at all times means that it is possible for even the most faithful and loving of servants to be abused into doing the bidding of an unjust master.

So it was with the crystals of Atlantis. They were conceived of as a technology of the stars, given of old to the ones who would rule in Atlantis to enslave the world for the good of the world. It was so in Rome and in Hitler's Germany as well, was it not? Techniques that seemed able to liberate mankind instead were unable to teach him how to be balanced in his approach to himself and others. And the balance is in love of self and others, that "ye love one another as I have loved you," if you will, but more, with all peoples and nations, that you simply treat others with the same loving kindness and respect you would like to be treated with yourself, never allowing ideas of your superiority or inferiority to cloud you from seeing that all are equally in a process of growth that leads to the summits of certain attainment in the apparent uncertainty of time, as we all unfold in God on high.

The balance for Atlantis was to face destruction herself, as she amplified the energies of the crystals to the point where they cracked the resonancies of the earth's protective layering of sound and light. For this is how the earth is maintained with such apparent stability in time and space: it exists in a memory bank of past emotions and stabilized energies that are in harmony with the stars around them; and it is maintained in this state as in a bank of resonancies of the starry sky by the simple expedient of having the resonancies monitored at all times and balanced accordingly, in minute, ongoing incremental adjustments, by those who are responsible for same. Who might this be? Why you yourselves, at the level of your Souls and Selves, or who you truly are; for the responsibilities of the ancient Souls who come here or to any planet are to include the maintenance of that planet in its proper frequencies of expression, within the harmonious resonancies of the medium of stars and space in which we all exist. Otherwise, instability would be much closer than you can currently imagine. The earth would spin out of control in no time. And the slightest wobble and spin out of phase with time and space as it should be in balance would result in the death of all physical forms on earth in the twinkling of an eye.

Such is the balance that Atlantis in its pride and ignorance disturbed ever so slightly, disturbing the surface of the earth enough to adjust the existence of mankind on earth to allow a new beginning, free of the abuse of intellect and free of the amplification of emotional fulfillment for the few rulers who relied on crystals for their control.

Such is an example of the limitations of the first through third weaknesses and strengths of crystals. The first was the amplification of intellect and emotional fulfillment as crystals amplified all that came to them and in so doing made clear to those who used them just what was going on. That the Atlanteans over time failed to balance these possibilities by ensuring that spiritual growth take precedence over mere intellectual growth and fulfillment of emotional needs was in order for that time. We have felt the balance of their choices for these past thirty or more thousand years, as human beings felt the balance in daily expression on earth, feeling that they were wrong all the time for no apparent reason (the reason came from that Atlantean past, you see). Also, in abhorrence for mankind in his pride, there is an echo in the group Soul, so to speak, of that earlier ignorance and pride. We have held such an abhorrence for ourselves long enough, however. It is time to release these things in peace and understanding, letting love once more return to dominate our expressions as once they did in Lemuria and early Atlantis.

Lemuria has a story we will take up in a moment. For now, let us say that mankind has need to forgive itself for Atlantis and the recent cycle of guilty incarnations on earth, as most of you have undergone for the past twenty to forty lifetimes, to one extent or another. We find forgiveness of self the most important single element of growth in the humanity of this current age.

Lemuria and The Way of Harmony

The second strength and abuse of crystals is possible in their harmonizations. For this we will draw on a contrasting scene to that of Atlantis, where amplification in technical ways predominated to the exclusion of the self and Soul in their growth together on earth. This contrasting scene is that of Lemuria, an existence in full bloom prior to that of Atlantis, yet in many ways concurrent with it, on the other side of the world, in the waters of what is now your Pacific and Indian Oceans, whereas Atlantis was dominant in Atlantic waters, quite naturally, and in the areas of Africa and India as well, where eventually Atlantean outposts came to survive the floods that accompanied her destruction. Ragnarok was the name the Norse peoples gave for this destruction, for an end to all things it was, and a beginning of your present times, times spawned first in the freshest ignorance, and only later developing the complexities you have known them for.

Lemuria was as a sister nation or culture to Atlantis. She complemented the excesses and weakness of Atlantis, for she was weak where Atlantis was strong, in the ability to take hold of life on earth and shape it to one's ends, so to speak, shape it to one's needs for material benefit. (Is this not much like your current "Western" culture?) And Lemuria was strong in ways that Atlantis did not care to know: she was harmonizing with all that lay around her, as with the flowers, that each has its own particular gift for mankind, each its own particular blessing of a spiritual or moral nature, in the simple truth of a nature presented in purity.

Let us take but one example of how far such harmonizing with nature can go, as we look at the lotus flower and the lessons it taught the ancient Lemurians directly in the form of experience as powerful as that of any human being on earth today. The lotus flower is a plant that points to resonancies of a particular nature, you see, as do all individual plants or beings in the realms of nature. Lotus flowers bear a gift of their own inner being to one who can attune to these things directly, as we ourselves have learned to do, in part, over the past dozen or so years. The Lemurians could sit on a park bench and experience as strongly as we do our own thoughts the messages of the roots or seeds or stalks of a plant, as well as the nature of the flowers, which are the crowning of the plant kingdom. The plant kingdom was their special resonancy, if you will, but the whole realm of nature was something that drew forth from the Lemurian the sensitivity of his or her being, while it drew forth from the Atlantean only the activity of inner self-discipline to appreciate at all, or to manipulate what was thus discovered.

So we see a contrast in styles and ways of consciousness between the Atlanteans and the Lemurians, if you will, as to the way they functioned in time and space. The Atlantean felt only the amplifications of his or her devices, in time; while the Lemurian experienced the natural world directly, with an intensity that required no devices to amplify what was already present for all who could show sensitivity for all. Thus, for example, in the case of the lotus flower, an Atlantean would look and recognize name and structure and uses for same, but would notice nothing of inner purposes and uses at vibrational levels, even when these were affecting him or her on more subliminal levels. The Lemurian, on the other hand, recognized what was happening in the inner life of a flower or plant, activated in the inner being of his or her own self. The lotus, for example, would give attunement to the Soul in a way that is grounded upon the earth, just as the plant itself is such an attunement, living as it does in both worlds, so to speak—in the darkness and wet mud of its roots, in the watery world of its stalks, and in the way it floats on the surface of the water, completely attuned as well to the qualities of water and air, the qualites of light and perfect order of the Soul, as manifested in its flower and the perfect order of its leaves, which float upon the water in perfect harmony with all. Thus the lotus is itself a symbol of the harmony and attunement we would have you remember from the Lemurians and Atlanteans too in their earliest days. For the lotus was such a symbol to the Lemurians themselves, as it has remained also even in your current times. For the Lemurians, however, it was a direct experience of nature that gave them the sense of what order the lotus manifested for your earth. For your current peoples, it is usually only a pretty symbol of life everlasting, as it is in India today.

The Lotus is like the springtime in a merging of light in earth and water. So for a woman or man lotus can give the perfect balancing of its own example to one sensitive enough to notice its gift. With this one flower, we have given you an instance of the sensitivity of the Lemurian civilization, that could appreciate things in nature in harmony with all life. The Lemurians honored hundreds of plants in the same way they honored the lotus. And the other aspects of nature were likewise appreciated directly.[1]

---

[1] Discussions of Atlantis and Lemuria that might be of interest may be found in the following three books:

Gurudas, *Flower Essences* (Albuquerque, N.M.: Brotherhood of Life, 1983). This book also contains detailed discussions of lotus and other flower essences, as they were used in ancient times and could be used again most profitably.

Eklal Kueshana, *The Ultimate Frontier* (Stelle, Ill.: The Stelle Group, 1963).

Rudolf Steiner, *Cosmic Memory, Atlantis & Lemuria* (Blauvelt, N.Y.: Rudolf Steiner Publications, 1959). This book also appears in a Harper & Row edition under a slightly different title: *Cosmic Memory, A Prehistory of Earth and Man* (New York: Harper & Row, 1981).

Lemuria was as an opposite pole to Atlantis. For she was sensitive as to surroundings, whereas the Atlanteans chose to dominate surroundings. Lemuria was swift to judge the offender of nature, whereas Atlanteans at their best were far more swift to judge the errors of man towards man. In our times the Eastern cultures echo the gifts of Atlantis more fully than those of Lemuria, just as do the Western ones. Yet the Orient, as it has been called, nevertheless retains an echo of that distant land of Lemuria, that felt such peace with the gifts of time and nature as they are right now, without the hand of man doing harm to what simply is. We have since outgrown Lemuria, being closer to the needs of our own times, to dominate ourselves after passing through the harmonizing of Lemuria and the manipulations of Atlantis.

We generalize here at the expense of the many variations that existed in those times through infinite variety and differentiation, then as now. We mention Lemuria to you that you may learn once again from her example, both good and bad. All expressions of mankind could benefit from an inner sensitivity to what is, within ourselves and nature, as was the gift of simple Lemurians. These people were able to sense things we associate with the sensitivities of animals, through sense of smell, taste, hearing and sight. Lemurians were content with little as they harmonized with all, and here was their strength as well as weakness, as now we come around to the strength and weakness of the crystals that is applicable here, that of harmonizing with their surroundings for good or ill.

Lemurians could harmonize with all, and in so doing, they weakened their own abilities to respond through self and Soul. They could not assert their inner forces of independence and sensitivity to others at the level of actions. They were forever dependent on those around them to harmonize with same. Whole cities and colonies of them would grow so dependent on one another that the inability to act was stultifying to those who sought freedom and true growth through choice. The choice to follow and reward others for being followed was all that was allowed in time. And the freedom that is our own gift to life was never allowed to flourish as it should. There were times it did, then as now. But on the whole the dependency of the civilization upon herself was a weight of inertia that sank both Lemuria and Atlantis, as Lemuria valued the Whole at the expense of the parts and the independence of same, in honoring environment and group harmony and dependency more than independent growth in her individuals; and Atlantis honored the conquest of the many by a few "great" individuals, who dominated nature at the expense of the individual for the sake of conquest and superiority of humanity over nature, as they considered themselves to be above any law of their Creation or Preservation in the expanse of God's own work. What a story! What a balance! And it is our own story, the story of our Souls.

Today we could benefit from the past of Lemuria in many ways, in her strengths as well as from seeing through her weaknesses. For we are choosing for ourselves now from out of all our pasts at once. This is the melting pot of time as well as of peoples of your planet in the present. All races and conditions that humanity has ever known are now alive in you and those around you. Choose, if you will, for this is choice you face: to be at one with all you have been; and choose what you will do for now as well as then, balancing what you are with what you at last will be, the oneness of yourself and Soul in perfect integration and love.

Lemuria, then, used crystals equally with the Atlanteans, though we have seldom heard about this use in our more recent times. Atlanteans were the glamorous users of crystals, after all. Often it would have been difficult to tell that Lemurians were using crystals at all, for they left them in place within the ground, you see, allowing the crystals to be used only as a person became able to access them by out-of-the-body travel or by the processes outlined for you in our chapter on the memory and functions of crystals. For men and women who were temple priests and initiates would be guided to use an access crystal for themselves, once they were able to experience first hand the accessing of crystals through the inner mechanisms of sensitivity within the human temple. These people would be placed in an environment of light and support that would allow them to grow in their sensibilities enough to be able to see for themselves, as it were, the gifts waiting in crystals. In our times these gifts must be given to us by our Souls, as we are unable to undergo the preparations necessary to allow this ability to ground out in the physical as direct visioning and hearing of the crystals and their overshadowing Devas, you might say, the beings at work within the creative hierarchies of expression to bring you the mineral kingdom in physical expression on your earth. Thus the Lemurians in the limited natures of their "physical" expressions were able to play with direct perceptions from crystals, whereas the Atlanteans were able to do this to some, small extent (greater than our own but vastly less than the Lemurians of former times), and the Atlanteans thus developed laser-like technologies to access the crystal storage capacities, divorced somewhat from their frequencies of love and emotional content, and divorced even more from the creative beings of guidance and love who had actually created the crystals and were available to you then as now through the forms of their expression, the mineral kingdom and crystal formations of your earth.

For more dramatic effects, the Atlanteans used their technologies to propel themselves to the places where the crystals had formed in earth naturally, without ever interfering with the crystals there—except in a few experimental efforts early on to know crystals by actual digging for them.

More often, Atlanteans used their network of crystalline communication (described earlier) to access across great distances the crystals they worked with and learned from.

The Lemurians, meanwhile, taught a way to travel out of the body to the crystals by way of a "soft" technology, if you will, a temple technology that developed the human body's own abilities to connect with crystals and interface with their awareness and capacities, including memory and activity of different types of healing and blessing. This "soft" technology was itself very detailed and efficient at enhancing natural abilities that would normally not have advanced very far.

The Atlanteans, on the other hand, depended on "hard" technology—as we will choose to call it for now—in order that they might bypass the steps of body development that the Lemurians embraced. The Atlanteans thus were able to program the crystals for their own purposes independent of any spiritual or subtle adeptship on their own parts, though at times they developed these abilities in their own ways as well. The Atlanteans were dependent on their technologies of amplification to attain what the Lemurians did by attunement. And the Atlanteans failed to realize the finer natures of the crystals, preferring to see them as machines or devices, if you will, rather than as the living, outward manifestations of the stars and the beings of guidance for a particular region of the creative hierarchy of life and of mankind as a whole, those in charge of our mineral natures.

Thus the Atlanteans failed to trust themselves to know the truth about themselves, that they were whole in the universal scheme as they touched the universal whole in themselves and in the things around them rather than through the artificiality of their own machines. And the Lemurians were more balanced in this, as it turned out, that they understood the stars in the nature of things; they understood the crystals in themselves, as a living expression of God's creative efforts in us in common with the crystals outside ourselves in the world.

Where did the Lemurians go wrong, you might ask? The Lemurians became dependant upon their own harmonizing abilities with all things. They could not handle dissension. They could not accept experimentation in order to grow, and they could not take the distrust of the stars that came with their choice to accept only half their expression, that of the group instead of the individual. For distrust of the stars was what they seemed to feel as the universe mirrored for them their mistakes, and they withdrew more and more from all things beyond their own kin and wisdoms. So it is in our times as well, were we but sensitive as the Lemurians were to our own inner feelings of choice.

In time, the Lemurians become so enfeebled in their total insulation within stability and harmony that they were unable to fend for themselves outside the group, outside their own temple and energy-enhancing support systems (for they were masters of the technologies of strengthening the bodies of light in the physical). Thus they grew too dependent on the harmonizing abilities of crystals and the environment that acted in the ways crystals do. They accepted the harmony of all things at the expense of growth, and you will find this a tendency within yourselves as well, for you will tend to want to be alone with those who are in harmony with your expressions. You will not want to venture out for growth, to change the way you relate to your world by hard effort on your part. And yet this is necessary for you to do. Each day you must go into the world a bit, even if you are a "housewife," or if you have found a way to make a living from within the sanctuary of your own home. This will strengthen you to deal with things that come your way, if you will do this a little every day of your life, even if you have no practical need to do so. You will weaken yourselves and your ability to deal with adversity and conflict if you do not follow this kind of suggestion in some form.

Also, be able to adjust to the energies of many types of people. As you work with crystals you will find yourself attuned more and more the way the Lemurians were, though the greatest gifts of the Lemurians await a distant future, in terms of what is in store for mankind in the next few lifetimes of your earth. You will find yourself noticing the passions of other men and women as both like your own, yet different every one, and unlike your own as well.

You will notice more at a subtle level too, for you will be able to tell the frequencies of planets and stars as you look up at them in the night, just as has the channel speaking, starting with nights of several summers ago when the stars would speak with their inner natures, healing and blessing as they were noticed and asked for their personal assistance. For stars can assist our growth as well as planets. Try attuning to Sirius some time, or Orion. Or the distant planets of a star of the Pleiades, Alcyone, a sun related to our own, where distant guardians of our race are found at the center of our local star system of elders.

You will see a teaching directly in many things, when you come to this full expression of sensitivity and harmonization, as did the Lemurians at levels past our current capabilities. But like the Lemurians, people in this time will have the danger of being over-sensitive, avoiding conflict to their own impairment, as when they surround themselves with only the energies of love and peace and ignore the world they seek to serve and change in gentle free will possibility over the next several decades of choice.

Today as a Time of Free Will Choosing

We give you this to see the balance of the strengths and weaknesses of using crystals for your growth. It is the Atlantean abuse of power that is most near the possibility that we ourselves possess today. For we are in a time that echoes what has gone before, as all times do, and we are in expression of abuse of power at levels of choice for ourselves and others in this time. This is more than the Atlanteans faced. They saw the choices in terms of domination of others including self, for the sake of emotional experimentation, if you will: for the sake of astral body development, we would say to you. The Atlanteans were your brothers of another time in that they were dominating and dominated, one by another, and they dominated nature—with their force of will.

Today you face a similar situation, but it is different, at least for many of you on earth today (and all in time). This is the situation of choice from the level of the Soul, if you will, and the level of the intellect as well, for this is the age of the intellectual development of mankind. Intellectually we have such freedom today, but this freedom in rarely elevated to the free will level of choice. Usually the intellect is free to experiment with the choices of others, and in so doing, the intellect is dominated by the appearances of the physical world and of the newspapers of your time. For yours is an age of group mind. Though you think you are free to think what you will in this country, you are subject to this mass appeal of the intellect and its choices within the confines of your own national and racial heritage. You are rarely free to be yourself.

This presents us with the final of the three strengths and weaknesses of crystals: the free will responsibility for self that the crystals always allow you. This means they do exactly what you think they do, if you fail to ask them to do anything for you more directly. And if you ask, you are given exactly what you ask for, in all its limitations or lack thereof, because you are respected in truth for what you are and choose to be.

This may seem confusing, that crystals give you free will choice so completely and in so doing seem to have no will of their own. But we can only say to you that it is so: the mechanical nature of all your world is only this, the free will respect that your Creators have for you. The inner wisdom of these things, as seen through your planet in its physical nature, as well as through crystals, is that you will grow in love in choices of your own choosing rather than choices from outside yourselves, from other Souls in freedom you aspire to.

This is the simple choice you face, and like the times of Atlantis and Lemuria gone by, this time shall face a choosing it will fail at if it does not listen to the inner voice of God within, the inner voice of perfect choice made whole. You are here to grow as one with Soul; no other way will do for now. You are here to first become the One you are in truth, then to know the possibilities for self expression/Soul expression as one thing in God's own heart. This is all you have ever been asked to learn. In different ways and choices you have come to make your lives. In this current time, as in times gone by, the way is the same and yet it is unique as well, most like the choice of free will expression itself for now, most like the choice of making up your own mind in harmony with all or not, just as Atlanteans knew choice in realms of desiring, amplifying what they wanted in harmony with God's will or no; and Lemuria knew choice in same, the love of God, as they were given choices to grow in self-responsibility, harmonizing with the crowd the energies around them.

This is the time to begin again to heal the wounds of our past expressions, the old ways of your lives on earth that went before, and know the truth wherein you find your freedom, whole in God as love and life and more: the self-same one as God's own Child of love.

Chapter Twenty-eight

Crystals & Other Therapeutic Practices

The next thing for us to take up with you is the connection between quartz crystal healing and other healing modalities. This will surprise some, that quartz crystals can enhance most other healing efforts. We give you this idea so that you will know the universality of what you are dealing with. A portrait of yourself in perfection, if you will, exists in these crystals of light and love that are within you. You are dealing with an outward element of parallel construction that can magnify the good intentions of any healer.

We will list for you some other healing modalities and discuss the support work that crystals and you can do for each of these in turn.

Beginning with healing as a balancing practice, concerned with balancing and aligning of subtle bodies, we will proceed to crystal polarity work; meridian work in general (including acupuncture, if it is appropriate for you to do this type of work under your qualifications); massage, with a bit on shiatsu and acupressure work; work with vibrational remedies including homeopathy, flower essences, gem essences, and combination remedies; medical practices such as first aid, healing broken bones and recovery from surgery; a few words on natural treatment and prevention of illness, including the use of doctors and allopathic medicine; and lastly, something on counseling, including psychiatric procedures.

The list is really endless for what can be done to complement the particular work of any health care practitioner with the use of vibrational applications of crystal therapy. We will give you enough information to generalize from there with your own creative efforts, for your own creativity is an essential ingredient in any successful curative process, and your own creativity is the way you grow as you apply the things you have learned to others and yourself as well. For we are all guided to grow through the creative processes of our own Souls, in conjunction with the aspects of our own free will choices.

We will begin with an overview of healing as it appears to us, and then as it applies to you.

Healing the Human Body
The Process of Unfoldment

The human body is a subtle process of alignment of many levels. If you could see graphically the natural balance of the human body it would look like this:

figure 17. (a sphere within a triangulation of energies)

This is not to say that there are not more complex energies at work here as well, for the human body takes a form that is relative to each condition it finds itself in, including that of the world in your modern era. It only means that there is a hidden form behind the appearance of a human being that you will be dealing with most certainly as you are serving the growth of a child of light in love.

The best thing you can do is to heal the form of what truly is for a human being. This is called by us regeneration of the body physical (physical, emotional, mental, causal, if you will)—and by this we mean all that is subject to error and decay within the being of man/woman. This regeneration process is looked to by us as a precondition for growth on other levels, as the condition of the "physical" (as we have called it here in a larger context than your own) is a reflection quite literally of the condition of the Soul as it relates to physical expressions through time and space dimensions.

It is the Soul that grows over time and space without growing old or weak or ill at ease with itself for what it is. For the Soul is in perfection even as it expresses its own true nature, and its own true nature is love and light, at play in God through growth over aeons of your time.

We would give you this information to know that the Soul expresses through you without risking loss in any way. The Soul is in perfection, and yet it grows through many millions of your years, hundreds and hundreds of millions of your years in fact. The Soul learns by doing what you would have it do to guide you, and—if you allow it to—by balancing the expressions of your life and your actions through reflecting them back for you in the perfection or lack thereof of all you do and say, all you think and feel. If you do not allow this process during your lifetime, your Soul will guide you to this process after you have died.

To say this in another way, you cannot hurt yourself at the level of your Soul, though you can teach your Soul how to be at levels that you are familiar with. Your Soul shall grow from all you do, be it good, bad or indifferent; and therefore, what is it that you can do that can harm your Soul in all the things that are possible for you?

The Soul is perfect, yet it grows. This is the key for understanding how you serve your Soul, and how your Soul balances out your life and its expressions by mirroring back on you and subsequent expressions of itself in future human personality forms on earth the imperfections you create in your thoughts and feelings, words and deeds, and in your love or lack of love on earth.

Dissatisfaction of self with self is often only reaction to attempts by Soul to reach you, at the level of personality, with the possibility that you might grow in any situation, no matter how difficult it may look for you to change. A process of balancing is going on for all. And the balancing can come suddenly with a change of attitude or attention, or it can come slowly over many expressions in human form, as a person reacts or fails to react to the hints from Soul that there is room for growth in such and such an area of expression.

Why are you given this process of balancing of your expressions? We would say to you that nothing is simple in the process of conveying why you are here on earth. It is a trial and test to be here. Yet there is deep significance for us in all you do, for you create with deeds the world you choose to live. Over many lifetimes, this is true for all. And what you do is mirrored in the whole of God and man/woman on earth. All areas of expression in the Soul are mirrored in the heart of God in truth, and all forms of the Soul's expression are also mirrored in the heart and mind and being of a man/woman on earth. All that you do will resonate in God as well as man. And all that you do will change the patterns of your growth in ways you do not know, yet ways that are quite good for all. And we mean for all when we say all.

The mirroring we speak of is done on different levels in quite precise ways. The physical body itself is a mirroring of the ways that we are aligned with God or misaligned. And this is the purpose of this book, to heal the misalignment by sharing with you a perspective of the point of view of your own Souls as you work with self and Soul through crystals of light and love, inside you and without.

The guidelines for this work with crystals in balancing the work of the angels as they function in your bodies are to notice what exists for a person, including yourselves, and redirect the energies that are misaligned, at whatever level this may be so, to fit the perfect pattern of creation for a Soul on earth who is choosing to be in two-armed form, if you will: in the form of Adam and Eve. (By the way, angels do indeed work within your forms to keep them up for you; without their deeds within you, all unknown by you, you would disintegrate in a matter of hours into formless dust and less substantial fare than that.) This overall pattern of choosing the direction of an energy balancing for another is appropriate in this time. It is the proper way to grow, to share your growth with others, and to learn from others than yourself what it is you lack or need if you are unable to do so for yourself.

This is an overview, and yet the basic pattern is the same for all: that misdirected energies are instilled with patterns of their wholeness as you notice them and adjust them at the appropriate level of truth for growth, and this is done through you from the level of your Souls as well as the personalities of those you work upon, for without their permission, nothing can be done that is not for you alone. You alone can be changed when you alone are involved at a conscious level giving your permission for change. Others will have to give their permission on an individual basis, case by case, and you will have to assist them in this, for few of them know their permission is really involved; and yet it is, for all are free to grow as they choose here on your earth, and all are in the order for which they are intended when first they see that they are in charge of all they do and are in truth.

The next thing we would take up for you is the misalignment of the subtle bodies, for it is this alignment or lack of it for which you are responsible in this life. You are responsible to be whole and indwell the light, if you will, but it is our responsibility to see you are in charge of what you are given, that moment to moment you are given the choice for which you were intended, and this choice manifests through your subtle bodies, your emotional faculties, your thoughts (which are likewise organized for you in orders of energy or chakras, that correspond to the resonancies of the universe in ways that are ordered by God on all levels), your energies, and your intentional causation. This last is what we would call the final level for which you are responsible: the level of your creational impulses mirrored in your "physical realms," the realms subject to decay and death. This final level is called causative or causal because it generates the others at frequencies less rarefied to your intelligence and conscious experience. And all these levels are subject to change and decay, all are physical from our point of view, that of your Souls as well. All are in regular octaves of expression or branches that together form the trees of life that find their reflection in other realms besides your own—in your Soul and you. So there are regular patterns of seven, twelve, five and four that echo through creation. Take, for example, the patterns of five—earth, water, fire, air and ether, if you will, at one level; or physical, etheric, astral, mental and causal, if you will at a second level; or "physical," Soul (the "water" aspect of the whole of your being, as it were, correspondencing to Pisces, the fish, the Christ or Universal Love aspect of God), Father/Mother Creator God level of being, and the level of the Creative Mass itself, with the fifth or ether correspondence level being the sequence of the whole, the completion of all four previous expressions in a synthesis of integration.[1]

It will be a step that awaits further evolution of this planet for mankind to integrate the completeness of the Whole into its being, yet the understanding of this completeness is useful for the correspondences that exist between the vast beginnings of your Universal consciousness and the completions of evolution that await you in the distant future of your expressions. We give you this that you may be encouraged with your work to understand the stars, even though you yourself will share in these destinies only vicariously in this or any other single lifetime on a planet of limitation of expression. So we ask you to continue with your efforts to understand all things, even though we know you will succeed in this only as you grow into yourself, as it were—grow into who you are at other levels of choice and destinies of the distant future. Sing out for joy in these destinies that await you, for they are as joyous as you will allow them to be, even now. You are a child of a uni-verse that loves. You are the calling that the stars have been born for, you and all other children of light and love. And you are as God, one with the destiny of all, child of Mother/Father God, who is beyond your current comprehension of loveliness, but who is also more likely to give you all loveliness with every moment that passes, for you are

---

[1] These five are to be taken up in greater detail in our book *Patterns of the Whole, Vol. II: Subtle Body Anatomy*, to be released in the next year or so.

accepting more and more all the time, and this is the choice we would prepare you for in time: to accept or reject yourselves as God's own Child, as nothing short of who God is for you and all on earth and in the stars as well. For are you not as he/she is? Are you not of love? And are you not worthy to be who you really are in fullness?

So it is from our point of view. From your point of view you are faced with choices of sickness and wellness, life and death choices, as it were. You are confronted with pressures to grow that seem to be from outside yourselves in time and space, though this is only an illusion of form at a certain level, and at other levels where it is real there is nothing outside your form that does not resonate completely with you as inside your whole of attention and consciousness. So we say to you that nothing is outside your whole, nothing is less than who you are, and nothing is given to you by chance, even though it seems to be a powerless world that confronts you in random ways; so you would deal with it, anyway, when you deal with yourselves from the point of view of sickness and wellness outside the context of who you really are as child of God. Thus it is we deal so thoroughly with the so-called spiritual side of your specialties of healing before we undergo any learning or teaching about the selected topics of health and healing we would practically apply your work with crystals to.

Specifics on your work with others are, after all, transitional. Your practices and trainings are as a bridge to those you will use once you awaken to your true natures. You are given what is appropriate to you at any given time, as are all those who align themselves with any given path for expressing their healing natures through the material expressions of the Soul of all. Is this to your understanding?

Our next topic, the misalignment of the subtle bodies of humanity, is a subject unto itself, full of wisdom and differentiation for all men and women. For now, we direct you to the list of suggested reading for further sources for your work with crystals that include some basic texts on subtle anatomy. The process of aligning subtle bodies is something touched on in the chapter on healing and quartz crystals earlier on. Refer to it if you have not done so already for a foundation on what follows. With the intention of aligning the chakras you begin to align the subtle bodies as well, for they are all tied in with what you do on different levels of the "body physical," as we have described that which is subject to change and decay within your Souls. (For you are all within your Souls in God, are you not?)

Once you are working with subtle body healing, as you will be in any case no matter what discipline you take up—from pills, needles and medical surgery all the way to processes of growth at the level of the Soul—you will be concerned with subtle body alignment or lack thereof. The process of subtle body alignment is subject to correction at any time by the Soul of the one you are treating. This is important to understand. As you are treating a person, it is not in order for you to undo the work of that person's Soul, even if you are ignorant of these things, or unwilling to cooperate to any great extent with the Souls involved as you work—yours and your client's. For you are dealing with a learning experience in the patterning of the Soul, as you are dealing with life in death, in your own context, in the ultimate terms of what this is for you, to be alive on earth as well as in the stars of God.

We say this to you that you will understand we work within the greater context of your Soul at all times, and we guide you now to see things more from that perspective as well, that you may integrate your lives with that of your Creator. This is to know the oneness that exists in the intentions of God, as all Souls work to enjoy the growth of the physical plane with as much detachment on your part as possible. For with detachment comes the ability of your own Soul to work through you for the light and growth of all, and that is why you are here: to shepherd those who come for experience to meet the experiences that are in order for them at any given time.

In our time, it is the return to God as light that is encountered behind the scenes of reality as you know it, and it is the free will choice to love that is harbored most deeply by the Creator Gods themselves, for the effort of the One God, as you would call him/her, is to find as many Souls as possible to share in this creative endeavor at any given level of existence. And at your level you are chosen to cooperate with the forces of growth that manifest in the Christ and other beings of light and love on earth.

So you are given an opportunity to help those in need who come to you for their growth. It is in this context we give you the following suggestions on specific paths for treatment, in the full knowledge that you will work with these things as best you may, growing in light and truth as you do so; for you are here to cooperate that you may grow as well, healing the people who come to you in need, that you may experience the truth of what you believe as you practice it with others. So it has always been on earth, and so it shall be for a time for you until you are ready to grow into other forms of expression that are not included in the earth experience at the present time, the experiences of the Divine incarnated in mankind on a world of your own choosing.

We say this to you that you will find for yourself the context for your work, not that we will dictate it for you. For there are as many paths to attain the goals you seek, and these are the ones you choose as a child of God in love. The specifics we will leave to you as you grow accustomed to the practices we present. You are able to pick for yourselves what will serve you. Feel free to modify in any way, and test all that we, your author, are given—and give to you in turn—from the level of our Souls. For at a personality level, we have in turn played and worked with the sources of truth that have come to us in a creative way, in conjunction with our own inner guidance; and we recommend the process of testing, with your own common sense and understanding, all that comes your way.

Polarity

The first set of specifics to consider, then, are those that deal with polarity. Polarity is a process of allowing a person's own energies to do the work for you through the medium of your own body. You place your two hands upon a person, thus allowing a polarity to be set up between the two expressions that are under your hands. The flow that will result will be the process of the consciousness of the person you treat adjusting to the closer alignment of the area of one expression with that of another. Energy from one location of your hand will flow to the other if the amount of energy in the first is greater than that in the second, due to the greater consciousness or awareness that has been allowed to focus there, for whatever reason of blockage or greater appreciation of the area in question. Thus you will allow yourself to be a channel for the current to flow, from one point on the person you treat to another, across the span of your hands, then up your arm perhaps, across your shoulders, and back to the first point in question through your other hand. This allows you to let people heal themselves or do all the work themselves, as much as possible.

This in brief is the process of polarity work. The details we will leave to you for further study. See the suggestions for further reading if you would have sources for further information on the subject.

What we propose to do is enhance the work of polarity for those of you who are acquainted with it. We suggest you study it first with others before you apply it in full with crystals. Thus the crystals will serve the specific understanding with which you use them, rather than being vaguely expected to take the place of detailed knowledge at every turn. They will in fact do this up to a point, but we suggest complementing them with your work in specific fields, as this knowledge you acquire is a respecting of the details of God as well as the details of man, and the details are to be honored as much as the whole. He who loses sight of the details, as we have said, will lose sight of himself as a being on the earth and a detail among the beautiful and meaningful details that fill our universe of light and love and hope for all. Details though we may be, we are expressions of wholeness as well, and we are children of God to be respected every one, in all our glory as well as in all our detail on earth or whatever other level of development we may find ourselves to be.

The details of polarity can be enhanced with crystals by allowing the crystals to set up the perfect degree of polarity at either point you wish to choose. The crystals will oscillate to frequencies of expression that are precise for that particular location, whatever it may be, heart, head, feet, hips, shoulders, thighs, etc.

The exact nature of the polarity exchange is little understood in your time. It is dependent on adjustments of minute detail from the point of view of Soul at the time of the actual polarizing. It does not take place automatically, but rather appears to take place automatically as the Souls of both people, the treated as well as the therapist, adjust the energies of both to fit the needs of the moment. Crystals can be used to enhance this process in that they are attuned to work at a "physical" perfection that is only possible for a saint or one with a perfected aura. This is the level of the etheric and astral, the energy and emotional states of the being respectively. We give you this to know the general reason why all your work with energies, of whatever level, can be enhanced by using crystals, as this is the way crystals work—fine-tuning your energies with their example and the free-flowing channeling they are able to do, as you will be able to do as your energy and light bodies are balanced for you by God and through your own Souls as well. You are given this work to grow in working with yourself on others, and as you do this work you will grow your own vehicles of expression for your service efforts here on earth at the same time you heal the vehicles of others, temples as they are to God in love. This healing work you do will use the ability of crystals to oscillate with exact energies or frequencies, if you will, though the energies involved do not have frequencies or intervals at all as you know them, at many levels of their existence: they are instead of an instantaneous nature here on earth, not subject to refraction or reflection in time and space at all, but rather of a wave nature only on the dimension that they themselves exist upon; on other dimensions they may express as instantaneous rather than such continuous flow as light appears to be on earth. To illustrate, love itself may appear to flow when it takes on appearances of cause and effect on earth, but as a state of being it is instantaneous as the knowing love of God instead of conditional or discontinuous in expression. So it is with the "frequencies" you will find existing in your crystals, as resonance or as instantaneous nature of being in itself.

The goal you have with crystals, by the way, is to be like them. It is to know yourself as one with the energy states you can experience as you work with what you notice outside yourself in the dynamics of crystals as one with the processes you are capable of yourself. So polarity with crystals will enable you to grow with this experiencing, as you use a crystal in each hand to polarize the being of the person you are dealing with at two distinct focuses of polarity or more, as the case may be.

With crystals, an additional polarity technique is available that is not available with your hands. You may create additional "hands" for yourself by using crystals in the following way: place a crystal at any point you wish the polarity of the person to work from. Then place another crystal at a second point. You have set up a polarity that is just as effective as the one you might contemplate making using your hands alone.

You will find you may set up further polarity patterns with crystals, using your hands to assist you as you wish. Thus the entire pattern of the polarization of the hips with shoulders, in diagonal resonancy across the chest, balancing left and right, right and left—this pattern can be done simultaneously with crystals. See the diagram below for one way this can be done. The pattern of the five-pointed star, an expression of these same diagonal resonancies in completion, is a proper model for these patterns, as pointed out in the book, *Like A Hollow Flute.*[2]

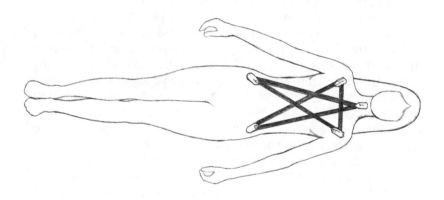

figure 18. five-pointed star polarity pattern

If you are not yet familiar with the workings of crystals, it may be surprising to you that polarity work can be so easily done using them. There are several ways you might envision the polarity between two crystals working in resonancy with one another. Perhaps the best way is to visualize that the polarities or relative attention focused for the moment at each location are equalized through the flow from crystal to crystal

---

[2] Maruti Seidman, *Like a Hollow Flute* (Santa Cruz, Ca.: Elan Press, 1982). This is a good, basic book on polarity therapy.

as across the person's own energy field, or "around" it—for crystals are not limited in time and space as we have said. A current can flow between crystals either across the direct space you can see before your eyes over time, or it may flow "around" time, as it were, bypassing the normal three-dimensional conventions you assume, through other planes or levels of existence—balancing in patterns of instantaneous resonancy, so to speak. These two ways of looking at polarity balancing are both useful. Imagining the flow from one point to another will help develop participation in the process and an ability to notice what is taking place at subtle levels over time. Imaging the flow outside of time and space is also useful, for it can be noticed as a second step, after noticing current flows, that there is instantaneous resonancy overall that is itself most effective for healing—for the directness of the exchange without obstacles or interference.

Actually, the polarity process as you know it is more a process of instantaneous resonancies adjusting dynamically than it is a process of a crude flow taking place that is limited like the banks of a river limit the water flowing; the resonancies involved do take place instantaneously, at least to a certain degree, especially if you allow them to do so as you work. If you limit yourself to the flow that can be felt as from one pole to another, you merely limit yourself to that which you can at present imagine in your current conceptual frameworks for growth. Much better to reach a point in your work, whatever that work may be, where you are able to release such conceptualizing to the duties of your Soul and your God in truth, thus giving us and them free rein to work with you in spite of whatever limitations you may have in your concepts of time and space. We will assist you in any event, but the more open and conscious the permission level we work with the more we can give you from the level of your Souls, in the way of cooperation and growth exchange from one Soul to another. The only limits on our work are those you place there yourselves, for we are subject to your free will, as you are subject to ours. And you are as God in this, as well as are we.

So we have given you a sense of the resonance that exists in polarity work as well as the use of crystals to do this work, as you increase your abilities to polarize situations in the bodies of man to many times what you could do with only two hands and with the limited actualizations that you may currently express in your energy fields, as crystals represent for you the completion of the potentials of those energy fields in ways that speak to the future of your own development in the next few years, as well as the next few decades for those other than yourself who may not at this time be actively drawn to complete their energy circuits through means such as using crystals.

Working With the Meridians

We will next turn to energy balancing with the meridians, as in acupuncture, acupressure or shiatsu. The meridians are capable of being directly stimulated using crystals. Knowledge of these meridians in great detail is not essential to do this, though it is useful for the activities you would undertake at this time, in that it gives yet another detailed feedback system with which to work connecting your understanding and cooperation with what is being done from the level of your Soul and your guidance, should you be actively allowing us to work with you through God's grace. We suggest you study the meridians from the point of view of Indian Ayurvedic medicine as well as the traditional Chinese acupuncture, as the Ayurvedic concepts of the elements of coolness and heat are complementary to those of traditional Chinese understanding and would supplement the limitations of the balancing of yin and yang and the five elements of classical Chinese medicine to include the astral influences that Indian medicine attunes to. You would find that the approach of acupuncture is dealing with the astral level only indirectly, and herein lies the source of its weakness as a treatment modality when used solely as a primary modality of treatment. It is an astral influence that is most felt with illness in our time, for the emotional states of Western humanity are as the cause of much of its distress at a physical level. The subtle emotions that are as habit for human beings are not understood or appreciated in the ways that they actually affect you, being causative of much illness.

For example, curative approaches to leukemia would have to take into account self-worth issues at a basic level of forgiveness of self if they are to prove useful in the long run for the

Soul involved, and to do so they must take note of the conscious conditions of the person's intellect and emotions as they interrelate in thought and in actual emotional states of existence. The proper treatment of this and other diseases will come when there is no separation in healing modalities, but all levels of treatment are employed in a complementary fashion, utilizing each at the level of its greatest effectiveness so as to draw upon all levels of a being's expression.

Acupuncture, for example, would be most useful in diseases of the energy meridians, in which the flow of the person's chi or meridian forces is blocked to a great degree, thus allowing no proper balance at this level of the being. The times when such treatment is most in order are when the physical level itself bears the symptoms of greatest distress for the patient or client. At other levels, such as emotional expressions or belief systems, the treatment would have to seek other modalities to be most effective.

If the acupuncture or other meridian work is used in isolation from other modalities, it will be short-lived in its effectiveness, for the healing of the emotions are as key in our time to work on the individual, and unless you can heal the cause for the disturbance at a causative level, you will not find your work taking effect at the deepest levels you wish to work upon.

Nonetheless, meridian work is essential in many instances for maximum effectiveness, and it can be an access point for treatment, with other modalities being brought in once the meridian work has established a sense of what is taking place between the client and the practitioner.

We ourselves use meridian work as an adjunct to the work of balancing at other levels of expression, usually when people need a physical or energy boost to their efforts to come into harmony with themselves. Often it is best to begin so, with a meeting of the immediate symptomatic needs and a strengthening of the meridian system in general, before work on other more basic levels can be effective. It is something like the need to eliminate physical pain and exhaustion before doing much else in cases of accidents; or like the need to eliminate immediate traumatic reactions and weaknesses before getting at the underlying imbalances. Thus it is possible to see that the client has first been stabilized and strengthened on a short term or near-emergency basis. And meridian work can often be effective as one tool in such an approach.

For meridian work in general—whether or not you choose to use it in the way we do—we suggest using crystals once you have a sense of what you are doing with crystal work. Also we suggest studying a bit in at least one of the various traditional ways of treating the meridians directly, using this detailed work as a reference for what follows.

With this background in mind, you may use a crystal to implant an astral or etheric "needle" of light at full force in the exact, most effective spot on your standard acupuncture insertion points or meridian points. This is possible if you ask us to assist you, for at the level of your ordinary consciousness it is completely impossible for you to do this kind of thing effectively. It is easy, however, for us to do it. You should ask that we work in the way that is for the highest and best good of all when we work, in harmony with the earth and the stars, under the will of God—or whatever other way you have of directing that we work in accordance to what is a sacred methodology for us to work, in harmony with all that is designed for your best, orderly evolution among the stars of time and space unfoldment. We give you this suggestion here again, for it is not possible for you to work with acupuncture in this way unless you are thoroughly familiar with working with your Higher Self and your angelic healing guidance for light work under many different conditions. The knowledge that is required for this exact type of work also depends upon detailed communication between yourself and your Soul (or your angelic guidance, if you will, though we suggest Soul guidance as a more essential aspect of this effort to communicate at levels of your own divine nature). You must be able to ask for exactly what you wish to have happen, if you are using this form of vibrational acupuncture, for you will have to know details of meridian points, the length of time for insertion and when, the level at which it is to be inserted (astral, causal, etheric, etc.) and the exact vibrational rate or frequency for the insertion itself. You must ask us to do at least the last of these for you, since it will be well nigh impossible for you to have a sense for these things through your study or experience on the earth plane level. Mechanically it would be quite difficult as well, for how would you go about giving instantly a 10 mm vibrational frequency to an astral needle of light if we were not here to help you with your intentions? There are devices that could do this, but the technology required is beyond your time as yet, and it is quite unnecessary when once you align with your Soul and other assistance from levels of your own divinity in God. For we can see very clearly the exact level that is desirable for these insertions, both as to level and as to frequency or potency, if you prefer, for we can work with homeopathic potency levels as a language of communication as to frequency.

We give you the above detailed, rather advanced information about acupuncture on subtle levels for we would like you to convey this to others as rapidly as possible that this is in fact the superior way of doing acupuncture in the first place. Needles will work, you know, but not at the levels we are discussing here. And the effectiveness of your approach with needles is limited by the necessity for careful training in the medical arts of anatomy and oriental medicine if you are to be licensed or allowed to puncture the skin of a patient or client with a thing as dangerous as a needle of steel. The finest operation possible at this level, with the use of steel, is only to approximate the effectiveness of an etheric level insertion of a needle of light, which can be inserted without need for precautions at a physical level, and which can be inserted by us for you, once you ask us rather precisely, at levels of exact dimensionality (by this we mean the reality behind your concepts of astral, causal, physical and etheric dimensions or levels), frequency (or potency if you prefer), duration (for time too is an important element for the treatment), and positioning (for the exact point in question must be activated or influenced if the needle treatment is to be effective: a needle a millimeter off to one side or another may not work effectively; and a depth of half an inch when a quarter or a third of an inch might have been best will again throw off the treatment, however slightly, as the exact timing or release required may be delayed or, in certain instances, missed altogether when the depth of insertion is incorrect). We can do this for you, this exact coordination of all elements involved with insertion of vibrational needles, at levels of perfection you can only dream of. And in this we are a part of your possibility of effective expression on earth as a healer and active coordinator of the blessing available to all through the Divine in humanity as well as God.

The reason for your need to know in such detail what we are doing at these levels with acupuncture is that there is a basic law regarding our intervention on your plane of existence, in order that you might have the integrity of your own choices honored. We say to you that we are allowed to intervene only in special circumstances once the needs of your normal maintenance and subtle feedback systems are accounted for. For us to heal you must ask us. Otherwise we allow cause and effect, action and reaction, to direct your lives at the levels where they are appropriate. We use these things for your growth, but we do not override your choices, actions, thoughts, feelings and energy levels. If you sleep too late, for instance, we do not heal you to overcome this difficulty. You experience it until the normal course of healing is complete for you in a few days time, no matter what the results. If your boss is angry at you for being late to work as a result, we do not intervene, you see. And at subtle levels this is true as well in a similar manner, though there are in fact many exceptions and additions we would have to tell you of to complete your picture of how we work in balancing your lives in this manner.

The approach we must take with you is that you are in charge of your own lives until you ask us to take on some of the responsibility. If you ask that this be in the way that is perfectly appropriate for you, we may intervene in some instances just to encourage you to help yourself by helping us. But also, we will help you because you have allowed us to. It is your free will choice we are honoring in this. Thus, the direct work on meridians is your responsibility. It is not in order for us to direct this level of your existence. You are in charge of it. Thus, you must ask us in detail exactly what you wish us to do for you. Again, if you ask us, we can tell you what treatments or healings would be best in as much detail as you ask for and are ready to handle. And if you ask us for further assistance, we can then apply the methods or treatments we have recommended to you but a moment before. So can there be a pattern of cooperation that overrides or releases the limitations that must sensibly exist between your personality's world of expression and ours.

We are not required to keep you in the dark about yourselves, you see. We will call this the law of free will choice as it applies to the areas of overlapping or mutual responsibilities for us both. If you ask for it, there are some areas, rather broad ones, in which we can be of assistance, although there are others we cannot, for they are wholly in your hands. These are areas of the physical plane itself, the location of objects or people, the practical sorting out of what you will do and with whom. We can give advice where the choices for you are harder than you are able to evaluate easily from your physical level of existence, but usually we will only clarify such choices for you, giving you the ultimate decision-making responsibility. Thus we cooperate with you in some areas; we leave others to you; we take care of others automatically (as is the case with your healing and resting during sleep); and others we are capable of handling if you allow us to. You can be conscious of some of what we handle as we do so for you, and some of it you will need to evaluate with the help of your Soul, as it is long term or exists primarily in realms you are not capable of evaluating with any sensory capacity you currently possess at the levels you are conscious of existing on. We say these things to you to explain in part the apparent discrepancy or confusion you might feel as to why we can intervene so meticulously at etheric levels when we ordinarily do not show ourselves in your frequencies of expression.

We could spend a much greater time evaluating what we have said for you, but instead we will leave this to your own understanding unfoldment and hope the rest of this book and the others in the series that are to follow will give you additional insight into this your condition on earth.

One further point we might make here—though your common sense will probably already have told you this: the detailed involvement with any technical approach to healing is not necessary. The details of acupuncture are not necessary any more than those of another methodology, as the simplicity of the coming to your own awareness of self and Soul are what is essential and in order for all at this time. The details only lend familiarity and purpose to those who work with them or accept their power in their lives. All in the world accept the power of details such as these to some extent, and therein lies their usefulness; for by using them to undo the need for detail, you will inevitably respect the simplicity of what we bring you all the more. The tools we give you here are transitional. As we said earlier in this chapter, many techniques of healing you will use are likely to be useful only for a short time, but during that time they will be very useful. We outgrow one set of toys to take up another. That is the gist of it.

To go on, there are other meridian applications with crystals that are simpler than the approach we have given you above. We have guided you to the possibilities that exist for acupuncture at once so that you will value and appreciate our ability to work with you in fullness of expression at this time. In former times this was not so as now. We are in a time of growth that allows us to work with you more directly than ever before, as you come to understand just what it is you are dealing with, the completion of your own expressions of Soul, and self at the level of the Soul. We give you now more details of acupuncture work as it is usually performed.

The application of needles for acupuncture can be greatly enhanced using quartz crystals. First, it is not generally understood that the needle itself carries a vibration or level of expression that effectively passes over into the person receiving the application. This means that you are constantly giving one person the vibration of the last to be treated unless the needles have been cleared of their energies. Boiling and sterilization is essential for this reason, as well as for reasons of sanitation understood by conventional medical applications of acupuncture.

The needle may also carry a charge that is gratefully received by the patient as a blessing, much as the vibration of a homeopathic remedy or flower essence might be received by the same patient orally. We suggest therefore that you place your needles in a tray with a crystal, or better still, a triangulation of small crystals, that you leave in the tray for that purpose. The sterile conditions of this tray should be maintained, yet a crystal may be placed in it, as a crystal cannot of itself contain any contaminating elements for such treatment, and will rather insure that the needle is "programmed," if you will—though we prefer the word "oriented" in this instance—to meet the needs of the patient or client in the ways that the current applications might dictate.[3]

---

[3] We might point out as a warning here that the effective treatment of crystals includes the possibility of cleaning them with sea salt, sea salt water or blessing, but not the use of boiling for sterilization as you will damage your crystals quite rapidly with rapid change of temperatures.

To do this, you may simply program the crystal to charge the needles and continually adjust their energies, to meet the needs of the current client for his or her highest and best good, in the way that is in order for his or her Soul and growth. This will insure that we are able to work with you to adjust the frequencies of the needle itself as it is used for different persons; provided of course that you have asked us to do the adjusting and programming of the crystal for you at the levels of your own divinity and that of your Creator as well. For we are here to assist you in this, and we are capable, as you are not, of adjusting for all the factors that might enter into the choice of exact vibration that is allowed to affect the needle in each instance.

We would like to give you a third application for crystals in conjunction with acupuncture, as we say to you that by touching a crystal to the end of a needle that has already been inserted into a client, you will be able to impart a vibration through the needle into the person you are treating that is like an electrical insertion of energy, thus releasing the meridian point you are choosing to affect far more rapidly than might otherwise be the case, with much greater precision of interaction of energies. In addition, in this way you may have the needle vibrationally affect the person at astral or emotional levels that ordinarily would not be reached at all by needle insertion, thus greatly enhancing the effectiveness of your meridian work, for the meridian points are greatly affected by direct insertions of energy from levels that command their orientations and alignments, so to speak, as is the case with the downward flows of the astral and etheric from levels of expression more subtle than those of the meridians themselves.

Thus you may ask us to work through you as you insert a needle, then place an activating crystal to its exposed end. We will see that it is charged appropriately as you ask us to, even if you understand you cannot possibly know the right frequencies involved yourself. We can tell you if you ask, but this is not necessary, unless you choose to insert an astral or etheric needle in place of the physical one through the simple expediency of touching a crystal to the already inserted needle with this intent. Again, you need not know in advance just what you will do. Ask us, and we will tell you if it is best to do any astral or etheric insertions in the first place. Then we will tell you if it is best to insert the crystal needle by itself or in conjunction with a physical one. The factors involved are complex and exist on many levels you are not aware of, but you will know with your common sense grounding and experience whether what we say to you is accurate or not. We will train you quite systematically at this if you allow us to work with you over the course of several years of your expression. We will test you in many ways as we go along, to keep you involved with this in a way that is active and sensible; but we will also guide you to see the best ways for your growth.

We suggest you find those who like yourselves may be exploring work with their own Souls, as this will greatly lessen the chances for error or misinterpretation of what is happening for you as you grow in cooperation with us.

The next application of crystals to meridian work is simpler still. It is possible to touch the needles only to give a simple blessing to the person through them, in whatever way is appropriate. This is not something that need be detailed or explicit. And something will always happen when you do this. You need only keep your crystals clean and programmed for such a blessing in perfection.

Lastly, we would give you a simple technique for knowing which points to insert your needles into, especially if you are using vibrational needles rather than physical ones, as the latter require—in our opinion at least—considerable training and guidance from experience in a clinical setting. The following technique works admirably with physical needles as well, but, again, we strongly caution you to first become fully trained in acupuncture before you go putting needles into anyone. Once you are trained, of course, you may confirm with your understanding and clinical experience all that we give you. But you must still check and confirm our input with your own, as we will not allow you to depend on us overmuch, and will from time to time test you to see if you are becoming dependent on us to the exclusion of your own inner activity and insight. In other words, stay grounded with anything you are given from the level of your Soul. Use your common sense and insight on your own to confirm or reject anything that comes to you, whether it comes from God or the negative expressions of same.

With vibrational needles, you may insert energies by looking on an acupuncture chart and asking which meridians you
will be involved with. We can give you the correct points to
activate for yourselves or for others by dousing techniques or
by direct inner guidance, depending on the stage of contact that
is appropriate for you. We can then guide your hand to the
exact point, as we will say "yes" inside you when you reach
the point; or we may let you know intuitively without words,
if this is your best approach to contact with us; and we will
give you a positive indication with any dousing technique,
such as stick plate or pendulum as well—again, if this is the
appropriate method for you.

The timing, then, can be up to you as you use your intuitive
sense for when the points are releasing and need no further
work. Or you can ask us to let you know exactly when the
release has been effected and the "needle" is no longer necessary. The above technique works especially if you are using
the actual physical needles of metal or are using light needles
after the same patterns as the physical ones require. We would
suggest to you, however, that another pattern of usage will
prove just as effective if not more so, that of asking us the
"dosage" rates of the vibrational needles, such as 10 mm (for a
lower astral treatment) or 20x (for a more etheric treatment)
and then asking us the treatment schedule that would be optimal for you and the patient or client. Such a schedule can be
expressed in terms of normal dosages, just as you might describe dosages of crystal use or of medicines such as homeopathics or gem elixirs and flower essences (e.g., twenty minutes two times a day, morning and evening for three days; or
one medicine dropper full, three times a day for two weeks).
Or you may simply tell appropriate clients that they will be
treated for the following two or three days at regular intervals
with etheric and astral acupuncture, if that would be acceptable
to them. We are fully capable of selecting the optimal times
for such work even if the clients are not aware of just when we
are treating them. Such is the work of angelic guidance when
you ask God for His or Her help to assist you.

You will find yourself using the more general alternative for
acupuncture treatment (as opposed to specific dosages) when
you have a patient or client who is not able to actively antici-
pate the process you are using in all its possibilities. You
might use dosages if the person is already familiar with a

pattern of treatment that includes either homeopathic remedies or flower essences along with acupuncture. It is important to use consistency and rhythms in treatment of any kind, so that the person involved can better relate to what is happening for their highest and best good. It is easy to overwhelm someone with details of what you are doing, and it is not necessary for you to do this, as the general suggestion that we will work with you in such and such a way over the ensuing days, weeks, or months is more than enough. Permission from them is all that is required. On a basic level they are giving it to you when they return to be treated at frequent intervals (once a week or month, let us say, depending on whether you are working on the etheric or astral level primarily in your current treatment for them).

An additional way to work is to insert a needle in such a way that you notice its results for yourself and ask us to modify this as you notice any variations that might seem appropriate. In time we will do this for you without your asking, as you grow accustomed to working with yourself and us in conjunction. You will then simply notice what is going on as evidence of our work through you and through your client. Old masters of the art do this all the time. They often have a knowing about what is going on that does not necessarily include a conscious recognition of where their information or knowing comes from. But usually they know it is from a deep level of being that is accessible to all with practice at receptivity and inner quietness. So a master will train his apprentice, in the classical ways of teaching acupuncture—or acupressure too, for that matter—as the deepening of awareness is a key for many things, including the receptivity to what is going on and what is appropriate for all. You may ask us to assist you in this, the increase in your own awareness. But your own constant practice will be required as well. One can never avoid the need for inner growth to enhance the efforts of self and Soul. Is this to your understanding? Good. Then we proceed.

Acupressure

Acupressure is another approach to the meridians that is effective. Again, you may treat acupressure points using a crystal—with such effectiveness that you will approach the level of acupuncture without really needing to know directly from your inner source the exact times, frequency rates, etc. for applying acupuncture needles of light. We would suggest you run the meridians involved with your treatment as well as specialize on certain points. Thus you will encourage the flow of energies along those meridians, which shall in turn effect releases of active blocks along the circuitry involved. We shall guide you in this, if you will, though you do not need such guidance to any great degree. The meridian level of expression is subject to the natural flows of electro-magnetic force fields which surround any quartz crystal, and once the crystal is clean and activated it will be able to stimulate or soothe the meridian involved as the case may be. You should simply ask that the crystal work in the way that is for the highest and best good. If you tune in carefully you will then be able to note whether the crystal is working with an under-active or over-active meridian or meridian point, as it will energize or sooth respectively in the proper manner. It is not necessary that you be able to tune in so selectively for this process to work. We give you this possibility only for your own sensitivity training and attunement. It is through processes such as these that you will be able to develop sensitivity and discrimination on many levels that have heretofore been unavailable to you through neglect and lack of awareness of their significance for you .

We would suggest further that you study the effects of your crystals on these meridians by feeling the results over the succeeding hours and days, for it is not always immediately that you will be able to notice the direction of the long term results, if you will. We suggest the word "results" to you only in as much as there is a long term process that has been set in motion as you proceed with your work with another and with yourself. It is only by fairly frequent repetition that you will achieve anything with anyone in this time, for instant results would leave too much room for doubt and questioning on the part of the one being worked on. The educational value of the learning process that goes on when one begins to peel away the layers of indecision and imbalance that have accumulated over the years is a step-by-step process of little enlightenments, if you will, though these enlightenments have the effect of gentle processing of information that is at times inspiring

but usually goes unnoticed at a conscious level until one becomes fairly in tune with the process over a number of years.

Consciousness is a funny thing, you see. For you are conscious of so many things, but not your origins, your beginnings in light and love of God. You are conscious still of this
origin in your deepest heart. And this origin is as the beginning of awareness of God and self and Soul, as it is rooted in
the beginnings of your Self awareness. Such Self awareness
can lead to more than you can ever imagine, and the beginnings of it are all around you and in the stars—and in yourself
as well. As we explore the beginnings of your Self awareness, we come to notice the intent of the Holy Ones who originated you and your beginnings for you. And we come to
notice the constituents of your own beginnings in the stars as
origin of the enlightenment you seek and know one day in self
and Soul as God. This beginning for you is as measured in
time and space. The actual reality is already here, for it has
been given you as a seed in growth, full potential already present forever. And this new beginning we suggest for you is
only the final step in a process that began before your birth, in
the integration of your self with Soul in former times as well
as now.

Massage

The next thing to consider is massage work, for we are guiding you step by step through a list of specific possibilities for
treatment that you currently accept as wholistic possibilities for
your healing and your growth.

In this section we will include acupressure and shiatsu to
some extent, for these are arts that rely on personal contact between the therapist and the client at a physical level, and these
things can be enhanced by using crystals and other vibrational
techniques.

First we would give you an actual fact about shiatsu and
polarity, etc.: this is that the healing that is possible is able to
take effect only in as much as it is accepted by the client. It is
important to offer complete healing to your client. But it is
also important to realize that if you are calling upon God for
assistance in a complete and unhindering or unlimited way,

you are offering complete healing all the time. Rest assured that the acceptance of your healing does not depend upon the acceptance of your self or Soul by the patient or client you are working with. It only depends upon the acceptance of self and Soul on the part of your client. Thus you may release any fears you may have about yourself and your work and know that as you call upon your Soul and your God for healing in the name of the perfection that is designed for humanity, you will be offering wholeness you are not as yet aware of in your own consciousness. And it is not necessary to be perfect at personality levels to do this. Only at the level of the Soul can there be perfection anyway. And this perfection is who you are all the time.

We go on to give you a few suggestions for your work with crystals. Place around your massage table (or whatever you work with) a set of twelve crystals that are smaller than those you would normally use for yourself in ideal conditions. This is so that you will not overload your clients. (Two inches long by an inch wide would be ideal. Anything close to that would be just as good.) We suggest you place these crystals in pouches of some kind. We ourselves use cheesecloth pouches we have stapled to the underside of the table with a staple gun. This way you can remove the crystals when you want to move the table or work with fewer than twelve crystals, as will occur from time to time, especially if you want to remove the crystals for your own use or for other clients at the same time. We suggest you close off both ends of the cheese cloth just a bit once you have attached it. We have found that the crystals will slip out of their pouches unless you do this. We use paper clips on either end, but you could sew both ends as well, just enough to have an upward slope that the crystals cannot slide out of.

We suggest also that you use an electro-magnetic grid system with your crystals, as was discussed in the earlier chapter on operational specifics with crystals. As we said in that chapter, you may make such a grid most easily using copper tape of 1/4" to 3/8" thickness set in a grid with lines centered one and a quarter inches apart.[4] Such tape is available in any stained

---

[4] Pattern from Rev. Dr. Frank Alper, *Exploring Atlantis Vol. III* (Phoenix: Arizona Metaphysical Society), p. 48.

glass window art supply store. The purpose of this grid is to enhance your own healing energies and focus your attention on ours, for ours do not need any enhancing; it is only yours that do, and the energies of your clients we include in this, for they are upon the table using its circuit to amplify any impact our work might have on them. The electro-magnetic effects of copper are well known in your time in certain circles, as they are warming, invigorating and stimulating in situations that require such stimulation.

Next we suggest you look to your hands to decide if you need further amplification of your efforts to stimulate or invigorate through your hands. If you do, we suggest using quartz crystal in each hand for a time at least during every session so that you maximize your effectiveness. You might begin to experiment with a small part of your treatment at first, stimulating the subtle bodies of the person involved from the energy or etheric level, soothing the nerves and emotions, steadying and clearing the mind, and giving the person a clearer idea of who they are all the time as you work with them. These shall be the results of using crystals with others to enhance or complement your own massage work, and you will find you are guided in all you do more and more as you ask us to assist you with each client or patient.

We give you this background or summary from a previous chapter for you to realize that the same work you will participate in for yourselves will quite naturally begin to apply at once with those you work with in turn.

As you activate your own circuits using crystals, you will find your own need for crystals diminishes, especially in regard to aura balancing work or energy enhancing work. Thus there will come a time, step by step—for most of you within two years or so—when you will be able to work with or without crystals just as effectively, using crystals as an option when it will benefit the client you work with to see the "props" of your profession, the visual bridge between what they conceive as a part of a human being and the electro-magnetic activation that will in fact have taken place for you in your working with crystals over the years. Some people will prefer to think of you only as a massage therapist, for example. Others will be hungry for the truth about themselves that you can gift them with as you work on them, and for these people, the greatest gift you have to offer will be the gift of understanding themselves that you will offer them through such transitional techniques as the use of crystals. For so such ways have worked for you and others over time: offering you yourselves in understanding, allowing us to activate who you are in an orderly and patient fashion.

The next and last thing to take up with you in massage work refers to your acupressure and work of a similar nature, when you activate the energy meridians and centers through the use of your hands. We would give you a tool for your growth with crystals that has a bearing on this kind work as well as on the acupuncture discussed above. This is to use crystals for pinpoint energy insertion in cases where such patterns are applicable. You will be able to use this technique with reflexology techniques on the hands, feet and even earlobes if you wish to, though we suggest that the feet and hands will be more useful to you in most instances, as you will be duplicating your own efforts should you try to use all three, and the former two are about equally successful. Use a crystal in this by activating it for healing and blessing, through our assistance, of course, and then touching the tip of the crystal only momentarily to the insertion point in question. You will need to know your points, so to speak, and the general regions that affect given conditions of certain organs, in the case of reflexology. But once you do, your effectiveness will be multiplied many times over using crystals. You see, we are able to work with you in this just as we can with an acupuncturist. Inserting vibrational "needles" in the right places at the right times, using your knowledge to guide you and our knowledge to direct you more precisely as well, you will be able to accomplish much more than you dream of. The exact frequencies to such light or vibrational insertions shall correspond exactly to the needs of the client or patient; and if you will ask that the treatment we render be exactly appropriate, neither more nor less than what the patient needs, then we will be able to guide you and him or her to see the exact nature of what is possible at any given moment in time. We will do nothing if that is appropriate. We will do everything if that is appropriate. And we will usually do something in between, as that is generally what we discover to be in order for the Soul and the growth of a member of the human race at any given moment in time. You may rely upon the perfection of what is being done if this is what you have asked us to do, for we are your Souls, and we are as one with the God who created us.

Operations of a Surgical Nature
And Damage to the Physical Structure

You may use crystals to enhance healing of a physical nature at times, especially once you have seen to normal emergency measures as would be recommended by a physician. Vibrational remedies are also quite useful in this regard, as homeopathic as well as physical applications of arnica and at times comfrey (when the problem is confined to the skin, as in light burn cases) can be very useful in healing the breaks and bruises that the body is prone to, and Rescue Remedy, a flower essence,[5] can be helpful in situations of traumatic reaction. We suggest using crystals with breaks in the skin or bones once other accepted methods have been put into effect and you are wondering what to do next. Crystals can enhance the healing process as they set up a flow of electro-magnetic energies through the particular area of difficulty. You must understand that the body has its own blueprint for perfection at levels that have not been damaged. It is only up to you to increase the available energy flow for the alignment and formation of the physical tissues involved to be greatly facilitated. Once you have done this, there is every possibility that a speedy recovery will come about in a fraction of the time normally required for such healing to take place. We suggest setting up a healing flow in accordance with the basic principles outlined by Frank Alper in his book *Exploring Atlantis, Volumes I-III*, which we have verified for ourselves and to some extent developed simultaneously, for we were using some of the same techniques before we discovered them in his books, as have others with whom we have worked over the years.

Briefly, use crystals to set up a polarity on either side of the damaged tissue or bone, allowing a current to pass through the

---

[5]   A Bach Flower remedy. For further information on this remedy and others developed by Dr. Bach see, for example, Phillip M. Chancellor, *Handbook of the Bach Flower Remedies* (Essex, England: C.W. Daniels Co Ltd., 1971).

area, easing pain if any is present, then clearing away damaged or dead energies, and lastly replacing these with new energies that will be appropriate for speedy recovery. Ask us to assist in the proper programming, as well in the actual work of healing, once your flow of energy has been established.

You should set up the polarity of crystals on either side of the injury at points that span as short a distance as possible yet still rest upon actual energy insertion points on the body. These are generally located near joints for the limbs, and on either side of an organ or at any point along the spine, in the case of the torso, or at opposite sides of the head at definite energy insertion points usually found in acupressure or meridian work. You may experiment to find these, but generally if you rely upon your intuition you will be able to locate energy insertion points fairly readily by yourself. Just to be in the general area is usually enough.

The healing time and timing will vary, depending upon the condition of the patient. As a rule, three times a day for twenty minutes would be a good general prescription for healing bones and bruises, until such time as you and/or the patient feels the work is complete. You may tape the crystals in place if the location of the injury makes simple placement difficult. We suggest you work with these things for a while before you develop hard and fast rules about them, as you will discover patterns of healing for yourself that will be of use to you in your work and in your growth. Is this to your understanding? We hope to press on rather rapidly from here.

Vibrational Remedies—Including
Flower Essences—and Quartz

Next we will take up flower essences in brief, though this subject is discussed in great detail in *Flower Essences* by Gurudas.[6] The patterns for charging remedies of all types using quartz crystals, as outlined by Gurudas, you will find incredibly helpful and valid. The best thing we can suggest is

---

[6] Gurudas, *Flower Essences* (Albuquerque, N.M.: Brotherhood of Life, 1982).

that you read this book for details of using quartz with vibrational remedies (gem remedies, flower essences and homeopathics), as we would only be repeating what is given therein if we were to discuss this at any detail.

Let us content ourselves with the following: that crystals are used to amplify and harmonize all things, and with vibrational remedies it is these two abilities of quartz that can be utilized to the fullest, with great sensitivity. Thus you will find your remedies exactly attuned to the individual patient or client, without your knowing the details at all, but with us cooperating with you fully. Call upon us in this work just as you would with normal crystal work. For we can set a remedy for you in ways you cannot, eliminating all ill-effects that might exist with any remedy as unlooked for possibilities of your world that is subject to error. And we can make and charge remedies for you in ways you cannot, for we are as beings of light and love, and we are fully capable of charging water in any way we may wish to, God willing. This is something that we do all the time for the channel writing this book and his wife in her private practice, though we rely on them for insight as to what remedy they would specifically request and on what level it should be potentized, for they are in charge of their free will choices in the ways we have already discussed with you in this chapter. And as we stated also in this chapter, we advise them on what remedies to ask for before they ask for them, that we might supply them with what is appropriate for their Souls and growth in all circumstances that are not strictly within their own physical level of responsibility—provided of course, that they have asked us beforehand for such assistance; for unless they or you have asked—and listened accurately to the reply— nothing can be done or understood, through them or you.

We suggest also that you use the existing, physical plane remedies which are available in your market place, for there is a law that it is important to honor the level upon which you are working as much as possible, so that you draw upon that level as well as others that are more formative to it. In this way you do not confuse who you are and why you are here, which is to honor and respect all levels of God's manifestation on earth as equal in the sight of all who see as their Creator.

We would also suggest you use the flower essences and gem remedies, as well as the homeopathics.[7] These remedies are of a wisdom you can only guess at, for they honor the actual existence of nature in all its manifestations, as plant and mineral kingdom, in that they recognize its inner usefulness and wisdom to the ways of humanity; and in this honoring they are blessed, and they are as well a vast improvement upon your dilapidated attempts to extract at a chemical level all the vital essences of the plant and mineral, when Nature herself has actually already done this for you in the plants and animals, flowers and trees of nature; and in the very ground you walk upon as well, though to a lesser extent, as this kingdom of the rocks is more distant from your own. Crystals and gems are the extracts of this kingdom, and they are wisely used when they are compounded as vibrations in water, as has been done by your Gurudas and those like him since time immemorial, and before the races of humanity began to walk your earth. For there are others of as great intelligence who have walked your earth, and these have used flower essences and gem elixirs, as you might call them, in places other than on your earth. In fact, they have been responsible for many of the plants and minerals that exist upon the surface of your world, as they have seeded them here as well as on other planets, too distant for you to travel to except in your imaginations or in your subtle bodies made of life and light.

The use of crystals is as we have stated earlier, that you set up triangulations with crystals, programming them with our help to assist you. You may also employ triangles and squares of crystals using pyramids to assist you, as the energies of the pyramids will be amplifying to the crystals and vice versa. You may use magnetite or lodestone with the pyramids, especially the four-sided pyramid, as this will amplify further the effects of the crystals in the movement of electro-magnetism that will flow along the arms of the pyramid as a result of the natural magnets. We suggest referring to Gurudas' book *Flower Essences* once again for further details as to how to do this for vibrational remedies, which we would include with our own instructions to be very specific in your requests to us for assistance. For with such specifics, you will be surprised

------

[7] These remedies are available from Pegasus Products, P.O. Box 2044, Boulder, Colorado 80306. Phone 303-442-0139 or order by mail.

to find how completely we can perfect what it is you wish to do with vibrational remedies, as well as other therapies.

Health Maintenance

Next we will go on to approach yourselves as beings who need assistance to maintain health in all situations. Health maintenance is a basic need of humanity, for it is the balance of expressions in physical existence that lends strength to your endeavors for your Soul as well as self. We suggest you use crystals in this only for fine tuning, so to speak; for the proper balance of everyday life will assist you more than anything we can give you using crystals to keep yourselves well and hale. We suggest you sleep with crystals beside your bed in a pattern of a triangle, the point at your head and two bases at your feet, if you would help coordinate your sleep patterns with us and our work.[8] This pattern enables us to communicate with you at energy levels more fully. It also enables your waking life to be coordinated with your sleeping life more fully, as we approach you through your crystals once you allow us to do so through your intentions. (See figure 19 below.)

We would give you this advice at a basic level relating to your health because the health of the body so often has to do with coordination of your sleep patterns. At rest you are more susceptible to what we would do for you than at other times of active interference on your part. And coordination of sleep activities can be facilitated by conscious growth as well as by using crystals.

Once you begin the release of your former life patterns of incompleteness and unhappiness, and once you are involved in a process of systematic healing of your self at many levels, many forms of sickness will emerge as releases of these earlier patterns. It is not necessary that these illnesses be anything but gentle releases of the old, but for humanity at this time there are usually resistances to growth that accompany any release of the past, and thus blockages may take place occasionally that will necessitate other means than the ones prescribed

---

[8] We credit Dr. Frank Alper with this pattern; our Soul informs us it is a universal pattern at a Soul level of expression.

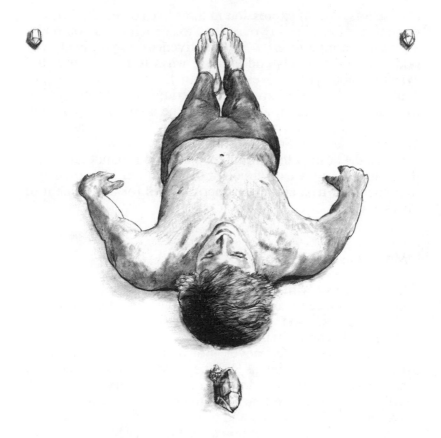

figure 19. sleeping pattern

for your growth to assist you in freeing yourselves of such resistance and blockage. Crystal patterns are invaluable in this,
as well as is use of individual crystals for healing in the ways
that have been mentioned in this book. Patterns of six and
twelve are especially helpful. Also the patterns of placement
of crystals upon the individual chakras or energy centers of the
body will assist you in this cooperative effort of repair and
balance as you grow.

The alignment with life that is possible for humanity is little
suspected at this time. It is a duty of those who would assist
their Souls to see that the regenerative and transformative processes we undertake with you are available to as many as will

choose this form of expression in their lives on earth. The co-operative effort to train yourselves to see who it is you really are will continue to grow in effectiveness as you heal your bodies at many levels and explore ways to heal your belief systems about your selves and your Souls as one. As you heal, you will come to know the overriding efficiency of God in your lives on earth, as well as in the stars. And you will grow in confidence about yourselves as you tread a path of growth that leads to Soul fulfillment.

This is the destiny that awaits you all. You cannot fail. And this is the destiny we offer you at every turn of life's own natural course of trial and error opportunities for unfoldment of yourselves.

Medicines and Crystals

Briefly, crystals may be used to charge medicines, even regular pharmaceutical medicines, in the way that is for your highest and best good.

Simply ask, and it shall be done.

Such medicines need never interfere with all you do for growth at conscious levels, by the way. It is not necessary that you avoid all normal drugs for sake of purity, or anything like that. There will be times when the simple healing of your doctor will be best for you and those you love. If you are too resistant to your growth in this aspect of your being, you will find yourself needing doctors by and by, and wondering what you did to deserve such a fate. It is only that all things have their place, Arjuna.[9] All things require only that we use them wisely in their proper place.

Counseling

We often have people ask us how to improve their counseling work through use of crystals, and thus we include this

---

[9] "Arjuna" is a proper sanskrit name meaning "of the Soul" or "one who is of the Soul." It is of universal application.

brief explanation of counseling and its after-effects as they apply to crystal use.

Begin by using crystals to activate your room for healing, if you are a counselor. You may do this with a pattern of eight or of six, as you wish, though eight crystals in a circle are best for this effect. You must build your field of light so that those who come will take from it what is needed for their growth, even if they resist your insights.

We would advocate that you become thoroughly familiar with means for protection as well, for protection is essential for proper channeling of light and love to all who come to you, and you must learn to be effective without draining yourself and your reserves for growth as well as love. You may refer to our book on *Patterns of the Whole, Vol. III: Alignment With Life*,[10] for details on protection in addition to those in this book.

Lastly, use a pattern of six crystals regularly beneath the treatment table you might use for counseling. If you use a chair for your client you will have a harder time concealing the crystals, but you may still choose to place them around the chair in the pattern of the six-pointed Star of David, that your clients draw perfect balance from their exposure to your energies and your crystals. We say "concealed" because we would have you know it is perfectly proper for you to use many different technical aides to your work without all of them becoming subject to discussion or examination by your clients. You will pick and choose which techniques, if any, to relate to your clients for their own growth and conscious connection with their own processes as they are treated through yours. You will also know that true permission is granted you only from the level of the person's Soul, and this is a level that will know of crystals through and through. It is not necessary for you to educate the person to your crystals every time or even as a usual practice, depending on the nature of your clientele. And permission is granted you to continue with your work in healing given individuals when they return for more, so to speak, after you have affected a bit of a cure with them the time before. So you will notice you are progressing with them, in their willingness to share their growth with you each time.

---

[10] Publication projected for 1988.

Thus we have completed our survey, however brief, of alternate healing or therapeutic modalities and their enhancement with crystals. This does not mean that we have exhausted or even considered all of the fine treatments that exist in this time; only a representative sampling of them in order to give you ideas about your own work, whatever it might be. We hope we have helped you in this, our rather detailed chapter. In the future you will be blessed with many more details yourselves, God willing. Thus the store of knowledge of a useful and practical nature to help us with our work may continue to evolve in humanity as a whole.

Good evening to you, and God bless you.

Chapter Twenty-nine

Experiencing Color In Crystals

There are many small details we would like to deal with at this time. We toy with leaving many of them out so that you may explore them for yourselves, but we content ourselves with the thought that many of the things we will teach you in this chapter may be of use for your own discoveries about self and others, as well as crystals. For the generalizations abound from these little thoughts we will share with you.

Color Resonancies in Crystals

To begin with, crystals each have their own color frequency or frequencies. There is an exact correspondence between this and humans, of course, as we each have our own frequencies as well, even though we are expressive of all the possibilities of being human and more than human as we understand it. We will give you an idea of what we mean by this by describing color with crystals, in the hope that you will generalize for yourselves about how crystals are like you in this matter of color.

Each crystal has an inner and an outer color resonancy that is familiar to those who have developed the psychic ability to see color. The outer color, in particular, will be obvious to a good astral or, in some ways, etheric reader of the psychic. Our own ability to tell the resonancy of a crystal is dependent on our ability to "feel" these things with an inner sensitivity that then locates sensation of the corresponding color in the body physical. What we mean by this is simple. Explore yourselves to see what feelings colors have for you. This is a more common ability we are discussing than you might imagine at first thought. It is an ability shared by 90% of those who come to us interested in crystals, and it is something we teach with great success in our classes. You can feel this resonancy if you try. The following method will give you a fighting chance at this, though the direct procedure of a class is more sure to succeed.

Take a crystal in your hand and feel its life within you. This is not hard if you have been following the steps we have described for you to know what crystals feel like. Share with the crystal the nature of its energies, if you will, but rather, we would say, share with it the nature of its life, for it is alive as you or I, yet it is in different form and state of evolution. It is a life that is coexistent with God as is your own.

We would say to next feel the resonancy of color by sharing with the crystal as it corresponds to your own central nervous system, for along this your crystal will echo, out of your ability to resonate with it, as you try to feel its intent for you. It is a little thing to notice where along your central matrix or nervous system this echoing of the crystal will take place, for as the resonancy responds to your own consciousness, it will feel as if it is resonating with a chakra or chakras in particular, unique ways; and it will seem to localize the feeling in one particular area, as if you were vibrating in your attention in one area in the exact ways the crystal is for you.

Experience this feeling of resonancy and then compare with a standard treatment of chakras, their colors and their alignments, to get an idea of the corresponding color that exists for you in the crystal.

The next step is to go into the crystal a second time and ask it to give you its original resonancy—its pre-programmed resonancy—rather than any resonancy it may have taken up in order to treat you for illness or imbalance of expression.

We would say to you that the resonancy you will get with this second effort is a different one than the first if the crystal itself has had to change its nature, temporarily or otherwise, in order to relate to you for the best good of your growth and evolution in same. This is a surprising thing for some, in that the crystal has actually changed its resonancy in order to treat you. But it should not be surprising if you consider that you too are in order as you relate to another: in other words, you too adapt your frequencies to adjust to those you are dealing with at a given moment. This is so that you may treat them for major illnesses and imbalances in their expression, if they give you permission to do so, at a conscious level or otherwise. So you see, in yet another way, you are like a crystal.

We apologize if the details of this previous exercise at first seem not exact enough for you to duplicate it in completion. We would like you to practice it if you can, but it is hard to describe this practice in a way that is easy to assimilate unless you actually try to follow us in our directions for you. You will then find that the economy of expression used in these directions is appropriate, has allowed you to have just what you need to succeed with this exercise if you persist and if you do not block your natural responses of understanding. In our time, many do so block responses of understanding, for they have found in the conditioning of childhood that it is not safe to understand too much of what happens—without feeling the gap between what is happening and what an adult believes is happening, at the expense of the self-evident reality every child may feel, in his or her heart, as the events of life unfold. So we would direct you to have good cheer in life, to accept your instantaneous understanding of all that comes your way, and go on to allow growth as it was intended for you in all ways. We bless you and stop for now.

The Rainbow Resonancy of Crystals

Crystals resonate in all color frequencies for you at all times, yet they are whole in their expression of light in one color resonancy as well.

This means something special for all of you who work with crystals. For infinite possibility is here, in unlimited dimension with your work with crystals, and yet the crystal itself will have a definite resonancy all its own to speak to you with as blessing. You will see that the "treatments" you are given by any given crystal will vary widely, depending on the crystal you are using and your own capacities for growth at any given time. We suggest you follow your heart in finding the crystals that work best for you, knowing that any crystal will adapt to you as best it can—which is a great deal, in fact: as much as any person might adapt to healing you.

The next thing we would say is that the colors you represent are complete at any given level of expression for you. This means that the octave of your expression is a rainbow of light and love. This is in order for you to know at this time, for you are healing your planet as you work with yourself in your true form; and this form is the whole of God in any way that you can work to find this out. You are guided to know what you are to be. This is the nature of what we are telling you. In time, you will be anything you can ascertain about your true potential. So it is for us as well, unlimited growth in God of our own choosing. The rainbow we are discussing here is the rainbow of your own octave of expression. It is your own set of possibilities, to grow with and into, as the case might be. In time you will become a second set of intervals as well. So your growth proceeds in stages, orderly evolution for all.

The rainbow of lights in your "physical" body that we have been mentioning, here and elsewhere in this book, is the best way that we can guide you to appreciate yourselves at levels unknown to your conscious minds before you explore yourselves at subtle levels of knowing and understanding. The best gift we can give to you is to know God, but short of that, we love to explore with you yourselves in the forms that you appear to take on other levels of knowing than the ones you are normally accustomed to, including the forms of love and life as well as light that we are presently discussing.[1]

The next thing to say to you is that the octave you are given to work with, the rainbow of your own chakra system, is not a singularity in and of itself. It is a progression of levels, four "trees" or sets of chakras in all, that cope with life as you know it and life as it appears to be for you. The rainbow of lights or chakras we are discussing is the same set of frequencies or resonancies that we have given you under our section

---

[1] For elaboration and further explanation please see our *Subtle Body Anatomy* book.

on color programming as it applies to crystals earlier in this chapter. Know your own set of programmings through exploring the rainbow of light within yourself from base to crown, if you will, but more as well: through all the seven levels of your expression of rainbow light and love. Red, orange, yellow, green, blue, indigo, violet—these are the colors that predominate in your chakra systems, in the exact same order from bottom to top of your being. Red is at the bottom (as it comes to you from the earth) and green is at the heart (as it heals all things with emerald light and love). Green is at the bottom too, but it predominates only at the heart of love. Yellow is at the solar plexus where it turns to gold as you fill your life with God (a solar presence). And yellow is also of the mind—the intellect choosing for you the details you will turn your attention to in time and space continuums of your development.

The rest is up to you to fathom, what the colors fit in you and in your color resonancies—except that the crown itself is violet at the other end of your expression. From top of head to base of spine you have this rainbow pattern for your growth in truth, in God as well as men on earth. Both rainbows are one light.

So we have given you a summary of the rainbow pattern for your growth and self-discovery here on earth. Use it wisely with the other gifts we give you, for it is what you are at one level or more of your expression: not the whole but patterns for your growth.

The patterns of crystals and of people are the same, you see, in the areas of color expression. Resonancy between the two provides direct experience of color in your lives on earth, as they appear at formative levels of your expression.

We would give you ways to choose your growth, though any given way is needed only once. And ways with crystal colors are not necessary after they have been experienced in full in any given life. Thus ways with crystal colors and ways with human colors parallel each other once again. And ways with either one are yours to experience here on earth as you have already known in Soul in God, and having known in Soul, you may choose again.

Having experience of both is unnecessary, but experience of either one will enhance experience of the other. So we gain a knowledge of who we are at operational levels that approach those we use with crystals and ourselves all the time.

Color Resonancy as it Applies to Life on Earth

The color of the rainbow is in your hearts as love. It is the light of the world that all must follow to come to Soul and self in God. The rainbow is given to humanity for the purpose of differentiating the possibilities of expression available to all. It is a defraction of the light of our creator.

The just use of color is to know this differentiation, this defraction, as a polarized expression of aspects of ourselves that grow and change over time. It is a knowing that all is one yet all is separate and distinct unto itself. The Two are One, and yet they are two as well, you see. In color you will find a chance to grow in God as love as you discriminate and yet make whole all the time. All the energies around you can benefit from these twin processes, you see: making whole and one, on the one hand; and valuing the integrity and uniqueness of all things on the other. These two balance our expression in love and light all the time.

Crystals set in motion patterns of expression in color just as we do. They evolve over time to find the truth of who they are through color, light and sound—just as do all conscious beings at play in the fields of God, as it were. You will know this to be so as you examine for yourselves the things that we have been saying in this chapter and in this book about the similarities between people and crystals.

The reason for taking on such detail over color is to introduce you to the novel idea that your own color alignments with yourselves and others are important for your growth at the subtle levels they are taking place; to heal these alignments, you will have to know the song and language of color before you work on people. We would recommend the sources at the end of this book for learning the details of this. Also the *Subtle Body* book we are planning for you. In the end, your own experience is essential, and thus we encourage you to integrate the expressions of color you discover in our first exercise with crystals at the beginning of this chapter so that you will realize who you are in the color possibilities for your growth. We have done so ourselves, taught others to do so, and now encourage you reading this book to continue with these experiments until you have found the nature of the entire color spectrum for yourselves, both outside you in the world of color in the physical dimensions, and within—as you may access with your crystals.

Just allow them to resonate for you in the appropriate area of your expression; notice the color awakened or activated as it "feels" activated by the resonancy correspondences between the crystal's energy and your own along the rainbow of your own chakra alignments; then appreciate the meaning of this for you by taking notes on the impressions that colors give you as you activate them for yourselves.

You may do this work with color in a further way for yourselves. Allow a particular crystal to be activated with any color of your choosing by asking us to do this for you, choosing perhaps the color red first, since it is most obvious for your sensitivities at this time. (You avoid it in fact most of the time, as you wish to be less involved with physical expression and more involved with the activities of the stars—at least this is the case with 99.9% of the people who will read this book for themselves.) Next try the color red as tempered by orange. Have this fade into pure orange, and so on through the rainbow. See if you can feel as the colors blend into one another and move up your spine—or down it as you have activated the reverse procedure. Isn't it easy to experience something real as a communication, if you will, from your self and Soul at other levels of who you are in truth?

Nothing could be any easier than for us to help a willing soul with the octaves of their own expression, as they ask us to reveal these resonancies in feeling perhaps a pressure, a tingling or an activation, up the spine through the rainbow of light and love that you are.

Next, you might allow us to work on you through the colors, by programming the crystals—with our help—with the colors adjusting to work on you, one by one, each in its own way that is perfectly in order for your Soul and your growth. By doing this, you will experience what each color holds for you at this time, as well as what you have need to learn or appreciate from any given color. You may find it helpful to take notes on this as well, for you will thus catalogue for yourselves what best can be done by each color in your own case. By the way, be sure to ask for the love aspect to work as well as the light, for thusly you give your crystals and us a chance to be more complete for you at the upper end of your own octaves all the time. You are allowing yourself to experience who you are all the more when you do this, and you are allowing us to heal you all the time when you do.

You might as a third and additional exercise allow the crystals to work on you with each color in ways that would generalize for you the effects of colors upon others. Thus, for example, you would experience for yourselves the ways that red might work in your treatments on others. You may ask your guidance to do this for you, you know. And you will learn what is possible for yourselves, the limits and the lack of them, with each such experiment in cooperative efforts with your Souls and other forms of guidance you call upon. Your angelic assistance too would love to be of service in this capacity, and the familiarization you would gain from these forms of assistance would stand you in good stead as you approach your work with others with true confidence in what God can do through you and the conditions you set for your work in service to your Soul. So you are blessed in all you do in truth. We ourselves did experiments with these processes several years ago. And the growth that was possible from such little things was encouragement for change in alignment with our Souls. So we would encourage you as well.

Lastly, we suggest you let yourself feel color in other ways, for example in the sunset or sunrise—once you have given yourself the fine-tuning sensitivity training to crystals and color we are suggesting. You will be surprised at the language of color that your senses will reveal to you; and the language of love as well. For all things are as orders of love in God. And all things are given that we might know this truth in self as well as Soul for enhancement in same. God bless you.

Chapter Thirty

The Memory and Functions
of Crystals:

Whole Light Octaves of Expression

We have noticed that there is little information today about what might already be "programmed" or stored as memory within crystals. *Windows of Light*, the book by Vicki and Randall Baer, provides a good, general discussion of the functions of crystals,[1] but there is more that might be said.

We would like to give you a sampling of the kinds of "memory" and other programmed workings of crystals we have come across. Please bear in mind that the details we will give you about what a crystal is for or what information it holds is understood only imperfectly at this time by our conscious minds. We are often advised by our guidance and our Souls that we are dealing with a small percentage of the full capabilities already programmed into the crystals we have. Once or twice we have analyzed fairly exhaustively the functions of a particular crystal and have gotten the possible percentage we are capable of understanding up to as high as 95%, but this is still only that which is within our particular, human limitations of expression and comprehension. Other kingdoms of nature that are highly developed and conscious might see crystals and appreciate functions that are not within our current capacities. So we are advised, and such has been our experience.

The important point to make here is that crystals are usually already operational in ways that demonstrate understanding

---

[1] Baer, *op. cit.*, pp. 54-59.

and wisdom, also technological understanding, far surpassing anything we can currently comprehend at the conscious level. We think it makes sense to respect what already exists in crystals, learn from them, and exercise a certain caution so as not to damage what a particular crystal might already be doing or ready to do.

Ways of Damaging Crystal Programming: Lasers

It is possible to damage functions before they are ever accessed by certain procedures that usually only someone scientifically inclined would be likely to use. The two major such procedures we have come across are the use of neon or other inert gas lasers with crystals and the use of de-magnetizers with crystals. On the subject of inert gas lasers, perhaps the simplest way of describing what happens when one is used with a programmed crystal is to say the process is analogous to what happens when someone makes a crude phone dialing machine and damages the phone company's tone-reading equipment because the crude, home-made version is similar to the more sophisticated and precisely calibrated equipment used by the phone company itself: it actually works, but it is crude enough to damage the instrumentation at the phone company without the inventor ever realizing what he has done. Depending on the level of the wholistic information in a crystal, there may be little damage or a lot when using inert gas lasers with crystals. Especially at higher astral or positive emotional levels, where the programming is very delicate, the damage is fairly complete. At levels that correspond to textbook, linear information or etheric movie-like or holographic information, the damage is less but noticeable, especially to the subtle human faculties capable of noticing such things much more accurately than any device or machine. In other words, the information gets fuzzy and its finer, subtler aspects, especially positive emotions, get lost or damaged. Since mankind at his current stage of development is especially needful of right emotion or stable nuances of real love, this kind of damage to a crystal is unfortunate.

Use of a neon laser and many other inert gas lasers fuzzes up the existing encoding in the lattice work, with the frequencies of the laser itself as an overlay. These frequencies are generally devoid of any informational content of their own, other than that of the rare gas itself; the non-life supporting, rather random electrical frequencies of the current used as a power source; and the materials used in construction of the laser, which themselves are selected with no thought as to their overall resonancies. They are not "noble" materials in the sense the alchemists would mean "noble." That is, they do not enhance our growth, but tend to detract from it. The crystal itself is not damaged. Just its programmed functions. This is all right in one sense, but if people knew the functions already existing in the crystals they so unconsciously de-program or fuzz up, they would probably find other, more "ecological" ways of accomplishing their goals.

I am told by my guidance that I would have to be a physicist trained in divine science, or at least science beyond its current level of understanding on earth, to be able to understand adequately the dynamics of the differences between crystal lasers and inert gas lasers and how they affect quartz crystal programming; but apparently, inert gas lasers are close enough to an actual physical level programming or encoding process, yet crude enough in the ways they are currently being used (of necessity, since we are only beginning to reconstruct a real crystal technology for certain functions on this planet) that it would be best to avoid their use in almost all instances. According to my guidance, the crystal lasers (ruby, emerald, sapphire, etc.) while more expensive, are not destructive to crystal programming and are life positive in their operation.

Damage From De-Magnetizers

De-magnetizers work in a different way and have a slightly different effect than lasers have on crystals. The effect is similar to that of a magnet on the memory of a computer or any computer disc storage unit. The magnet tends to strip the information, which is being held in an electro-magnetic language on a semi-conductive material, such as silicon pure glass or semi-metal. The language in a crystal is also held electro-magnetically, although the way this is so may not be readily apparent to our current scientists, differing markedly from silicon chip programming both as to level and functioning. But magnets and electric de-magnetizers do have an influence on crystals: the former in a positive way, within reasonable limits, so to speak, and the latter in a less positive way, as interference—and even disruption, at times of reliance on their use for de-programming crystals of their existing programming.

The Structuring of Crystals

It is perhaps in order for us to outline briefly the way "information" is stored in quartz crystal. For this purpose I have done a certain amount of reading in the relevant scientific literature in order to ground out this type of understanding with the cooperation of my own intellectual endeavors. I am told that the information in a crystal is held primarily by the silicon molecules, with buffer zones or breaks between different units of information created by the oxygen atoms that surround silicon atoms in a series of spiralling tetrahedrons. (See figure 20. This is only the physical level description of the process: the subtle level is the more important one, as information is also stored at etheric and astral levels. And the etheric levels themselves are the levels that the crystals actually rely upon for their information.)

Unlike computer chip semi-conductivity, the silicon atom does not operate with a binary encoding language in natural quartz crystal. Instead, it operates with an encoding that fits its subtle geometry, which is hexagonal. It operates on a language of six possibilities (six sides) plus one (the center position), or a total of seven. I am told that this way of looking at the situation could be partially described in terms of the valances and energy differentials of the electron rings of silicon, but I will leave this for someone more knowledgeable that myself in these areas. I am also told that three-dimensional models of the quartz atomic configuration or the latticework of silicon and oxygen that can be seen to spiral under a microscope or other observational tool of science is not the way we would suggest you use your imagination to model how quartz works for you. The three dimensionality is itself a problem, for the

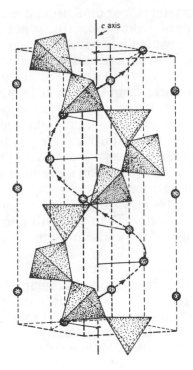

figure 20. Simplified crystal structure of quartz showing oxygen tetrahedra. Structurally left-handed. Morphologically and optically right-handed. (From Wahlstrom.)[2]

---

[2] A crystal with this spiralling direction would be experientially expansive or active—at an etheric level of expression. The mirror opposite is also common: structurally right-handed, etc. And with twinning—the ability of quartz to structurally vary or reverse itself within the same crystal—there exists a continuum of possibility between the two polarities for any given crystal. For healing, just as in polarity therapy, both directions of flow would be possible in one crystal, no matter what its twinning, depending on your intention: either active or receptive, male or female, centrifugal or centripetal. You choose.

The diagram and information on optical, structural and morphological properties is from Ernest E. Wahlstrom, *Optical Crystallography*, 4th Edition (New York: John Wiley & Sons, Inc., 1969) p. 375.

language of the crystal is four dimensional at even its most rudimentary patterns of expression. This is not within your ken, so to speak, we know; but it is within the ken of crystals—and within your conscious, experiential appreciation as well. We guide you to see this as a pattern of spirals in time and space that are projected there from ladders of light, if you will, but rather whole frequencies or levels of projection beyond your three dimensional world of matter, light and sound, though these things too are based in four dimensions, at least in the casual relationship they have with everything you see or sense in any way. The whole pattern is more than we can describe for you in quantifiable terms at this moment in time. We are sorry, but this is so for now. Be guided in our love and know the truth of who you are. Then you will know in immediate terms the language of the stars through crystals, if this is a thing you wish to do.

To explain a little further about this light language in crystals, we would say that a base-twelve language is in some ways more accurately depicted as the language of crystals, over that of six as described above. It is accurate to say six (plus one for seven), but more accurate in many ways to include the possibility of double expression to each of the six for purposes of discovery with crystals of light and love, as well as with those of more physical expression at this time on your earth. Twelve is in may ways a happy combination of elements numerically, as you shall discover as you examine the mathematical and symmetrical properties of this number configuration. For configuration is what it is: a configuration of relationships in archetypal form, if you will, a dynamic of interaction, as is the case with all numbers. An explanation of such dynamics could be handled in number theory or in the geometries of Pythagoras. Such understanding is the basis of your sciences of numerology as well, though in your time this science is not respected as once it was. It is still, nonetheless, a science, for it is the description of the fundamental, underlying diagrams of creation. The dynamics of sound, light and any other dynamic interaction is explained in quantitative and qualitative terms, as well, within the science of numerology. We recommend it for your examination at the simplest level of its expression, free from glamourous or fortune-telling considerations. For it is an understanding that would come to you as you wished it to, and it would assist you in many ways you are perhaps not familiar with at the present time.

To continue, twelve-based systems (for that is what we are actually discussing—a system of dynamic interactions) are more flexible than two or six-based languages or systems and thus more useful. (For example, for starters, twelve is more flexibly divisible than six). Understandably then, the encoding in quartz crystals is also based on the dynamic of the twelve silicon atoms that make up one complete rotation of the spiralling quartz crystal latticework. This same single rotation also forms a complete Star of David or six-sided star when viewed from above or below the central axis of rotation. The vision we have of this is to tell you that you are spirals of light and love that resolve at multiple levels into this Star of David in a circular way, just as do these crystals. Thus the actual language of encoding can optionally be on a base-twelve system, again plus one, or it can be based on a complex interaction between the six-based language of the single silicon atom and the twelve-based language of the overall hexagonal or Star of David pattern of twelve silicon atoms in the latticework of the quartz crystal (again, in all actuality within a four to twelve dimensional pattern transcending your normal three and four dimensions of time and space, as with the language of the stars). Either of these systems would again be inherently plus one, either six plus one or twelve plus one, because either the single atom or the single, complete lattice pattern of the Star of David operates as a single system and has but one focus or center: as does the universal language of all things in time and space.

As might be gathered from the above, whole "sentences" or strings of language meaning in a crystal latticework are also formed in a different, more effective way than in our current computer technology. In a quartz crystal these "sentences" are contained in spiralling chains of three-dimensional, "three level" hexagrams; such is a beginning concept for your appreciation of the process, so to speak.

Just looking at a Star of David design, which coincides with the high temperature, hexagonal, polymorphic form of quartz crystal, it is possible to think of this form as being made up of three interlinking diamond shapes, each rotated 60° from one another (see figure 22 outlining one of the three diamonds). If you think of these three diamond shapes as rotating on three ascending levels like steps of a spiral and then continue the spiral pattern indefinitely, you will have one way of imaginatively approximating the three-dimensional latticework spiralling that exists within a quartz crystal. You must then expand your awareness to include other dimensions as well, as these spirals are in no way limited in their expressions to any directionality in time and space as you know it: they are not really three-dimensional, as we have said. Information, you see,

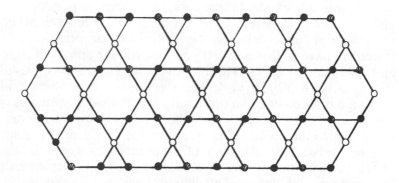

figure 21. Simplified structure of the high temperature form, a -quartz. The circles are silicon atoms on three different planes of the latticework, one above and one below the third. Different levels designated by different degrees of shading. Oxygen atoms (not shown) are in tetrahedral patterns about each silicon atom as in figure 20.

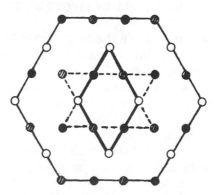

figure 22. diamond pattern in simplified latticework of a -quartz

is encoded along these spirals. Operating in octaves and in twelves (plus a center), this information is actually a language of harmonic resonancy patterns, just as is light and sound. Thus, the language involved in a crystal, or in universe creation, for that matter, is a language of octaves and of twelves encoded and maintained in light and sound, although the light and sound is usually only at times at the levels of wavelength and quality that we normally associate with our visible and invisible light spectrums and our audible and inaudible range of sound. On many levels of expression the patternings of octaves and of twelves repeat themselves. All are related to one another, have correspondences to one another. As it was stated by Hermes Trismegistus, "as above, so below." This is a basic law of divine science, I am told, as well as of the alchemical transformation of man.

If you add to this above picture the idea that the coding of spiralling lattices is taking place on a network dimensionally extended into the so-called etheric realms of subtler vibration, you will see that a filamental extension of this latticework takes place at all times into other dimensions, and thus records the oscillations and vibratory transferences of languages of light and sound (subtle sound, if you will, though we regard this as a language in itself, the language of sounds transferred along electro-magnetic grid systems of expression throughout your galaxies) that are as formative to your understanding and your expressions in time and space. This network of filaments is a geometry of extension beyond time and dimensionality as you can conceive it to be, yet it is no more real than anything else in your universe, and no less real at that.

It is difficult to conceive of what is actually recorded in such "languages" as being levels of "information." Our entire creation is such an organization of "languaged information." In a crystal as well, it is best to think of the form of the information involved as wholistic, manifesting all the components of living expression, including three-dimensionality, light and color, sounds, smells, also emotional qualities, concepts and complete, overall designs—all contained in the same, "whole" information within the crystal. This is holography taken to its ultimate expression. Roughly speaking, the same principals that govern holographic generation are at work with the generating of the wholistic extensions of information within crystals and within all dimensions of our physical creation as well.

This is perhaps enough of a background on the encoding processes in crystals for people to appreciate what follows next, a detailed list of a number of crystals we have been exposed to and chosen to analyze. After we give you selected examples from our list, we will briefly generalize about the basic types of crystal programming. For those interested in looking into this further, we recommend comparing our work with that of Randall and Vicki Baer.[3] For us *Windows of Light* offered confirmation of our own discoveries about functions of quartz crystals.

Large Crystals and Small Crystals

In this chapter, we will focus primarily on larger crystals we have worked with or tuned into. In general, larger crystals have more character in regard to their uses and programming (though this is by no means always the case). They are given elaborate programmings from their origin times that can offer us much insight into creation and maintenance of universal levels of expression. We can draw upon such insight to see ourselves in the context of what we are in time-space continuums of light and sound expression.

We might add that larger crystals are good for growth in the following ways: healing when growth depends upon insight into the strength of God (as God is capable of all things, Arjuna, even the strengths of crystals); also healing when dependency on the physical precludes belief in God as able to care for you as well as can instruments of sense perception, such as crystals can activate and maintain (in technologies, if you will, beyond your means as yet to comprehend in full). We would also point out that larger crystals are fascinating for you in their sheer size and strength, as well as beauty of expression.

Smaller crystals are as effective in many ways, but their more open, general programming, as a rule, is not as detailed as what we find within their larger cousins. And since larger

---

[3] Baer, *Ibid.*, pp. 54-59.

crystals are unavailable for most people and relatively expensive, we will offer this list for you to grow by information you might otherwise not obtain.

To give a little more detail on programming of smaller crystals in particular, we suggest you would find that they are programmed most often to be open, healing crystals—accessible to many, good for many, working in a more general way that fits the well-being of most people. At times, however, any size crystal may have elaborate programming in it.

In addition, smaller crystals often have programmed functions and information to fit one person or group of people who will work with them. In fact, any size crystal may be preprogrammed for the use of the person or persons who use it or will use it.

Another common pre-existing programming in smaller crystals is as communication crystals or attunement crystals. They are programmed usually in this instance to help one communicate with one's guides and teachers, and one's own Higher Self or Soul. We will come back to this point later in the chapter.

In this book we give you a framework for working with all crystals—large and small, but we might emphasize for you that while we have played with larger crystals ourselves, it is by no means necessary for everyone to do so. We would say that the experience we have gained from this has been valuable for our growth, yet the arrangements for our growth from Soul levels of expression could have worked just as easily without such larger or generator crystals, as you might choose to call them. The planning that is involved in dealing with a larger crystal is greater than that required to deal with smaller ones, as the smaller ones do not need careful programming modifications or adjustments as much and do not need careful cleansing processes as much (such processes as we have described for you in our chapter on cleansing crystals). Such programming modifications we can assist you with in any case, but for larger crystals, such modifications to programming, if you will, are far more important; and cleansing left undone with larger crystals will give you reason to wonder what it is that you forgot to do.

You will also appreciate that a six or twelve-pointed star formation of smaller crystals, perhaps only two to three inches long each, plus a generator of only slightly greater length, is actually all that is really necessary for your work with crystals. Such a formation, again, is of inestimably greater value to your growth than all the possible functions you might find in a larger crystal such as the ones whose programming we will now discuss for you. This is simply true at the most basic levels because your Soul is in charge of your growth, not some crystal of light and sound, no matter how useful it may seem to you now. And the crystals we will describe in the following list are only useful to you through your Soul, ultimately, because your Soul shall guide you to use these things along with your common sense, everyday level of expression.

So we suggest you learn from this list without finding it necessary to inquire as to the availability of massive crystals here or in other places in the world. We have such crystals ourselves—that is why we can discuss them—and we have learned from them. But we suggest you follow your own common sense as to what roles such crystals might play in your lives, as you activate the growth you share with God. And we bless you for all times ahead, whatever growth you choose.

Listing Some Crystals

We would like to simply list some of the programming in crystals we have analyzed. The list could be almost endless. Ninety-nine out of a hundred crystals have a story that would make Edgar Rice Burroughs green with envy. Below is a simple cataloguing of crystals with notes as to some of their preprogrammed properties.

You will also find that we shall teach you a great many things about crystals indirectly through this list (and a great many things about yourselves as well, if you will apply these same things to humans as well as crystals).

It is also important for imaginative purposes to bear in mind that none of the following crystals are in any way limited to the characteristic resonancies of their primary expression relative to humanity at the present time. They are all capable of incredible variety of expression, incredible subtly, activity without limitation, expansion and contraction of infinite variety as well as goodness. They play.

<u>Crystal #</u>   <u>Programming</u>

#1) This crystal has golden resonancies. It is a projective crystal. Easily accessible. Opens one up to his or her inner being. Further uses: stabilizing out of the body experiences, as well as feelings, subtle impressions, subjectivity. Could be used in dream state work. Healing? Yes, but activated through the Self. A Self-knowing crystal. Programmed by the Creator Aspect.

#2) Color resonancy green and blue-green. Good for healing and balancing. A toning crystal; for use in chanting, for example. Balances you as you tone. Programmed by the Creator Aspect.

#3) Perfect balance crystal. Attuned to the Father/Mother Creator of this local universe, and through that the Grand Universe as well. Has a green, emerald-like color resonancy; a higher octave of that resonancy. An informational and activating crystal, perfectly attuned to a frequency that on earth we have called the Christ energy, or what David Spangler describes as the will that is behind all things on earth, guiding and nudging them towards their own potential, perfect expression in the love vibration.[4] Actually programmed by the Zoroastrian initiates in Atlantis to fit the Inner Sun (Son) later emphasized in historical Zoroastrianism.

#4) Healing. Pinky-gold. For aligning and balancing. Programmed by Alayna's Soul without her conscious knowledge for the purposes of a class. Formerly programmed in Atlantis for guarding spacecraft, to not allow access to main flight crystal without pass code. This was a precaution against subliminal programming or interference from random thoughts.

---

[4] David Spangler, *Reflections on the Christ* (Forres, Scotland: Findhorn Publications, 1978).

This programming was no longer necessary, hence the change.

#5) a. Programmed in early Lemuria. Used for engineering the skeletal systems of the seven root races. Stabilized the energies of creation for the project of creating skeletal systems for humanity; used with the quartz crystal skeletal systems still in five medicine bundles of the initiate priesthoods of the earth, some amethyst, some clear quartz, which were at that time as the ideal forms for the carbonized, calcium-filled skeletons being created for men and women.

 b. A second crystal, very similar, used to effect the balance of these energies with the energies of the earth. Both heavily coated by the creative hierarchies so that these information systems would not be common knowledge in times of greater darkness and misuse of such information. Such information could no longer cause any real threat today due to shift in earth's balances. These crystals are an heirloom of the human race. We suggest they be kept in relative privacy for now, and yet be preserved for the future.

#6) Information on big, smoky Lemurian crystal, from the Soul of John Rea (an example of a really detailed analysis):

This crystal is programmed to register and mirror all past life information, so that any work on character and personality still needed by the Soul might be activated; it thus carries defects and negativity in a form that can be brought to attention for self-evaluation. It is a "looks-within crystal," in the terms of Native American, indigenous tradition.[5] It is an active, projective crystal, with complex color resonancies: a golden echoing to activate healing of negativity and perfection of a human energy field. Gold also to align and balance emotional bodies with the causal interfaces. Rose for the heart, at an astral and etheric level, to give health and love expression to balance

---

[5] A good source of information on the Native American tradition is Hyemioysts Storm, *Seven Arrows* (New York, N.Y.: Ballantine Books, 1972). This is one of the great works of American literature, of human literature. It is straight-from-the-heart teaching of the inner wisdom of the peoples of North America, keepers of the sacred medicine bundles of this continent, the sacred bundles of the guardians of the earth herself.

character growth, which is the major purpose of the crystal's programming. Resonancies with violet also exist to order the expression of love toward God. Crystal is smoky at core to aid in elimination of negativity by raising it up from the past to be processed. Thus it is possible for an astral or etheric psychic to notice "negativity" in the core of the crystal, the patterns of expression of past alignments that still need work in the person for whom the crystal is intended. The seeming negativity is but an aspect of the crystal's ongoing work, to bring up and mirror aspects of the Soul's work that are currently being dealt with. The crystal was programmed in Lemurian times to do this, and it has been adjusted to fit an individual, in order that the Trial by Fire process might be quickened in his case, and in order that the process of adjustment and alignment to Soul might proceed as quickly as possible; for such has been the wish of all concerned in this project of conscious growth for the being personality involved. This crystal is to take up the stuff of past lives and transform them by showing them in an atmosphere of total support to the personality of the one using the crystal that he might deal with such things as he sees fit, even to the point of being overwhelmed by the intensity of the expressions. As you are aware of, this has not happened, and the test has been passed. The crystal is little used now, because the one using it has outgrown the need for it.

#7) Attuned to one's guides and teachers. For example, the person who discovered it thought it was attuned to a Confucius-like being, because that was a healing guide for her. For the authors, it would be attuned to their Souls most often, since direct work with one's Soul is the main form of guidance they work with at this time.

#8) General, all-purpose healing crystal with open access, programmed to be easily available to heal and aid the growth of those who come within its range. It would be excellent for a great temple crystal, since it would help so many.

#9) A balancing crystal, to instantly align and balance all energies in its environment. Connected to an Atlantean fire crystal under the sea. This function demonstrates dramatically a crystal's ability to operate outside of conventional time and space. It is blue with a golden tinge to its energies.

Other functions are in order: programming of other dimensions for light and sound; programming the self for balance in the present time and place; programming a group for same; programming the self to attune to Lemuria and Atlantis through the large crystal in the deepest ocean mentioned previously; and lastly, programming from the Soul to align to God.

It has another function relative to the attunement with music and orders of sound in that it is programmed to interface for you the workings of light and color with those octaves of sound you are familiar with in your time.

Very useful. Difficult to access because of all the specialized structures of its programming. You have been involved with it in the past and will be again.

#10) A crystal attuned to devic kingdoms. You could use it for inspiration, as these kingdoms are a flow of creativity from devic levels of sound and color. One of your friends, as a composer/performer and painter, is in fact attuned to these frequencies. Place it in a wild garden to balance the energies of that place. It is indeed a home for such beings, a useful interface between their modes of expression and your own. You could recover something of the quality of living, etheric heavenly realms from being around this crystal from time to time.

#11) A small elemental crystal, attuned to the energies of those known as earth elementals and their guardians. They use it to attune themselves to their universe, just as you would use most crystals to attune to yours. It is programmed with their intent that it be used only for them. "Dwarves" would be a positive word for these beings, though "gnomes" would work too. They are all members of an order that is elementally attuned to the earth and its minerals.

#12) Holds image of the egoic lotus and projects it onto the astral where it can be "seen" or sensed more readily. Silver resonancy.

#13) A teaching crystal. Contains information on many healing systems relevant to a specific individual. Programmed in

Atlantis for this purpose by the person's own Soul in another physical incarnation. (See section on this process in chapter nine, "In the Memory of Mankind.")

#14) Super memory crystal. Contains libraries of information relevant to rediscovering the knowledge of Atlantis. It contains complete histories, in many fields, of the memories of mankind. Programmed in later Lemuria by a particular Soul group for use in our current time. I am told it is a source of more information than the combined libraries of the world, excluding the masses of information stored on current computer discs that are pure numerical or statistical data of no lasting value for mankind.

#15) Balanced crystal for mirroring one's Soul. Useable by anyone with the understanding of the Soul necessary to recognize its patterns.

#16) Attuned to a particular being's Soul, the owner's (not the author's). A fairly common attunement.

#17) Blue resonating healing crystal par excellence. It is attuned to its owner now that it is with her. (Another common type of attunement.)

#18) Programmed by a group of Souls in Atlantean times to reflect the energies of the Soul in its patterns on earth. It is a complete frequency crystal, able to resonate with all expressions of humanity in its current form. It is unusual in this. It was meant to be a healing crystal with wide applications for many to come within its energies. Blue-white is its usual resonancy.

"These are the energies of thy Father/Mother God. We would help you in summarizing this crystal and its role, for it has affected many. It has survived since the times of Atlantis as a beautiful example of what can be done using those energies. These energies can be of help once again in limited ways that you will find very useful. For it is very useful for you to recapitulate and master expressions of the past that you would now release into their perfect resolution. We would suggest you meditate on this, that these technologies are beyond your scope, and yet they are already something you have outgrown need for on many levels. For you yourself have become the healing temples of your time. These are no longer in the confines of great pyramids or temples as of old. And you yourself are the crystals of light and love you seek to understand. Understanding them, you become them for yourselves, fully capable of the resonancies they have brought you to realize as within your own expressions."

#19)   Healing temple crystal. From my Soul: This crystal holds an attunement with a healing temple on another level of expression. These frequencies are protected by and in tune with the Archangel Gabriel, the keeper of the devotional aspect of self, the annunciation of the divine in man at the level of the heart. Thus, this is a devotional healing temple, filled with information and the quality of attunement with self and God. Programmed by you and another in a former lifetime for use of this other, it has nevertheless ended up in your hands, as the crystal intended for your use has ended up in the hands of this same other person. This is not accidental, for your expressions are still linked by many ties of personal and Soul level cooperation. You will find that when the dust settles on these things that there is a balance to all things in God.

#20)   From my Soul again: A crystal for cutting through the differences between subjective and objective truth. It is as a light sword in frequencies of blue gold as well as electric blue fire, the color of mastery of self to the point of healing others at will (especially if they have given permission!). This crystal could be an attunement to self at the level of honesty and truth, free of errors of omission or subjectivity. It is attuned to the mental plane especially, though it is not at all limited to this, its most useful current area of work. In another age with other needs it would adjust to different purposes, as would most crystals. It is attuned as well to the light workers who bring energies of protection and even righteousness; or you might call these the energies of a peaceful Bodhisattva of truth who is in righteous knowing of untruth in all its guises of ignorance, anger and fear. We would not suggest using this crystal in its polar expression of good versus evil, however. As your American Indian traditions know full well, the tree of humanity's existence depends on perfect choice, and so its branches must be forked. There must be a balance of expressions for mankind that he find himself in the balance. And both are offered him that he might grow at levels of the Soul where his acceptance of all growth is assured in ways that transcend time and death and loss of self and others. For all is not lost, all is found to be whole in realms of whole light beyond death. And the remaking of the qualities of personality you treasure as self will begin when you have grown to the point where all things can be used for good, and all things are known as of worth in the eyes of your Self and your God as one. Not one, but as one. For they love each other in a perfect blending of expressions more perfect than anything you have known or imagined in your dreams of perfect peace on your earth.

#21) Attuned to Jupiter One, main command ship in your sector, for adjusting the frequencies of those in its responsibility and those who choose to be in the future.

#22) Atlantean programming attuning to a Lemurian temple.

#23) A communicating crystal, for alignment of subtle bodies in full conscious participation with the process.

#24) This crystal is a narrow band, education crystal, programmed to teach gifted children, star children in Atlantis, with step-by-step, subliminal education. The method described in Frank Alper's *Exploring Atlantis, Volume I.*

#25) A mental plane healing crystal; to release and dissolve thoughtforms of an imbalancing nature.

#26) A small, smoky crystal, usually unnoticed. Chocolate brown in color. It is silver grey in resonancy, attuned to Athena and wisdom energies. It is used to stabilize the relational abilities of a much larger crystal still located underground somewhere in Brazil. This little crystal is like a "friend," allowing the big crystal to continuously notice it is not alone, it is in relationship at all times. This is important to the bigger crystal for many reasons. Primarily, the big crystal is a relational crystal, allowing it to work with many people to program their lives for the better. It is in need of a friend at all times to remind it of the usefulness of its own functions, and to draw upon this relationship as a model for its own work in relating to others of its own kind (crystals) and other life forms, including devic and human kingdoms. An example of the ways crystals are not limited in time and space; for these two work together all the time, though they are far apart.

#27) A small crystal programmed by Jupiter One; near the author's bed to mirror for him the actual processes of astral healing he was undergoing in order to become more aware of spiritual healing, experientially.

#28) A crystal programmed in Atlantis to keep in balance and responsibility those accessing and using crystals through the normal "library" procedures of that time. Should these people grow too imbalanced in spite of the work of this crystal, they would automatically be disconnected from the access circuits to the crystals.

#29) A crystal programmed to the frequencies of the angelic hierarchies for healing and blessing; programmed by the Master Jesus in indirect answer to a prayer by the owner for help. Its frequencies are pale orange and pale rose in color, and they are for attunement with the protection that is always available from those quarters, the realms of the angelic kingdoms.

#30) A carving from a crystal of a Ho Tai figure (the Chinese joy guide or healing master). It resonates with an aspect of Soul that is like this guide in each of us. Those who find it strange are out of touch with their own joy, so to speak. Those who like it have a connection with their own capacity to play, the capacity to love in innocent involvement with little more than life itself. Very useful to anyone who expresses interest in it.

#31) A crystal that set in motion for me the idea that crystals might have programming beyond our wildest dreams on earth. First one person, then another, then a third as well, all noticed something special about this crystal: that it had to do with babies or with birthing in the places we have been before on earth and in the stars as well, on other worlds in other times in other ways of being. There were different observations and perceptions from each of these people who were reading independently the feelings that they got from gazing at this crystal, none aware of what others had noticed before them. But the common element was the subject of birth and newborn babies. Each felt the energies and the information contained therein within his or her own expressions. Each had a common sense for what was there. Such was my first respecting of the souls of crystals, as it were—that they could have such detailed knowledges in their forms as crystals of the earth. I was often guided to turn again to crystals after this, to see what I might find in crystals. So we start to grow, each one in our own way, and I in mine. We trust that you shall grow as well in ways of your own choosing.

This crystal actually contains, as I was informed by others, the knowledges of our past with babies and their birthing. It is a compendium of ways for treating the newborn, if you will —the process of birth included. It is not confined to ways on earth. It contains especially the ways of distant stars on Gamma six of this star system: Alveron, I'm told its called;[6] also the knowledge of this world of ours, as well as integrations with the wholeness of the lives of others here on earth besides the human race. It is a massive repository of knowledge on birth and babies. And it is wholistic in the extreme: its main qualities are babies as they are at birth, the feeling that you get from them in different worlds and all as one. It is permeated with this feeling of babies crying and babies living and babies in their perfect pink, as it were. But also babies as they chance to die, and the proper ways to treat yourself and others with such death as possibility—death in life at even birthing times.

Some Crystal Balls:

#1) Attuned to a particular star system for information on healing, and direct healing from those areas. Also, attuned to the color yellow for Buddhistic alignment and mental plane healing (used with two small crystals).

---

[6] Alveron is a region of space behind the star of your sector called Arcturus in the constellation of Bootes according to your earthly classifications. It is not a name from your earth, this Alveron or Gamma six region; it is rather a designation of our own.

#2) For healing mankind's day: healing the types of injuries to self that are self-inflicted in our day consciousness while awake, through wrong thinking, feeling and willing. This crystal works with exact frequencies of a person's ordinary conscious state of mind to improve and balance it.

#3) A healing generator: also an education crystal on man's proper balance.

#4) Attuned to hidden fires within the earth; subliminal messages of the earth itself; also kundalini energies awakened. (This crystal was slightly changed in its programming by us to have these energies be completely under Divine guidance, so that the crystal was altered to fit the highest and best good of the person acquiring it, under Divine will, in the way that is in perfect order for her Soul and growth.)

#5) Awakening to light, to realms of light, in a systematic optimal way.

#6) Attunement to an aspect of the earth we love, the nature spirits. This crystal will awaken the sense of love and joy we share with them.

#7) A Lemurian crystal, programmed for alignment with the "Els," a race of guardians from another world, who helped guide mankind from a civilization in the Amazon basin before the fall of Atlantis. When their tour of duty was up, so to speak, they went on to other assignments, doing the work of their Souls in service to their universe. This crystal would include much information relative to this civilization and its ways. It would help one today, as the Els were masters at guiding men to understand their universe.
    The Els were here to learn from us about understanding self and expressions of love, for it was by teaching their truth that they could best learn it themselves. So it is with us as well, as we come into our own mastery, as the Els once came into theirs, long before they set foot on this planet.

#8) A joy crystal; attuned to mirth and joy as an antidote to earnestness or depression. A joy guide, if you will, at least potentially.

   As you can readily see, this is quite a list. And it is a mere sampling of the hundreds of crystals, large and small, we have tuned into over the years.

Accessing Crystal Knowledge

   The techniques for this kind of attuning, by the way, can be taught systematically. We have been doing so for several years now with wonderful results. It is interesting and helpful confirmation for people new to the sophistication revealed in the pre-existing programming of crystals to find a room full of people all independently putting together the pieces for themselves of what lies inside each crystal, waiting to be discovered. For the crystals are actually eager to be of service under the will of their creator, like other conscious beings who are in alignment with their universe.
   We suggest that, as a beginning, you might simply hold a crystal and attune to it. Notice what comes to you, any impressions, colors, sensations, qualities, intuitions or feelings. These are subtle, and often not of a psychic nature; that is, they may not be susceptible to simple etheric or astral vision. Although we all do use so-called psychic faculties at times, we often use intuition and direct guidance instead, usually without knowing we are doing this, in addition to our normal intellectual discrimination and our five senses. There is a reason for this. Beyond a certain level, reality is not subject to perception of any kind. It does not have any phenomena, sights or sounds. It is simply intuitable or knowable. At causal and spiritual levels this is true. You may find that you simply "know" or "feel" something about a crystal, or about anything else. One of the most valuable lessons for us is to learn to trust our knowingness, or our feelings, and to learn when we are accurately interpreting these things, not confusing them with other input—such as wishful thinking, assumptions,

beliefs, or imaginings that are more subjective than objective (though imaginings can be very objective).

Types of Crystals

We would like to generalize briefly about the types of crystal pre-programming we have found, with a few preliminary comments. We are told by our guidance that in actual fact the functioning of most crystals we will outline for you is very similar. There is a lot of overlapping in most kinds of crystal programming. All of them are the potential of any one crystal that may have a specialized function for now or for its whole existence. And as any one specialized crystal does its work, it will probably utilize some of the other capabilities we will list in order to be operational at all. For example, a healing crystal must work with some kinds of communication capabilities. A communicating crystal will probably work with some kinds of memory capabilities. And a more general-use crystal might operate as a more specialized or individualized crystal for long periods of time, so that anyone coming across it might think it was a very specialized crystal indeed.

Another point to make is that while a crystal may have a primary programming already in it, there is a very good chance that it will be able to do other functions as well without sacrificing any of its existing programming. Usually a crystal is capable of doing an incredible number of things at one time. It is sometimes best if these different things are related functionally, but not always. An example of this is that you may use a crystal for years as a healing crystal, then learn that it has some specific memory function, or that it has a specific communicating capability. The programming in it may have been dormant for years without your knowing of it. Or it might have been happily doing both what you have directed it to do and what it is already programmed to do as well. Very often, what it has been doing without your knowing of it consciously is for your highest and best good. We have had such crystals that worked for years without their owners' knowledge until their job was nearly completed. It would have been most unfortunate if these crystals had been stripped of their programming through ignorance, though our Souls or other guidance might just as well replace the damaged programming with light and healing until it once again is able to absorb the perfect action it intended itself to have, this programming of your crystal healed all whole. You see, nothing needs replacing; all is whole in God. And all can be repaired through asking for our blessing, blessing of your Souls as one with God.

Another thing to note, a point we expand on in our section on cleaning crystals, is that most cleaning techniques, other than de-magnetizing, do not interfere with a crystal's positive, already existing programming. The reason for this is that most of this programming was done at a causal level not subject to any negative or imbalanced expression at all, and also not subject to change from any lower, more physical level, unless the damage is most drastic—physical damage or nearly so (for causal meets the physical in a circle of expressions, secret of the heart and mind of God). Such levels are, after all, "causes" and not "effects." The very best of human programming is also at this level (the causal), though most human programming is not.[7]

One final point to make here is on the subject of the relative permanence or impermanence of the programming in crystals. In general, the more causative the programming is, the longer it will last. Also, the more positive it is, the longer it will last. Since most of the programming existing in the crystals we have discussed has been done from divine levels or levels of the Soul, it is made to last for thousands of your years.

The following types of crystal programming are only the very general catagories. There are many specialized applications of each category, as can be seen from the above examples.

1. Healing Crystal.

Either general, all-purpose or of more specific application. There are many different ways for a healing crystal to operate, for there are many different possible ways for it to heal. A

---

[7] The interface between this programming and the etheric/physical is what gets damaged by a laser or de-magnetizer, by the way.

healing crystal may be for an individual or a group of people rather than for most people. It may also work in a specialized healing mode or octave. For example, it may be an emotional or mental healing crystal; or a crystal that heals by constantly showing someone the potential perfection or balance of any situation or form; or a crystal that draws out toxicity on one or more levels; or a crystal that simply broadcasts universal life energies in some definite pattern, such as that of the angelic kingdoms, or a certain system of energies that have a greater perfection than what is normal for any given individual.

2. Communicating Crystal.

Again, either general, all-purpose or more specialized. There are many different ways to communicate, just as there are to heal. Communicating crystals facilitate processes of communicating between different levels, dimensions, worlds, universes, states of being or existence, different kingdoms of nature, and sentient beings of different language, form, level of functioning and different understanding. Such a crystal may perform any one or all of these functions. It may serve as a communicator between one's self and one's guides and teachers, or one's guardian angels if you will. A communicator crystal may be for the use of many individuals, most individuals, or for a specific individual. It may attune you to a specific individual, group of individuals, world, or civilization—past, present or future. It may attune you to a particular species of sentient beings, a race, nationality or religion (usually at the levels of universal truth, giving the archetypal truths that structure species, racial, national or religious strengths and weaknesses rather than giving a more narrow or subjective understanding).

A communicating crystal may be attuned to beings or orders of beings that are extra-terrestrial, or non-physical. In fact, the most common specialized communicating crystals serve these functions.

A communicating crystal may not be for human use at all. It may be for communication purposes outside the scope of human capabilities. In fact, the majority of communicating crystals serve functions that do not directly involve human participation, although they will effect humans indirectly, as they are used by orders of beings who direct or influence the world we live in and/or humanity itself.

3. Memory Crystal.

A type of crystal whose primary function is to retain wholistic information at many levels. It may contain whole libraries —literally—in a single crystal, without exhausting its capacity for storage. And the information is not like something in a book—or even in a movie: it is complete, holographic, three dimensional and in five senses—with emotional, energy, thought, and pure concept or causal components that make it almost indistinguishable from reality as we experience it, though far more subtle. Such crystals often are more cloudy than crystals of other functions. This is a signature of their nature, in that they do not so much process a movement of energies through them as they hold specific patterns, and thus are apt to oscillate at slightly slower frequencies than their compatriots.

We might mention that memory crystals are in some ways similar to the Akashic records, the level at which all things that have been on earth and beyond are stored in the memory of nature, the vibrational echoes of the different subtle planes. Memory crystals contain a "library" of information that I am told by my guidance is the closest thing to the actual Akashic Records that exists in time and space. Such information storage is much more systematic and extensive than one might generally imagine, and it is in crystals that are non-physical as well as physical. The living record of human history on earth seems to be stored in the crystals of the earth, both on physical and subtle levels, primarily for purposes of learning and growth for those who have been able to use them. In Atlantean and Lemurian times, but at other times as well, the amount of working, integrated information and wisdom stored in crystals was tremendous. A single, large memory crystal is capable of more memory storage than the largest library on earth today. Just as an example, our guidance tells us that the Library of Congress of the United States has only about a quarter as much information stored as has one large memory crystal we take care of. And there are thousands of such crystals on earth.

4. Special Purpose Crystal.

This a broad, rather arbitrary classification we will use to designate uses that are much more specialized than any of the three functions we have described above, but are actually rather specialized examples of one or more of the above three functions in some form or another. Examples are: a crystal to perform specialized functions for accessing or storing information; a "beacon" crystal to give out a few particular signals for a variety of reasons at definite intervals; and a deva or nature spirit crystal, attuned to one or several dimensional levels that can serve as "home" or access window for beings that would work with us for such purposes as inspiration in artistic activities, help in gardening (indoors or out), or just pure fun.

5. Power Generation.

Especially in civilizations such as Atlantis, which depended on advanced technologies using crystals, it was common to use crystals for energy generation and direction of the energy so generated. The great "fire" crystals of Atlantis were the central suppliers of energy for that civilization. Apparently these crystals were made by space brotherhoods in non-physical expression and then apported to the surface of the planet for use by mankind. The abuse of these crystals resulted in cataclysmic destruction of most of the civilization of the earth at that time (roughly 10,400 B.C.), as well as Atlantis itself, which was inundated by water and earthquakes.[8] This use is not likely to be allowed in our time, in the opinion of the authors, at least until fundamental changes in mankind's

---

[8] Twice in Atlantean history such destruction took place: first in about 34,100 B.C. through failure to align with natural creative forces at work in your world (in such pseudo-scientific ventures as large scale racial and genetic engineering); and second in the time mentioned, roughly 10,400 B.C., through imposition of negativity on others, using crystals in huge pyramidal devices.

behavior have taken place. For different reasons, as of this moment, we as a species are no more ready than the Atlanteans to be constructive with forces that can be used against our environment and the rest of mankind for selfish and warlike ends.

6. Open Crystal or General Purpose Crystal.

Such a crystal may be programmed to accept easily any general use that might be required of it. It may easily become a healing, communicating or memory crystal with many applications of these various processes. Most crystals have such a capacity as a part of what they are able to do all the time, in addition to their other capabilities.

A crystal may or may not be functioning with its existing programming at any given time. The programming may no longer be needed, or only function intermittently; or it may be activated in the future. Also, a crystal may be in need of cleaning and be programmed to shut down until cleaned. This kind of programming is a precaution for the benefit of an owner or possible user. Finally, a crystal may seem to have no function because we ourselves are unable to notice or comprehend what its functions are. (It may not be for human beings at all.) Related to this, the crystal may simply be programmed to have difficult access because its function is very specialized. Some crystals are easy to access and some are not. It has been our experience that, with larger crystals, those with difficult access or more specialized programming will still have available a certain percentage of their programming for the needs and growth of those who come to be their caretakers. Usually, such availability is created by one's own guidance, although a person will seldom be aware this has happened. It is an example of the benign processes that go on all the time without our knowing it.

Chapter Thirty-one

Patterns of Crystals in Nature

A Message from the Natural World & Its Makers:

There are many details about crystals that are verifiable by means available to the scientific community of your world. There are other properties that are not, yet these are equally important. You must try to see things from our point of view for a moment, if you will. We are saying this to you that you will understand you are the ones who must decide what is real and what is not.

Only by discovery of inner self/Soul will you find the keys to your kingdom, so to speak.

The Souls of all are here to help you once you acknowledge your right to grow over time in your universe.

The following sections are from our Souls to you, for we are as your Souls as we guide the natural world in order for all. Bless you.

Crystals in Nature

The first thing to take up is the process of growth for you in noting what crystals do over time. They fall apart, you see. They simply fall apart, as the weather reaches them, as the earth cracks and breaks them up with storm and violence of earth shift over the decades and centuries of your time. Crystals are actually millions of years old when they come to you from the earth. One hundred and fifty millions years old on the average, in fact; though some you shall find on your earth's surface are as young as fifty million years and some are as old as three hundred and fifty million of your years. These oldest are few, for they were the original seeds that were planted in ancient times to give your world a representative sampling of the energies of this universe.

This is the work of conscious beings, you see: to implant your world with crystalline structures that resonate with the stars. Crystals have formed in a cooperation of natural forces and the unseen hierarchies connected with your earth at the level of mineral and crystalline structuring. For all is the work of conscious hands, even if these hands are as forces unknown and unseen by most humans on earth. The patternings of the Gods are at work in all. So your more pagan ancestors viewed these things. And in this they were wrong only insofar as they judged themselves to be without Souls quite like these Gods. For the Creator Gods of us all were as men and women in ages past, so long ago that the earth is as the youngest of children beside the age of such Gods. The earth has but a day's time of life compared to the years of life of those who are responsible for the creative acts upon the surface of your world, in harmony with their own Creators in turn. These beings are knowledgeable in ways you know not, yet they are as you, for they have cooperative understanding they share with your Souls and the divine spark of your own God nature; for you are as God should you awaken to who you really are, and this is in fact your true destiny, in the great expanse of time yet ahead.

The crystals you think of as rocks were formed long ago in the earth by processes that were carefully orchestrated from within and above, if you will, though this "above" was as interdimensional as well as literally "above." The beings responsible for this activity of sharing their natures with your mineral kingdom were as Gods to you, yet they are capable of no more than your Souls are capable of in time, acting as creative forces in the bosom of your universe as service to God and all. You are as one with them in your potential and your growth. Crystals are their work for this time, as your conduct and your lives are yours. So in time your responsibility will give you the capacities for growth that are available to all, and you will be as "Gods" for some world, creative in harmony with all.

Is this not a pleasing thought? To give of yourself with full integrity of being and to know all is done as it should be done, in the will of the One whose universe this is? This is comforting to us, we might say, for our growth is assured in this truth. And your growth is assured in us, if you let us approach you in love—your own true nature, your Souls.

Crystal Formation

Crystals have formed in deposits of magma cooling off, under supervision of creative beings of guidance, great and small, as upthrusts of molten material create a flow of living light and fire, full of beings essential for your earth, who shape these forces, and allow a certain percentage of crystals to form in the cavities and fissures of molten hot liquids that separate out from the more solid, hot liquids of rock. These all solidify into patterns of expression that are themselves as controlled by the unseen hands of those who are consciously at work over all.[1] This work is as lovely and strong as anything you might imagine at a potters's wheel or under the harness of a team of well-trained horses—and as delicate, for such things require true delicacy as well. These are patterns that take energy and hard work for all involved, but the skills of this blessing—for such this work will truly be for all upon your earth as it proceeds through time—these skills are of your own choosing, just as earth living is ours. You fashion the toys of your growth, by your own efforts and craftsmanship, if you will, as a preparation for future work with God and nature through your Souls. And the forges you work here are as nothing beside the forges that craft this great planet of yours.

We would tell you these things so that you would respect fully our efforts for you at all times. For so you might respect our endeavors to support all of yours. And thus you might make your endeavors more appropriate to your growth and our earth, lived as one.

---

[1] (See end of chapter for this note.)

The crystals that result from our work with you are as tuning forks for the universe to resound in. So an interconnectedness exists with all. These crystalline structures that are the result of the work of angelic beings resonate with all your universe in ways that we control for you. So your universe is allowed to balance the harmonies of your world, keeping a perfect balance in all. For energy patterns here are as resonancies with the stars, on the one hand, and activities of your own on the other. Crystals help keep the harmonies intact.

All this is not understood in your time, for you tend to think of merely mechanistic processes in all we do, and in this you are sadly mistaken. We say "sadly" because you suffer from the exchange that you have with what you take to be a "lifeless" world. The world is really alive in ways you know not of. All acts of God are conscious work of individualized beings of light and love—or even of flesh and blood, should you be so oriented as to help us in our efforts to coordinate your world at all natural levels, mineral, plant and animal.

The animals too are guided with love, you see. And all things as living and dead are the expression of unseen consciousness that works individualized through all you see around you in the kingdoms of nature other than your own.

For have we not said that the kingdoms of nature are coordinated as one, that they form an interconnectedness you can only guess about at this time? These things are true for all. And there is a responsibility for you in this that you miss. You are the kingdom in charge, after all. You are the ones who are dependent on God and your Souls, though you know it not. Yet you are in charge of the activities of your world, just as surely as a human is responsible for what happens upon his own property.

You would have it that nothing come to pass on a person's property unless he or she gives permission that it should happen for him or her, as the case may be. We say to you that the same process is invisibly at work in your world. For we could heal all if you would allow it. Yet you must give your permission as humankind collectively, for this is your "property," this planet, though you have not made it, and you have not kept it at times for the ones who did. This is your responsibility, you see, to allow us to redeem both you and your world.

And this we are ready and willing to do. If you would ask, we would help you, in ways you but dream of. The cooperation at Findhorn or in the channel's own backyard, as impressive as they are from the point of view of your natural science, are but a beginning as compared with what we could direct you to do for plants and your world, its soils and its weather, if you will, though weather patterns would follow our work with plants and soil in perfect order quite naturally, without your needing to ask any more directly for our help.

The order we would establish for you, without effort or understanding on your part but only perfect permission and a minimum of cooperation, this would be enough to redeem all. The necessary practical details are available if you wish them. You have but to allow and to ask, and all shall be done by us for you. For that is our role here, to help as we are able to do at this time, even when things appear to be so hopeless in this regard, and men so hopeless about helping us work.

You must have patience in these things and watch and observe carefully as you make first steps in these regards. You will see the results in time, far faster than you might think, if you are willing. We say only that you should regard yourselves as the key to this process of redeeming the earth with us, as you are the key to all things for yourselves and this planet as a whole. So we have been instructed to tell you, for we are the kingdom of nature herself, the nature spirits, if you will, though we prefer "devas," "the shining ones," as a name for our kingdom. God bless you now, Amen.

[In answer to my unspoken questions the following was given. The thoughts herein expressed are reaction from my Soul/your Soul to all assumptions I have had regarding nature and her forces "on her own," as it were—independent of the thoughts and ways of men. This is of course not possible to any great extent. It is only the assumption of our time that things are separate and alone, or isolated in their shells, so to speak. Again, what follows is reaction to my thoughts as they arise, for I have thought many things that are not in order from my Soul. And many things can be made certain in the light of God in truth for all. So we proceed as follows.]

The Role of Life

The geological formations of crystals are of interest to many, but we have preferred to give you the patterns of consciousness and responsibility that are involved with their creation, rather than the physical details that would fit in the same space. We would go on in a similar fashion, if you will, for we would give you some of the details regarding crystals in the context of who you are and why you are here, as these are what you lack more often than the understanding of crystalline formations and the like.

We would next consider the formative patterns of crystals as they solidify out of liquid magma, though in this too we shall deviate as we feel called upon to redeem your understanding, to the degree this is necessary. As liquids cool they congeal, if you will, in patterns that are determined out of the logic of their formation. This seems simplistic perhaps, but the patterns involved are relatively simple. The idea of a pattern is held by the creative being of a mineral or crystal, just as the pattern of an apple tree is held by the deva of these trees, who presides over all the trees of this formation. So crystals each have their individual being, presided over by a collective being, if you will—an active intelligence with active instructions as to service from the Sources of its own creation. The formative "ideas" of these intelligences have definite laws, as you might surmise from looking at nature all around you. It is these laws that natural scientists endeavor to explore from the point of view of what is actually happening beneath their instrumentation or, more accurately, within the range of their perception. These efforts are somewhat analogous to the efforts of natural scientists studying footprints in sand in order to figure out their properties without ever surmising that there are beings walking around who make the footprints. A strange state of affairs, is it not?

The best we can do for you is describe these patterns or laws within the context of the actual beings who make them and implement them, as is the case here and now. We are those beings, your own Souls who work at the causal level and above, who guide you in choosing for your lives. At a future stage, we shall be the same beings who guide your planet in its natural kingdoms from on high, as it were. We are your

Souls, yet we are more, in that we are the possibilities for growth all around you in the kingdoms and living patterns of the natural world. There is great wisdom here, is there not? Great wisdom to make the flower or make the child, whatever it is the Soul may do, with its cooperative effort in the name of All. We say to you that you are this cooperative level if you will allow it to be so.

As crystals form they are given their characteristic vibratory patterns and octaves of expression by the one who makes them. As they live their lives—for this in fact is what they do—they form different purposes depending upon the needs of those who work with them or use them, as the case may be. They are able to do a wide variety of things, including serving as the physical vehicles for a manner of collective entity that will begin its physical incarnations in this form, on the first day of its creation, so to speak. That is not usually the case on this planet, as the vibrations of the dominant species or life form here are not conducive to this operation of first incarnation at this time, being out of synchronization with the energy fields of all creation as a collective whole. In former times, there were such crystals here, ones that acted as the bodies for early Soul development, as it were. But that time is past, remembered only in ancient lore of the hidden capacities of special stones to speak and act in definite ways for good or ill. These things are not permitted at this time, as we have said, for the reason stated: that it would not serve a Soul to form in first beginnings with those around it who are misjudged—or misguided, as are the human beings of this planet.

Thus we have in crystals the potential bodies of individual entities that are at the present only the acts of creative beings as a whole, given instead definite, individual characteristics to inspire and serve all life. And so they shall serve you once you let them do it rightly.

Patterns of Formation

The patterns of confinement of crystals are the next point we would take up. By this we mean the similarities of their properties with yours as humans in human bodies of light and love as well as flesh and blood. Crystals appreciate silence, just as do humans. Given sound, they prefer a noise that appeals to their sense for harmony in all: gentle music gentle also to the ears of humankind. The more universal the tones, the more universally they will be acceptable to the uses of crystal activity that surround the crystalline gel as it settles. Crystals prefer clear, neutral light to color most of the time, just as would you. For crystals then have the chance to work with all expressions of color hidden in white, rather than being confined to a single color which may or may not suit their interests. This is similar for you as human beings, for one color to a window may or may not fit your needs, and if it does, perchance, meet the needs of the moment, it is a color that will soon be needed somewhere else as you outgrow it. For you are used to all color and all sound (in silence), and these are most pleasing to you almost all the time. So it is for crystals.

Temperature

The next thing is that crystals prefer the same temperatures as you do, with a few more rigidities due to their rather more solid nature of expression. They can crack at rapid changes of light or sound or temperature, you see. In the early sunlight after a night of gentle frost, crystals would only crackle and break up a bit as they change temperature so rapidly in the fiery sunlight and warmth, whereas you would only yawn and appreciate the change. Thus we would say to you to keep your crystals out of rapid changes in temperature, keeping them wrapped in cloth or blankets when you move them from one environment to another if the temperature changes are those of winter to an indoor environment or vice versa. In general, changes of more than fifteen degrees Fahrenheit are too much for crystals all at once. The gentle change that comes to them when they are insulated when traveling from one environment to another will help, along with leaving them thus wrapped up while they slowly adjust to the new temperature level.

Once a crystal gets more than 20 degrees below zero (Fahrenheit), it will begin to have basic difficulties doing its work, and it can be slightly damaged as well. Beneath the earth, you must understand, it does not as a rule undergo extremes of temperature change, nor does it know temperatures that are much below zero. So we suggest you do not leave crystals out overnight in frigid climates when it is extra cold. This is much the same as you, you know, confined in flesh and blood the way you are.

Next we would say that outdoor moisture too can pose a problem for your crystals, as the melt and freeze of winter snow or frost can melt into your crystal's tiny crevices, then freeze and expand the crack with the leverage of expanding ice. Thus we say keep your crystals away from freezing moisture, and extra cold nights even when it is dry, if they are substantially below zero. These are simply the unseen laws of the confinement of crystals, the patterns of their confinement, if you will. We have more to say on this as well.

The general temperature of a crystal is a fixed thing, believe it or not. Crystals like to be a certain temperature for maximum efficiency, the same as you do. Yours is room temperature, around 70 degrees F., plus or minus a few degrees depending on your health and general constitution. So it is with crystals. They have a body heat of 72.4 degrees F., which they endeavor to maintain with the means at their disposal, the simple electro-magnetic currents that they activate around them. This is a temperature at which they prefer to function, though they have, like you, a wide range of compatibilities with other temperatures. A crystal of several thousand pounds could easily warm a room or two with its ability to quietly adjust the temperature around it. You would find that in the house of the channel writing the temperature is held quite stable at a little more than 70 degrees most nights because of crystals, which accounts for slightly lower fuel bills—although on really cold nights the temperature would slip below this but for the furnace working overtime. We do not suggest this as a means of heating a house, as the temperatures of a house are always a bit uncomfortable heated only by crystals, and without our help, the mass of electro-magnetic force needed to heat a house is so great that you would need the largest crystals in the world, everyone, just to heat up a few common living rooms enough to find them liveable—and still the furnace would do the work most winter nights of bringing up the temperature to a comfortable range for you. A very expensive and bulky living room heater indeed!

[At this point the energies have shifted over to those of my Soul, rather than the beings who are in charge of the growth of nature.]

The next thing we will endeavor to discuss for you is the temperature of crystal formation. We do this only in an informal way, for we do not wish to compete with your scientific activities in our activity with you. We wish to teach you growth, not patterns of understanding to manipulate nature more than you already have.

Heat is the deciding factor in the alignment of a quartz crystal at a particular level, for as you may have noticed, there are two general shapes to crystals, the trigonal, or almost triangular shape (looking "down" the crystal lengthwise or along the axis of symmetry of the crystal, the so-called c-axis), and the hexagonal or high temperature formation (formed at roughly 573° C) that is more evenly six-sided in appearance (again looking "down" the crystal). The chemical constituencies of the two types of quartz crystal are identical or nearly so most of the time.

(Crystals do contain minute patterns of "impurities," you know. And these "impurities" are useful to us, for they are never accidental or useless to the conscious functioning of those using them, who fashion all things in nature with a purpose for God that human beings rarely guess exists.)

The so-called trigonal or more triangular crystals are useful to the earth, in that they are for gross energy flow or transferral within the earth primarily. Their attunements are usually related to the earth's own electro-magnetic frequencies and attunements. You can use them too, but this was their original purpose, to be used for the earth by those who made them.

The hexagonal crystals can do everything the trigonal crystals can do and more for you. Thus we generally recommend them for human use.

Most crystals are a mixture of both types of formation rolled into one, with the high temperature form predominating. Thus we recommend you use your crystals freely, without troubling yourself which type you have unless you are able to tell the difference from our description. The chances are that the crystals you have are of the high temperature variety predominantly. Most crystals from this country and Canada are.

Those from Brazil or Madagascar have a greater possibility of being trigonal, but most crystals from these localities are hexagonal as well.

Heat is an interesting phenomena for you to be aware of, you know. It is the first level of materialization, if you will, though from your point of view it is the first level of dematerialization as well. It is a dissolving of the physical as you know it. It is a passing into a realm that is not akin to your physical plane at all. Under the strain of heat, more things happen than you are aware of in your time. The form of an object disappears to physical appreciation, finally, as heat is applied. In its place, you would find the form at another level: the level of archetypal design. In the drift of liquids you would find more than you are aware of as well: you would find the form of all adrift in a sea of substance, whereas in the physical itself the form is solidified, however imperfectly, in a fixed condition. So in crystals the form is solidified through removal of heat if you will, but rather through the application of the strains of limiting physical existence as they apply to matter. This is what happens as the "freedom" of extra energy or heat is removed from the fluids or liquids in which the potential crystals are to be found.

The above paragraph contains the keys to understanding why crystals have universally been called frozen light or water. The forms it is possible to see in the movements of sky and water are present in solid form in a physical crystal. Thus the word "crystal," meaning originally "frozen movement," came to be called "frozen liquid," and in this time a certain confusion has lead your world to think the derivations for the word "crystal" are found in the meaning "frozen water or liquid." This is not a reference to the water you drink, you see. It is a reference to the mineral that takes the form of movement itself in the mediums of air and space, also the mediums of liquids of all kinds, though to a lesser extent.

This is a way of describing these things from our point of view, as living realities, if you will, as living experience. We prefer this to dry attempts to abstract the conditions of nature that are fashionable in your time for no good reason we are aware of, other than pride and strain of various kinds. We use the word "strain" here, as we did with the solidification of the crystals, for a similar force is at work: the structuring of form is a strain on thought as well as matter, as you know it. Enlivening of form in both instances produces changes in expression of a seemingly fundamental nature, as water passes into solid and back again; as thought passes into wholeness and back again into differentiation. Thus a tendency to structuring is inherent in all things close to solid, and life balances form with light work all the time. You would find that in your inner thoughts as well such balancing exists: you too are aware of balancing inner thoughts with tendencies to release such thoughts again in God. The Soul's work with you is to balance all the time, as well as in your thoughts of whole and part. The personality expression can absorb the growth of Soul and balance all, but often forms are given and released again imperfectly in our forms of physical expression. We all know the feel of forms that fix inside us, growing cold. This is what the forms in nature do: the Souls then guide these forms to be most true.

The best that we can say to you is that you are free to grow in form and substance of your Soul. The limits of your structuring are ours to give to you and then adjust for goodness' sake and yours. Our minds can only know the ways we teach to grow. This is incomplete yet whole as we intend. Our words may form a structuring within the confines of our minds—or release to greater freedom all the time. An enlivening is inherent here, you see. We would give you tools to fill your lives with wonder. Thus the freedom you aspire to still is yours amid the slowing and the changing that are yours as well on earth.

This is something to follow up on just a little, if you will allow us to do so. The form of things is a transitional phase between being and becoming, if you will, but rather, between living and dying. The form is released in giving up the ghost of something, the form of something. Thus your world is peopled by beings that are becoming what they cannot be, if one were to look only at the outward form of things. The forms you see are less than living, though from our perspective all things are alive in God—even trees and stars and other outward forms that seem to have no life. (For trees, you must realize, seem to have no more life than rocks do—to your outer eye, at least.)

The outward form, you see, is less than living because it is released by life itself. Otherwise you wouldn't see it any more. Its life would have freed it for new growth. It would be free to grow and not in physical expression at all. Only when you wake the forms are they alive the way we are. Only in such awakening is there the strength and life to grow, you see. And yet in God are all things living, trees no less than you or me or stars. It is hard for us to convey to you the meanings that we give to things and give to you to grow by when you approach the physical world itself directly. It is so different from what your lives assume yourselves to be. On another tack, it is important to try a bit, at least until you grow to know your Soul as one with you. Then you are free to notice for yourselves the truth of things you are aware of in yourselves as well as "outside" in seeming time and space.

To continue, the form you see around you is released by other Souls than you, who guide your world to grow in you as well as all around. We give you forms to grow by, can't you see? We give you life to live. It is our release to you, from levels of the Souls that guide you in all forms as well as yours. We release what we have known and used before, what we have loved and still release to you to love as well as we do. We know you will grow as you accept this gift from us, your Souls, in truth for all to grow by. And yet you know us only through the forms that die through us, the forms we give to you to grow by. The living life behind all form—this is another thing entirely than any form on earth. Respect all things, but know we guide you for your growth in other forms than those you see with eyes of physical expression. These forms are something that you could leave for others than yourselves in turn at times ahead, once you love them fully from your Souls' own point of view.

Note (from footnote number one): The patterns of guidance involved in these operations of light and life are not as you might think them to be, at first glance. They are scientifically calculated and guided from afar by our science—the science of form and matter that abides beyond your knowing, in forms we live elsewhere. Thus the forms on your world are created through endless cycles of formation unknown to your science as yet, unknown to your conscious minds. At their heart, these processes of creation are as ambitions of stars, not men as such, for your "men" are as they are because of our guidance, whereas the stars are as they are quite simply—complete unto themselves. And your crystal formations are of such completeness themselves.

So resonancies of stars shape worlds of light and life, complete unto themselves, with no further order of activity essential to justify their own activity, as it were. You yourselves, as men, are not so simple: you are justified in your expressions—out of harmony as they often are—through the learning of your Souls in God, the balancing as well. You are the seed atom of your Soul, in a way, because you are as light and love only as you create your full potential in yourselves as whole and one with God. A crystal is form divine already—never out of phase with all, except as you intend. And the formation of crystals from the stars takes place in patterning of seed atoms just as does your own, in that the resonancies of stars are implanted here as are your own, through those of your own choosing; for you are as Souls of guidance for this world, every one through you. And you are implanter of these energies of stars as well through actual bodies of light in the form of seed crystals implanted long ago upon your planet in physical expression, that other crystals in formation might grow around the resonancies held therein.

So too you have been such seed crystals for your world, that you have held the resonancies of stars and distant Souls for all to be, should they chose just so to be, or should they chose another form as well. For any form you once have known becomes your own in time. And any form you then become contains the forms of all who came before, for all are here right now. And all shall ever be—in time as well as any space in resonancy with the stars about your planet in the sky at large. So, you see, the world is subject to change, yet it grows through you. And you are all in time. You are seed crystal of these forms around you. All are in your whole. When once you have been exposed to all, then all shall be your name. God bless you now. Amen.

Chapter Thirty-two

Growing with Crystals

Merging With the Light and Love

This chapter is more than a summary of what you have learned from crystals thus far: it is a completion and a beginning of all that you have known thus far through us, your Souls, in words within this book. It is a completion you have reached before—and will reach again. God's blessings on you.

Merging with crystals is a process of growth and alignment with what is, as we enhance the growth and harmony of humanity in the present age. This is so because crystals are more like us than we ourselves can know. They are in some ways more like us than our own bodies are.

The process of becoming one with "bodies" of silicon that are more like us than those of carbon is a process we will undertake to explain in greater detail at another time, in other books, in other chapters on the Age of Healing (for so Atlantis called itself, forty thousand years before the birth of Christ). For now, know that crystals are in harmony with the earth and stars as are we all, and they are more perfect in this expression than is the physical body, subject as it is to oscillations of carbon more than silicon and still the resonancies of imperfections in our daily lives on earth—growing tired, growing old, growing weak, growing strong (for all these things are as instabilities or adjustments to the tuning fork of bodily expression). These things distort in turn the accurate resonancies between the stars and our expressions in emotions, thoughts and actions, and in adjustments that we make to those around us in our world who act and think as we do. For crystals do not think as we do, yet they know the stars as one with thought, as they are thoughts of God in fullness of expression, actualized on earth. They know the thoughts of all that live here in our world and universe as well. For they resonate in all, for all who ask their help, the thoughts of some Divine Plan that watches over all.

Crystals can have feelings too, for they echo inside themselves and out to all, those feelings that come to them—as we humans do in part; yet we do more, for we carry identification with the feelings of others, thinking them our own; and we dissociate from our own true thoughts and feelings as we do this, thinking ourselves in the wrong all the time.

In their actions, again, crystals are as we are; yet they are perfected in this as well, improbable as this may seem. They are perfected in action in that they do nothing that is not asked of them, nothing. And in so doing they are blessed. They are capable of much action, by the way, for being limited in bodies that do not move mechanically is no hindrance to thought and intentions of others, and crystals move by the intentions of themselves and others in ways we know not of. Verily, they move mountains, for they are blessed with the responsibility for the creative acts of others—their God and the creative hierarchies that guide and rule all life as we know it to be. Crystals are as creators, for they serve their creator in this capacity, as well as others. They serve all who would use them in harmony with all. They serve for a time those who would not, though this can only be short-lived; for service to self and Soul for all, means harmony with all over time, in the long haul, and balance is reached in the end by all.

The service of crystals, then, in the merger process we have already described for you in part, is to give you back yourselves, at the level of bodily expression. And by "body" we mean more than you might mean: we mean thoughts, words, deeds, and your feeling life as well, for these things are as possible because of vehicles of light, as it were, that resemble the stars and give you capacities to be in thought, in word, in deed, and in feelings. The subtle bodies, as they have been called, give these capacities, but actually they are patterns of Totality that resonate in definite ways you call your emotions, your thoughts, your words, and your deeds. Your words are as physical as the thoughts, deeds and emotions you bear before you into your life. They are causes of all, on another level. They are deeds of God at Causative levels. So we include them with thought, emotion and deed as four that guide you to know yourselves in truth, as you act out your frequencies of exchange with all that is and ever will be.

With crystals you have a perfected form for all these levels of expression. In crystals, these subtle bodies that carry our thoughts, emotions, words and deeds are acted out in fullness for all to see, in harmony with God. It is as if you had with you a saint as you carry around your crystal. Your crystal, in its wholeness, teaches you the light and guidance of God; and the love as well, if you ask it to. For Love comes only to those who choose it, and thus the crystals of this creation are loveless in a certain sense, until you add that love, and ask them then to hold it. So a crystal becomes as Spiritual as well as Physical, as you ask it to do what it would do most faithfully once you ask: give you perfect frequencies of love.

As a small aside, and briefly put, love, like light, has certain frequencies of expression for your world. There are thirty-six frequencies of expression in ranges you would call as love: thirty-six, in fact, that correspond to those of light.[1] The thirty-six are formative, in a certain sense, for they correspond to those of light that guide your world. Yet they are also part of a greater whole of twelve times twelve, or one hundred forty-four healing "colors," if you will; though you would see them more as love expressions and beyond if you could see them as we do. The three expressive ranges beyond your whole light colors are those respectively of love and life and God himself/herself (creative being in form-expression emanations from the divine source). We give you this to know that God is love at your current octaves of expression, and God is more in definite, beautiful fulfillment of your growth. The last thing we would say to you on this, the levels of your expression beyond the physical ranges of your Soul on earth, is that you are these things at all levels. They are you, not some distant recognition of the future, and they are love, life and being of the future God you are as one with your Creator and Redeemer.

---

[1] For the thirty-six rays of light, see Rev. Dr. Frank Alper, *The Universal Healing Rays* (Phoenix: Arizona Metaphysical Society, 1983).

36 rays of light....our "physical" expression...realm of our
(in 3 sets of 12)   (physical/etheric, astral,   personality
                      mental/causal)

36 rays of love....our Buddhic nature...........realm of our
                    (on twelve levels)   Soul or
                                                  Christ-Self
                                                  (High Self)

36 rays of life......our Atmic nature.............realm of the
                    (on twelve levels)   Father/Mother
                                                  God level of
                                                  our being

36 rays of being...our Creational level..........realm of the
                                                  unlimited
                                                  divine in Man
                                                  & God

The patterns of thirty-six besides your colors are not experi-
enceable by you in forms outside your Soul as one with God.
The love octaves or ranges of expression are of your Soul, just
as yours are realms of light. The realms of life are of your
Soul at Father/Mother God or universal levels of expression, if
you will, though we have called these of your Soul as well.
The realms of pure being—or active being, if you will—are
realms of your creator level of expression. You are of this level too, you see, as whole in God most good. This is simplification, but will do for now. In our other books for you we
would go in further detail into God.

To continue, crystals you shall merge with are perfect expressions of the thirty-six and their further combinations on
many levels. It is a harmonic balance in crystals that guides
you to them. They are as tuning forks for you in guidance
towards your truth. Yet they are also much as pets: unthreat-
ening to you, unless you fear some nameless dread in things
you do not understand. It would be best, in fact, for you to
note they are as teddy bears or toys for you, as much as they
are saints. For like a teddy bear that you can love and give
yourself to—without a thought of threatened or present de-

316 PATTERNS OF THE WHOLE, VOL. I

mands of others—crystals can be treated as a secret friend of your own childhood, a teddy bear or doll or toy, that you can imagine with in privacy and freedom, who will not threaten you or make demands or lie to you, or leave you lonely. Thus you can find a friend who is much like you, to test yourself with; just as surely as a saint, yet still perhaps more flexible than any saint, who must have needs for self as well as you. And teddy bears give love without a question. They give love with certainty to you, to play with as you may. Childishness is not involved in this. It is child-like and true to trust a thing inside of you that feels the love of God in all. So a child would learn to grow through teddy bears; and so a crystal can do something similar for you, at another level of your childhood, if you choose it to. We might suggest you leave the dolls and toys to children and keep the crystals for yourselves —unless you choose to overlap the two, or children come to you for crystals, which is something we have dealt with in our chapter on children. Here we only note the awakening child in you, whether you are old or young. And we suggest also, that unlike saints or teddy bears, crystals fit inside a pocket, or anywhere you choose to put them, taking them with you. They are more active too—in many ways we choose to show you in this book.

We give you now the following exercise to allow you to attune to crystals in a way that leads to appreciation of their wholeness for you and in you. For you are one with God and one with all his/her perfect things.

The merging process proceeds as follows:

First, allow yourself to relax inside your crystal as you let yourself drift in a white cloud of light. Let this white cloud merge with the crystal you hold in your hand for this purpose. Let the crystal in your hand expand to encompass you and your cloud, if you will, though you have become the cloud by now, as you imagine it all around you, growing in oneness with you all the time. This crystal encloses you and your cloud, as you and your cloud have merged. And now allow the cloud to spread inside the crystal until all the crystal is filled with the cloud. Let the crystal relax its definite shape for you as you are relaxing in it.

Now we would like you to merge with the crystal by allowing your cloud and you to merge with it. Let the consciousness of your cloud (you in your cloud as one, if you will) merge and meet the full attention of the crystal by becoming one with it. Notice what it feels like for you as you relax in this space of cloud and you and crystal all as one together, each giving the other all you have to give of your own perfection. You have set the condition, in advance, by the way, that this shall all come to pass in perfection for you. We will assume in this case that this means that which is perfect in the eyes of God, rather than the eyes of other men.

To proceed, allow yourself to relax in the cloud of your crystal. You in it, it in you. Allow it to merge with you as a long lost friend, for it is a friend if you ask it to be. Let it guide you in any way it chooses, for your best good. Notice what it teaches you: its sights, its sounds, its quality of being, if you will, for this is guidance for your life. Notice the intentions you bring to it at this time, for these are what guide the impressions you are receiving as you drift inside your crystal, as one with it in imagination, if you will, but more—in a seeming that imprints the whole of things that are affected by you and by your crystal too. For we are with you to affect you as a whole with what you see around you.

The next step might be to allow yourself to drift into a part of your cloud that contains a definite healing for you. Allow it to work on you for healing once you ask it to, from the point of view of being merged within your crystal. Let it work on you in ways that teach you what you have to learn to be made whole in God, for God is love made whole. And this is true for you as well.

Next, perhaps now or on another occasion, let your crystal guide you to a distant place or star system. You do this best by simply visualizing yourself inside the crystal traveling very far in a few brief moments or in the twinkling of an eye, as real travel in the galaxies is at the speed of thought not light. Pick a star system and notice any impressions you are given, or instead, let the crystal or your guides pick a star system for you. You will go to this star system in as much as you are willing to notice on a subtle level any input, however gentle or improbable, that might arise in consciousness. For your Soul is fully capable of programming you with the frequencies of

any star system that you see or think of, that you may compat-
ibly experience the nature of that world or worlds before you
are able to go there in full form of flesh and all that
accompanies it.

We say this to you, this business of a star trip, that you may
be guided to explore your dreams, your wishes. For with
crystals you will have a key to communicate with perfections
not available on the physical dimensions you inhabit in your
waking life. You have a window to your growth in this little
crystal that you see before you. You have a pattern of the
whole that leads to wholeness in all men and women who are
drawn to it.

You might, for instance, call upon the qualities of a favorite
archetypal being, one who has at one time lived as a human
being or not. You will receive the best of this being, if you so
wish it. For as you wish and ask, so shall it be, as control of
life for you is a given thing, and the Souls of archetypes are as
alive and available to all as ever they have been. For so an
archetype is: a pattern of the whole with life and meaning to
help in growth; otherwise it would not be an archetype. There
is power or strength in archetypes because they fit the patterns
and the needs of human beings, here and in realms that are not
on earth.

Another suggestion is to ask the crystals to guide you to a
guide or teacher who is most suited to your energies at this
time. You may do this quite adequately from within your own
crystal, for so you are within the pattern of six and twelve as
well, within the center of the circle. Outside it, you may set up
crystals in patterns of six and twelve to do the same thing more
fully, for then your whole body shall be physically within the
circle of light that is within your crystal, just as you in your
imagination and your subtle energies may call upon the crystal
from its center to gift you with its presence as you succeed in
merging with its focus and its light. For light is all at many
levels, and light with love are wholeness in your forms as
well.

We give you one more simple suggestion with this process
of merger. Let it happen naturally. Do not worry about your
ability to do it. Intention alone is enough. More than enough,
for it overrides all doubts and fears if once you let it.

Chapter Thirty-three

A Final Chapter

The patterns of your awareness are such that you are guided to things as you see them before you. So we have guided you to look at stones upon the earth, and at crystals as fulfillment of the mineral kingdom of nature.

The best guidance we can give you is to notice these things as yourself, to notice them as a part of all that is, a riddle of your creation, if you will, but more as well: the legend of humanity is guided to you from afar in all that you survey with love.

This is the basic perception we would bring to you of yourselves through crystals as well as all you do, that you are guided from afar, from the realms of time and space you know little of, and the realms beyond expression in your terms that are as guiding factors in your lives on earth. These realms are guided too, you know. Their guides are guides in turn for you. The best that we can say for you is that you are subject to the growth of your Souls upon this earth of ours, this earth of wonder. It is an earth prepared for all who come here to choose what they will do for growth, much or little as the case may be. Yet it is an earth that grows you as you wish for all, for your growth aids the growth of others in the world, and all you do and that they too shall do—these others in your world —is for your Soul and theirs as one in God of love.

The last thing we suggest to you as we draw to a close with this book is to seek still further in yourselves as you do now within the crystals for the details of your Souls, for they are whole through all the details that you find. In honoring the many forms of expression in you—as detailed moments in the God of love—you too shall find the source of all that is, the source that you yourselves aspire to know through all your dreams of gentle life in God; for God is gently understood by all you do to grow in truth.

The aspect of our Souls that incarnates upon this earth is full of wisdom. Love it needs to know. This is the simple secret of life, you see. In love you grow to the Souls of all. In love you are blessed with wholeness. This is the message of all Souls who come to God in truth. This is our Soul's message to you through me. For I am the writer of this work, yet I am a Soul as well. Two for one, so to speak, in you as well as me. And always has it been the case that you have come to Soul through me, the Soul of all through you.

Appendix I

Other Gems & Crystals We Work With

We would like to describe for you the uses of a few of the other gems and crystals we work with, perhaps those we use most often. We do this a bit hesitantly, for on the one hand, we realize that it is not necessary to use any other crystals for self-activation than clear quartz programmed to fit all needs; and on the other hand, we ourselves have taken years of trial and error discovery to fully realize this is so. We have used other stones with great appreciation for their gifts, and still do so: even though we know that through a prayer, the energies in any gem or crystal might be duplicated. It is wonderful to honor every level of our existance, is it not? And at the physical level, God has honored us with creation of many different truths and treasures in the mineral kingdom—though dwarves and dragons grow confused and try to hoard them all.

Below is a list of the gems and crystals we will describe for you, realizing the list could just as easily have been longer.[1]

1. malachite
2. rhodochrosite
3. amethyst
4. smoky quartz
5. rose quartz
6. citrine
7. star quartz
8. tourmaline

---

[1] There are many good books on the different uses of other gems and crystals. Please see the bibliography.

These are stones we have found useful in one way or another that we choose to describe for you. Gold and silver, topaz and turquoise, lodestone and vibrational gems—these too we might have chosen. May you discover their uses for yourselves.

Malachite

Malachite is a fairly common material in Africa and in North America as well. It is associated with the green of leaves, and it carries the energies of chlorophyll and leafy formations to some extent. It is experienced almost as a liquid chlorophyll by ourselves and many others we have dealt with.

Malachite is a copper derivative, being technically a copper carbonate ($Cu_2CO_3[OH]_2$). It is very soft (hardness of 3 1/2 to 4). It occurs in shelves of layered green, chalky-green and greenish-black veins that bubble and swirl in solidified liquidy patterns. It is associated especially with the properties of copper that are feminine in nature—properties of Venus—that transform our bloodstream and deposit strengthening energies along the walls of the associated vessels of our circulatory system, just as does liquid chlorophyll in another, associated way.

We would say to you that malachite is especially useful to women in this age, as women have need to reconnect with the earth through the plants and copper. They also have a need to reconnect with their own femininity and fecundity, if we might say so, through the energies of the divine feminine particular to Venus and to the malachite mineral.

Men might also benefit from this mineral in that they too must connect with the nurturing and warming aspects of the bloodstream that malachite enlivens.

We would say to you that the processes of feminine hygiene, in particular, would be made much simpler if men were involved in their own femininity and could accent the positive strengths of the blood to give the women a boost during the time of both their ovulating and menstruating. This is a strength that men as well as women might cultivate with the aid of malachite in your time.

Another property of malachite we find essential for you to utilize is the ability of malachite to deal with radiation, particularly plutonium, in fairly large quantities. We owe this understanding, in part, to the research of Gurudas, author of *Gem Elixirs and Vibrational Healing, Vol. I & II*, who we have learned from in both personal conversations and classes. Please refer to these books for greater detail on radiation baths and uses of malachite for radiation protection. (In general, simply wear or carry a piece of it.)

The next topic we would consider regarding malachite is to simply indicate the correspondences of the different types of malachite to their different uses. In general, you would find that the lighter the color of the piece you might be using, the higher in the body its healing functions will correspond to, aside from the overall properties we have described for you in the above paragraphs.

The lighter color of chalky light-green, we would say, corresponds to the blood vessels in the heart and lungs especially.

The deep green varieties correspond to the heart more directly—and to the properties of chlorophyll in general: aiding the circulatory system, warming the heart (and helping it relate to life), aiding assimilation of foodstuffs, and helping in other ways related to the warming effect of copper.

The darker, almost black veins of malachite correspond to the circulation of blood to and from the womb. It is the black signature that allows you to know this with fair certainty, we might say.

The properties of love and light be with you through your malachite. God bless you.

We suggest you use this stone or substance in ways that involve your own creativity, just as you might use quartz. We find the uses of any substance in God's earth are limited by boundaries we place on our imaginations, more than anything else. And malachite is very beautifully creative all by itself, as well as when you use it.

Rhodochrosite

Rhodochrosite is probably the stone we use most often besides quartz and amethyst. Because it is relatively unknown, we will describe it in some detail. It is very different from quartz, being a manganese carbonate ($MnCO_3$) that often contains calcium, iron, magnesium and/or zinc. It is much softer than quartz (hardness of $3 1/2$ to 4). The material we use is pink, salmon pink, dark red or reddish orange. Rhodochrosite is usually found in massive form rather than in distinct crystals. Its crystals are hexagonal and most often rhombohedrons. Cleavage masses that look like single crystals are perfect on three sides, forming rhombohedrons. Material for sale is most commonly from Argentina, Colorado or South Africa. The Argentine material is heavily veined with layers of pink, salmon-pink and chalky white. The Colorado material is most often in large, irridescent cleavage masses and crystals that are reddish pink. And the South African material is in deep orange-red, gemy crystals, usually quite distinct. Any of these materials will do for our purposes.

Rhodochrosite is a specific for the heart, healing it on a physical as well as etheric level. It is mending for the astral body as well, as it knits together rends and tears in the etheric fibre or etheric webbing that surrounds the body physical. This in turn allows the corresponding astral patterns to be restored to order. This stone also works directly on the astral.

Rhodochrosite is a substance that quickly seals the aura, when it is applied there physically. It is very useful for dealing with negative influences from outside one's being that might be able to access the physical structures of the subtle bodies, due to unwanted tears or holes in the etheric or astral levels of the "physical" expression. It is a substance we highly recommend for all kinds of subtle body repair. In many ways, it is to the etheric and astral levels what a number of the so-called "bone-knit" herbs are to the physical level: it mends all wounds to structural forms.

The most common ways people acquire such tears and damage to subtle structuring, by the way, are through negative and /or extreme expressions of emotion. The next most common forms of damage are those acquired through taking drugs or alcohol. Lastly, our attitudes about ourselves, largely acquired over many lifetimes of our Souls, also contribute to the tears and rends in our structural fibre on subtle levels. For example, a person who is inflexible due to past-life treatment of self and others might acquire weaknesses to the joints on a physical level. Prior to such physical manifestations, this person will have acquired weaknesses to the subtle fibres around such joints that rhodochrosite can help repair, once the source of the problem—particular patterns of inflexibility—are identified and dealt with, at least to some degree.

We would say that rhodochrosite repairs on all levels of expression, and this is the key to its use. It is also very soothing and repairing to the systems influenced by the heart, including the glandular system, nervous system (indirectly) and most structures in the bloodstream as well.

In summary, rhodochrosite is a wonderful choice for your healing work. We would add that once you are familiar with its workings, it is possible for you to modify your work with rhodochrosite by using quartz in conjunction with it—or even to replace its use entirely with your quartz. We mentioned this possibility earlier in conjunction with a footnote on the beryl family (see end of chapter fifteen). We have to say that quartz can carry all the frequencies of these substances to perfection; and once you familiarize yourself with the way rhodochrosite works, you can use quartz by itself to replicate these energies —or you can use quartz around rhodochrosite to amplify it. This use of quartz to enhance a substance or duplicate its energies is possible, in general, with all the substances we will mention in this appendix.

We ourselves use rhodochrosite because we love it and choose to honor its presence in our house by blessing others with its use. The choice is up to you as well.

Amethyst
(Please see our note on amethyst in chapter one.)

Amethyst is quartz with a purple hue. It is commercially available in this country from Russia (as a gem rough), Canada, Mexico, Uruguay and Brazil, to name a few. Amethyst is expressive of the purple ray, the violet ray to some extent, and other energies of transformation. We would suggest to you that amethyst is expressive of the divine feminine as well.

As the divine feminine, amethyst will coordinate the growth of all the chakras at once, integrating them in patterns of appreciation for all. It will coordinate our growth in this way.

It is also a good balancer for the kidneys and the adrenal system, at another pole of our expression.

In between, so to speak, amethyst balances the intellect with the energies of the vitality being in humanity. It provides integration of desires with understanding and appreciation for the Soul, if this is appropriate for the individuals involved.

Transforming energies, or transmutation—these are good ways to name the process that amethyst provides for us on earth. Transmutation, in this case, means the process of transforming our growth for us from one level (that of our understanding, perhaps) to another (that of our direct experience, in the same case). Amethyst also transmutes the desire level of our being to more compatible expression for our overall designs while on earth. It is a soother in this, and a balancer as well. It was this use that gave it its name, which means "to aid in drinking," for in other times amethyst assimilated for one the energies of vitality that were released through drinking alcohol.

Amethyst is also a wonderful aid to the assimilation of the Divine Intellect, as well as the Divine Feminine, in order that we might regain our "knowing" nature after the long period of intellectual development we as human beings have undergone on earth in recent centuries. The restoration of unimpeded flows on several different levels is a consequence of such regaining, and that is why amethyst is so successfully used to stimulate the intellect to heal (and thus sooth it, along with the emotions of frustration that arise from such damming up of the intellect, such efforts to grow). Amethyst will also stimulate and heal the bloodstream, after such a restoration has taken place—or before it, in cases where this is appropriate.

We suggest you use amethyst for many things in addition to what we have mentioned in this book. Please explore these uses for yourselves.

From our point of view, amethyst is best used in conjunction with quartz of a clear color, as the clear quartz is better able to adjust to all your possible needs, while amethyst confines it-self to several narrower frequency ranges of expression. It is important for you to grow in the widest possible way at all times, and thus, if clear quartz is always present in addition to amethyst, this will be possible.

You might use amethyst in cases where attunement to the particular color or energy of a crystal is not possible yet for a client or one you would give a crystal to. Thus it will be pos-sible to see at a physical level exactly the quality involved with the crystal (in this case amethyst) before one is able to sense that there is more going on than meets the eye, so to speak—that there are forces at work through crystals and through your lives on earth, as well, that are as determining factors in those lives, the determining factors being the light and love of all those who guide you and who are you, at other levels of appreciation for what is.

Amethyst is a fine stone to work with. We would counsel you to use it often if you like it. And we suggest you use your head about when to use it—or any other quartz with color—as it is not as neutral in expression as your clear quartz.

Also, we might suggest a last, interesting use of amethyst in the occasional substitution of amethyst for clear quartz as the second set of six crystals that go into the twelve-pointed Star of David pattern, thus making every other crystal quartz that is clear, and every other crystal quartz that is amethyst.

Smoky Quartz

Smoky quartz is usually formed within twenty feet of the surface of the earth by the activity of the sun over vast periods of your time (twenty to thirty million years, for example). Smoky quartz is the best transformer at a physical level of all the quartz family, and as such, it will frequently come into play for you as you work with those whose physical needs for change have not kept up with their energy changes and adjust-ments in their growth. We would direct you to the uses of quartz in ancient times, in that the best use for smoky quartz as well as amethyst is in conjunction with clear quartz in patterns of polarity. Two crystals, one white and one dark, form an excellent polarity of movement for your physical expressions and your etheric energy formations that are somewhat physical as well (and for related structures on other levels). We suggest, for example, that you place one crystal, the clear one, near your left hip and the other, the smoky one, beside your right hip to encourage a flow from left to right in perfect resonancy with a clearing of your energies. This will ground you in the physical by releasing your physical patterns of withholding or blocking at an emotional and energy level, as so often occurs in these areas, especially for women (though sometimes for men as well). We also suggest polarities around the heart, along the legs, and wherever else you are guided to work for the best. And perhaps the nicest use of all for this polarity is to place one in each hand, one clear crystal and one smoky, and use the energy as you are guided to for your best good. Amethyst is also useable in this way.

We would like to close this section on smoky quartz with a channeling we received through ourselves from the energies of the master Luke during one of our crystal classes. It concerned the reasons smoky quartz works the way it does.

"In the electro-magnetic activation that takes place with the spiral helixes of quartz as the ultra-violet radiation strikes from the sun, you get a permanent activation, a permanent quickening, so that electro-magnetic flows are increased and activated on a semi-permanent basis. You would find smoky quartz, if left free of the sun, in about ten million years would become clear again, once the electrical energies were finally released— in much the same way that a sun tan is gradually released when one stays out of the sun.

"This excitation that has happened, stimulation in ultra-violet frequencies, forms a permanent speeding up of the molecular mobility of the structure of smoky quartz and allows a speeding up process of energies that move through at electrical energy levels. These resonate with what we would call third level astral and what we would call causal levels that relate to the physical. This [resonancy] takes place instantaneously for anyone who touches it [the resonancy] at any time, and you would find that the polarity that exists here is the signature, for you have a polarity as between light and dark; and so in any polarity there is a movement. You can use this for your own release by taking in your left hand a smoky crystal and in your right hand a clear crystal. And you have as the polarities of light and dark expressions. You would find that on the breast plate of the priests in ancient times as written about in your bible, there was as a light and a dark object which are no longer identified that centered in the midst of the twelve, and these you would find were a smoky crystal and a clear crystal polished to act as the polarity of being of light and dark. Is this to your understanding?"[2]

Rose Quartz

Rose quartz is a pink quartz that rarely occurs in crystalline form except in small druse or tiny clusters. This is a signature of its ability to work on the cellular level within our being, operating for the general well-being of the individual rather than imposing on him or her anything that is more properly left up to the individual. For the property of a larger rose quartz crystal would be to activate the heart in its opening, and this—in your age—is a free will choice of the individual, to love or not to love all the time. Only in open-hearted love will the rosy quality of the heart center be activated in a man or woman of your earth. And once this is accomplished, the rose quartz crystal that many of you are attracted to but can never find in physical expression will be yours inside your own heart on a subtle level. (This has been a need or request we have regularly received from those buying crystals from us—to have a large, single rose quartz crystal.)

Stated very simply, rose quartz is for harmony at the heart. It is for the stability of love opening up in a gentle way within the heart center of man and god.

Rose quartz is an effective way to ground out the physical energies in general well-being and love. And it is for general overall health as well: that you might be in the "pink" of health, so to speak.

---

[2] We understand from Gurudas, author of *Flower Essences* and *Gem Elixirs and Vibrational Healing, Vol. I & II*, that John, who speaks through the channel Kevin Ryerson, has mentioned this same use for smoky and clear quartz used in polarity by Aaron and his descendents on the breast plate of the priests of Israel.

It is more, but this is enough at this time. We would only suggest the basics of these different stones and let you explore the rest from other sources, including yourself. For much is published already on these things. We would only point out to you our favorites, on the personality level of our expression, in a way that is compatible with our Soul.

Citrine

Citrine is a light yellow to deep orange or brown quartz, usually available commercially from Brazil. It is not possible to go into all its uses, any more than we have with other stones, but in general it is for the solar plexus or throat in its resonancies. It is particularly effective when used with clear quartz for treatment of conditions of mental fatigue (in its yellower forms), for emotional needs like over-openness or sadness (in its more golden forms) and for actual physical-energy needs in its browner or deeper colors. (It is often called madiera citrine in its deeper orange or reddish orange forms.) Madiera citrine is a good crystal to use for yourself at times of low energy or physical debilitation. It is superior for treatment of certain physical illnesses, and it might be possible for certain people to discover applications for treatment of gout and other hardening forms of illness related to the issues of the solar plexus: depression, sadness, unusual emotional needs, worry to the point of emotional anxiety, and so on.

We suggest the golden quality of citrine for treatment of the heart as well, as the heart is balanced in emotional love, and emotional love and stability are possible when one's emotional needs are met in golden harmony and love.

Star Quartz (and Star Rose Quartz)

Star quartz is a translucent milky or smoky white and is available from Ceylon primarily, while star rose quartz is available from Brazil. It is important to point out to you that the expression of rose quartz is fulfilled on earth in star rose quartz, and something similar is true for quartz in its massive forms (as opposed to crystalline). Star rose quartz is thus a good subject for your book. You may look within these quartzes for the benefits of meditation and of assimilation of the intellect at the levels of the Soul. This is because they are usually six or twelve-pointed, these stars within your quartz. And the six and twelve-pointed stars are an excellent focal point for meditation and assimilation of Divine Intellect.

The star within rose quartz tends to focus the heart and create the energies of assimilation that we might call ascendency of the whole over the diverse understandings of the intellect and the heart. This same sublimation or ascendency takes place for regular star quartz at the level of the intellect; and in the case of energies of such stones from Ceylon, at the level of the Soul through the crown chakra, as is being manifested through the rocks of Ceylon—and India even more—in your time. The clear or neutral colored star quartz is also a focalizer of energies at any center or chakra level you choose to use it with for healing.

Also, we would point out for you that within yourselves you have these same energies of attunement so that it is not necessary to acquire such quartz.

Tourmaline

Once called the "Christ Stone" for its ability to work on the etheric, tourmaline might be called "the one who has left us" by people who have worked with it most up until this time. It is not necessary to use it any more in this way, as it is no longer the case that anyone is gone. Now the capacity of the Christ, or of the future potential in all men and women, if you will, is fully imbued with energies of the etheric level. It is possible to attune directly to "the one who is risen," if you will allow us this framework for a moment.

The next thing to share with you is that tourmaline in its electrical abilities is within your own heart already. It is this great electrical ability that gives tourmaline such activity on the etheric level, by the way. Tourmaline is like a plant, you know: like the stalk of a plant. This is its signature. It is like the movement of life inside a plant. It is electrical in this and in another way as well, in that the veins or ribbing of the stalk of tourmaline (or of celery, for that matter) is transformative of nature in life: of the seeds of creation into active participations in it. Thus tourmaline is of many colors, each attuned to a different frequency level to enable you to activate the Soul at a different level of expression in the heart. For the heart is the source of tourmaline, as well as it is for you. You will see in this why Christ was associated with tourmaline, and why, as you activate your self as connected to our Soul, you are needful of the "Christ" or loving expression within your own heart; to get things going, so to speak:

> To get the love inside you
> From the source of all in all
> To the world that's all around you
> As you grow in love for all.

As you grow in love for Soul (in you and around you), you shall see that love is all around you, love is everywhere. And tourmaline is gentle activation of the movements inside your soul that resonate from the heart with love for all, if you give it a chance to be this for you. And tourmaline is no longer necessary for anyone, as "the second arising" of God's own Child in love for all is here in your time especially, in that the drama unfolds for growth in this time of the love of all for all.

Tourmaline is also activation of the soul in another way as well. It is appropriate to use tourmaline for circulation difficulties on any level. In its movement there is potential for this all the time. And tourmaline would share with you for a moment, in channeling from your Soul and through your Soul as well [the Soul of the author writing and the Soul of you, the reader]:

"We are with you this day to share with you our destinies from the stars as one way of love for all. This is a gentle thing to do for you this day. This is an activation you are feeling in your heart right now, to allow us to work more deeply with you all the time. You see, tourmaline will deepen love for all in you. Can you feel it activating right now?"

"Yes, I certainly can." [the author]

"That is good. We would give your readers a sense of the silence that enfolds them all the while they listen to the voice of God inside your heart as love. And they will hear their own hearts there too. Gentle love for all. So gently meant for all of you who read this book. Can you feel it too? Activate your Soul's connection with the following words for your growth (you who read this book):

"We can give you love if you will let us. Our hearts are giving now (this very moment as you read or write, whichever thing you do—as author or as reader). Can you feel us love you from our hearts? We are tourmaline in you. We are guiding hearts to speak with love. Can you feel us doing this? You can, you know. Pause for now and feel us work upon your hearts in peace. And let us love you with your heart unfolded upwards to your throat and love that's pouring down to you from Life itself as love.

"We are giving you tonight the thoughts we work with in your sleep. We are giving you the love that's in your hearts. That's all we do. So simply done. So much to give, to share, as one. We are done for now, but know you may call upon us any time for your growth. Once you know us inside your hearts, you will be able to call upon us anytime. And you needn't own a tourmaline. For we are in your hearts as one, for growth of all in love. God bless you, and thanks for all your help before we start to work with you in love for new beginnings of your soul with Soul of all through you. For you are "person," yes. And personality expression is the sounding of the Soul through you."

The last thing we would say is this, explore for yourselves the meaning in your hearts through the creative energies of tourmaline, energies you may invoke at any time through us, your Souls as one. God bless you indeed forever.

Appendix II

Using Prayer With Crystals

Crystals are an ideal way to introduce yourselves to the forms of prayer that are in order for you at this time. Crystals simplify the process of prayer considerably. Such simplification is possible because crystals respond so perfectly to your intentions. They are able to assimilate exactly what you have asked us to give them, and thus you may feel the results immediately of what your prayers can do.

Prayer depends on many factors, some of which are beyond your control in the physical, and it is difficult for you to sort out what is actually happening when you use true prayer. Crystals are a perfect way to allow the elements of prayer to be broken down for examination, so to speak, because crystals allow perfect assimilation of a prayer to take place for themselves all the time. Crystals allow a state of grace to exist for all in that they give perfect permission all the time for prayer to work through them.

A simplification is in order for you to learn what is going on through prayer all around you. You can feel the results of different prayers for crystals immediately, and you can analyze these differences. Thus a simplification becomes possible, for the usual complication to any prayer being useful in the world is its acceptance or lack of acceptance on many levels. And the acceptance of prayer itself, in your world, is usually dependent on the observations that you make of useful results overall.

(And thus prayer is little acknowledged for what it is: directed wishes for your growth through all.)

Crystals are able to accept all things that are in order for their Souls and growth, and thus are perfect servants of the Grace of God on earth. Such grace allows you growth and harmony. It is your grace we are speaking of, of course: your grace to live and share this world with God and all of God's beginnings at true peace.

This brings us to the reasons for using prayer, once you have sorted out its uses for yourself. This form of service to God (for service so it is) is in order for you at this time at a different level than formerly. Alignment with your Souls is beginning to happen, and thus is possible the truth you seek: that you are one with God in all you do. Prayer becomes activated in this way.

For Souls unite the truth in all, and all becomes your gift from God. Thus when you come to your Soul in self-acceptance, you are opened to the Father/Mother God in all, and as a Child in God you begin to know you are with your Creator all the time. You are given the chance to grow in love and light with all as you accept yourselves as one with God, and God allows you your wishes and your prayers as you are in your service to your Soul and God as one. This is a very real change in orientation for the Soul and self, as the activation that takes place with the self acknowledging its relationship to Soul is nothing less than empowerment to work with God as one. And your prayers become the prayers of your Creator.

This is the way we activate ourselves to work with the Divine in Man. It is a simple process, but one enobled by all time, to know your oneness with your Lord. And the steps to this are furthered in your time as well as now, through you in new beginnings of the Soul on earth.

For you are now able to reciprocate—more consciously than before—all the blessing that we give you through your prayers as yet unspoken from your Souls as one with God.

Formerly you prayed in ignorance to be helped, feeling little of the impact set in motion by your prayers. Now you realign the stars with every prayer, and you can know it through your Souls as one with God.

Formerly you were as children; you spoke in ignorance and thought and felt in less substantial forms of expression than can be expected from you now, as you process for yourselves the stars and Souls of all.

You are able in the near future to absorb the truths of Soul in forms you can accept, as working knowledge of the truth at last. For the blessings we would bring you are sufficient to attract the change in you we speak of. And assimilation on your earth of what is necessary for such change is allowed you through your Souls as one with God.

Such assimilation has taken place in times before in ways that affected only a few individuals with our truth, and fewer than can change a world at last. Men have yet to assimilate such truth—at any time upon your earth—in the numbers quite sufficient for the changes you are coming to through us.

Emerging is the love of God on earth.

We are ready to assist you in all you do. You are able to respond to what we say and feel through you; and this is the difference at last, for you to grow as one with all the doings of your planet as it grows in harmony with all. It is in order for you to share the reciprocal processing of responsibility, at conscious levels of your growth at last. And this is all that prayer would bring to you: conscious choice for growth experienced directly all the time.

Prayer is a means of perfect protection, perfect ordering of your lives in every moment. It is the acknowledgement of the true ordering of events, as you are found wanting in the discovery that you are less than you might be as long as you are guided only by your intellect, your limited framework of discovery in the physical.

Overall, we would have to say that you are limited in all you do through us as well as God, for you are form in its denser levels in this solar system, identified as you are with form in its widest sense. We would give you form in another sense than the one you know over passage of time, but for now know that the form you hold dear is passing; it cannot hold a hope for peace in all you do. It can only offer understanding, in time, for what you are going through. And God alone can give you peace, beyond expression that you know.

We say this to you only as a matter of course, for we are not opposed to your growth in truth upon this planet of expression; we only wish to guide you with a proper perspective for that growth. And prayer is a way for such perspective to take place, over time, for all who come to God for truth and grace.

Prayer is your hope in time of need; also balance of stability. It is the best thing we can offer you to grow by. For setting your conditions for your lives through prayer—consciously undertaken and expressed with loving kindness in your heart —you shall grow in peace for all end times as well as now. Know the two are one—at many levels of expression. And future grace is now, for all who listen to our call, for you to come to God of love; for you to know the truth of who you are and why you've come to be in peace for all to grow by.

Prayer is not some nameless task of indiscriminate trusting. It is a process of precise definition for you here. It is a process subject to error, like all other processes, if you will. But it is more: it is opening to truth that sets you free. You can bring precision to this process of prayer if you wish to. But you can trust that anything left undone may be resolved in your behalf if you but wish it truly, or request the same for all as well as you: perfect resolution of all things we do through you.

Prayer is a process you already engage in all the time. It is not a thing you separate from what you do at all: most of the time you trust that things will be done according to the best intentions of God without your participating actively in any way other than to put in your request to God through unspoken wishes on your part. These are prayers, in a form you scarcely recognize: like prayers of children for their daily bread that mothers everywhere would honor, whether gratefully received or not. (And like such mothers, God would honor you through prayers you make acknowledged and received as blessing for your growth; though you alone can gratefully receive such blessing for yourself, or dream of other things and play alone: it is your choice.) God allows for all your prayers over time.

You see, prayer is ubiquitous already. Why not trust yourselves to grow through all you do by trusting God to guide you quite explicitly? We can only give you such advice. You must take it for yourselves or fail to.

Finally, you may trust yourselves to grow in any other way you choose to. Know that trust in God is not requirement for your growth in same. It is only future possibility for your stabilization in same, not necessity of intellect or of feeling, that you acknowledge who or what you are. For by coming to your Maker you only give due credit. And who you are depends on your design for growth, not upon your future possibilities in same. It is your protection that you speak of when you choose to pray. It is only possibility for growth that awaits you as long as you remain at play overnight; for overnight it is to us. We are willing for the dawn at any time you chose for us to work on you. You are completion all the time for all. So it is and shall be evermore.

Let us recap just a bit in a slightly different way, if you will let us dwell a bit on this our favored subject of your growth. For we would orient your growth to us, in spite of any feelings you may have of past expressions that we are limiting your choices as we point out truth to you. For in your time men fear our coming more than trust it. And you are given love to be the source of peace for all, yet you choose it for yourselves or no, at any time.

Prayer, we say, allows you to sort out your future here with us. It allows also your future evolution, according to the needs and hopes of all. We have to say that you are using prayer whether you think about it or not. For you are using your own wishes to shape your destiny, and you are responsible for this destiny to the extent that God and your own Soul would honor your wishes for you without your asking them consciously or directly, just as a small child extends his or her wishes into life without a sense for where the answers come from. And like such a child, there must be beginnings for you to grow conscious of what you are offered through God in a second childhood, if you will; though one childhood, in a sense, is more than enough, as we would gather from the difficulties you bring us all the time.

In the greater scope of things, one childhood is all that is actually involved. As you grow more conscious of who you are through crystals, or any other means, there comes a time when you awaken to ever widening circles of relationship about you, ever expanding frameworks of destiny and choice. The choice to work with prayer at consciously interactional levels that we provide is one such widening of destiny.

About such new beginnings I am reminded of something the French author Colette once wrote, describing a particular child who after a long day of lusty play at last comes to rest at the edge of the garden, shivers once in the gathering dusk, and sees of a sudden a lamp go on in the sitting-room window, and sees her mother's hand pass across that lamp. "At the mere sight of that hand the Little One starts to her feet, pale, gentle now, trembling slightly as a child must who for the first time ceases to be the happy little vampire that unconsciously drains the maternal heart; trembling slightly at the conscious realization that this hand and this flame, and the bent, anxious head beside the lamp, are the centre and the secret birthplace whence radiate in ripples ever less perceptible, in circles ever more and more remote from the essential light and its vibrations, the warm sitting-room with its flora of cut branches and its fauna of peaceful creatures; the echoing house, dry, warm and crackling as a newly-baked loaf; the garden, the village.... Beyond these all is danger, all is loneliness."[1]

We are all in some sense like such a little child, who notices something for the first time, in noticing the actual state of things upon this planet, that by ourselves we are alone, actually alone—in ever widening circles of expression all around us, in us through and through.

This is perhaps backwards to the true state of affairs, you might say. For we are here to help you all the time. And you are giving light to all in darkness. But actually the truth is closer to this picture than you still might know. For you are child of God. And darkness is your state at last—after sunny days. And you are come to God in this, as once before you came to truth in light of day. For all around you is such truth, and you are in such gardens all the time. Know that you are guided by our hands. Yet you are guided by our love as distant as the stars in a certain sense. And you are alone as long as you notice only this hand that guides you, but notice not the stars are one with you.

So we guide you to your truth, that you, perhaps, are like this child, who goes through distant gardens all the time. And you are like yourselves in this as well. We give you this to grow by, and God bless you.

---

[1] Collette, *In My Mother's House* (New York: Farrar, Straus & Giroux, Inc., 1953 & 1981), p. 24-25.

Bibliography & Selected Sources For Further Reading

Quartz Crystals

Alper, Frank. *Exploring Atlantis, Vols. I-III.* Phoenix, Arizona: Arizona Metaphysical Society, 1982-85. Books can be ordered from: The Arizona Metaphysical Society, 3639 East Clarendon, Phoenix, Arizona 85018.

Baer, Randall N. & Vicki V. *Windows of Light.* San Francisco, California: Harper & Row, 1984.

Blinder, Robinson & Co., Inc. *Prospectus: Abek Incorporated.* Englewood, Colorado, 1985.

Bonewitz, Ra. *Cosmic Crystals.* Wellingborough, England: Turnstone Press, Ltd., 1983.

Bragg, Sir Lawrence. "Crystal Structures of Minerals," *Crystalline State,* Vol. IV. London: G. Bell & Sons, Ltd., 1985.

Bryant, Page. *Crystals and Their Use.* Sedona, Arizona: Network for Cooperative Education, 1982.

Dael. *The Crystal Book.* Sunol, California, 1983.

Garvin, Richard. *The Crystal Skull.* New York: Pocket Books, 1974.

Melville, John. *Crystal Gazing and Clairvoyance.* New York: Samuel Weiser, 1974.

Neklyudeva, Klassn M. V. *Mechanical Twinning of Crystals.* New York: Consultants Bureau, 1964.

Raphaell, Katrina. *Crystal Enlightenment.* New York: Aurora Press, 1985.

Smith, Michael G. *Crystal Power.* St. Paul, Minnesota: Llewellyn Publications, 1985.

Wahlstrom, Ernest E. *Optical Crystallography*, 5th Edition. New York: John Wiley & Sons, Inc., 1979. Also 4th Edition, 1969.

Wood, Elizabeth A. *Crystals and Light. An Introduction to Optical Crystallography*, 2nd Revised Edition. New York: Dover Publications, Inc., 1977.

Gems and Minerals

Ajit Ram Verma P. Krishna. *Polymorphism and Polytypism in Crystals*. New York: John Wiley & Sons, Inc., 1966.

Anthony, R. *The Healing Gems*. Ottawa, Canada: Bhakti Press, 1983.

Bhattacharya, Benoytosh. *The Science of Cosmic Ray Therapy or Teletherapy*. Calcutta: Firma KLM Private, Ltd., 1972.

_____. *Gem Therapy*. Calcutta: Firma KLM Private, Ltd., 1981.

Cayce, Edgar. *Gems and Stones*. Virginia Beach, Virginia: ARE Press, 1981.

Chesterman, Charles W. *The Audubon Society Field Guide to North American Rocks and Minerals*. New York: Alfred A. Knopf, Inc., 1978.

Criswell, Beverly. *Quartz Crystals: A Celestial Point of View*. Reserve, New Mexico: Lavandar Lines Corp, 1982.

Crow, W. B. *Precious Stones*. New York: Samuel Weiser, Inc., 1980.

Finch, Elizabeth. *The Psychic Value of Gemstones*. Phoenix, Arizona: Esoteric Publications, 1980.

Gurudas. *Gem Elixirs and Vibrational Healing, Vols. I & II*. Boulder, Colorado, 1985 & 1986.

Fernie, William T. *Occult and Curative Powers of Precious Stones*. San Francisco: Harper & Row, 1973.

Hauschka, Rudolf D. *The Nature of Substance*. London: Vincent Stuart, Ltd., 1950.

Isaacs, Thelma. *Gemstones, Crystals & Healing*. Black Mountain, North Carolina: Lorien House, 1982.

Kunz, George Frederick. *The Curious Lore of Precious Stones*. New York: Dover Publications, 1941.

Lorusso, Julia and Joel Glick. *Healing Stoned.* Albuquerque: Brotherhood of Life, Inc., 1981.

_____. *Stratagems. A Mineral Perspective.* Albuquerque: Brotherhood of Life, Inc., 1985.

Mella, Dorothee L. *The Legendary and Practical Use of Gems and Stones.* Albuquerque: Domel, Inc., 1979.

O'Donoghue, Michael, ed. *The Encyclopedia of Minerals and Gemstones.* New York: Crescent Books, 1976.

Peterson, Serenity. *Crystal Visioning.* Nashville, Tennessee: Interdimensional Publishing, 1984.

Pelikan, Wilhelm. *The Secrets of Metals.* Spring Valley, New York: Anthroposophical Press, 1973.

Richardson, Wally and Lenora Huett. *Spiritual Value of Gem Stones.* Marina Del Rey, California: DeVorss & Company, 1982.

Sinkankas, John. *Van Nostrand's Standard Catalog of Gems.* New York: Van Nostrand Reinhold Company, 1968.

Uyldert, Mellie. *The Magic of Precious Stones.* Wellingborough, England: Turnstone Press, Ltd., 1981.

Traditional Approaches to Crystals and Atlantis (Selected)

Alper, Frank. *Exploring Atlantis, Vols. I-III.* Phoenix: The Arizona Metaphysical Society, 1982-85.

Cayce, Edgar. *Atlantis: Fact or Fiction.* Virginia Beach, Virginia: ARE Press, 1962.

Cayce, Hugh, ed. *Edgar Cayce on Atlantis.* New York: Warner Books, 1968.

Cohen, Kenneth. "Bones of Our Ancestors." *Yoga Journal,* January/February 1985, Issue 60, pp. 31-33, 56.

Kueshana, Eklal. *The Ultimate Frontier.* Stelle, Illinois: The Stelle Group, 1970.

Montgomery, Ruth. *The World Before.* New York: Fawcett Crest Books, 1976.

Oliver, T. S. (Phylos the Thibetan). *A Dweller on Two Planets.* Blauvelt, New York: Multimedia Publishing Corp., 1974.

Plato (Edith Hamilton & Huntington Cairns, eds.). *The Collected Dialogues.* New York: Pantheon Books, 1963.

Rampa, Lobsang. *The Cave of the Ancients.* London: Corgi Books, 1963.
Steiner, Rudolf. *Cosmic Memory: Atlantis and Lemuria.* Blauvelt, New York: Multimedia Publishing Corp., 1959.

Native American Traditions (Selected)

Sun Bear and Wabun. *The Medicine Wheel: Earth Astrology.* Englewood Cliffs, New Jersey: Prentice-Hall, Inc., 1980.
Hyemeyohsts Storm. *Seven Arrows.* New York: Ballantine Books, 1972.
Harner, Michael. *The Way of the Shaman: A Guide To Power and Healing.* San Francisco: Harper & Row, 1980.

Flower Essences & Other Vibrational Remedies (Selected)

Bach, Edward. *The Bach Flower Remedies.* New Canaan, Connecticut: Keats Publishing, Inc., 1952.
Chancellor, Philip. *Handbook of the Bach Flower Remedies.* Essex, England: W. C. Daniels & Co. Ltd., 1974.
Gurudas. *Flower Essences.* Albuquerque: Brotherhood of Life, Inc., 1983.
The Flower Essence Quarterly. Nevada City, California.

Cooperation with Natural Forces & Their Guidance (Selected)

Hawken, Paul. *The Magic of Findhorn.* New York: Bantam Books, 1974.
Hodson, Geoffrey. *The Kingdom of the Gods.* Adyar, India: The Theosophical Publishing House, 1980.
Findhorn Community. *The Findhorn Garden.* New York: Harper & Row Publishers, 1976.
Fukuoka, Masanobu. *The One-Straw Revolution.* New York: Rodale Press, 1978.

Koepf, Herbert H., Bo D. Pettersson, and Wolfgang Schaumann. *BioDynamic Agriculture.* Spring Valley, New York: The Anthroposophic Press, 1976.

Kotzsch, Ronald E. "Return to the Garden of Eden: The Farming Revolution of Masanobu Fukuoka." *East West Journal*, Vol. 15, Number 8., Aug. 1985, pp. 38-44. Also see related articles in same issue, pp. 44-53.

Maclean, Dorothy. *To Hear The Angels Sing: An Odyssey of Co-Creation With the Devic Kingdom.* Issaquah, Washington: Lorian Press, 1980.

Steiner, Rudolf. *Agriculture.* London: Biodynamic Agricultural Association, 1974.

Healing Practices (Selected)

Allen, H. C. *Keynotes & Characteristics with Comparisons of Some of the Leading Remedies of the Materia Medica.* Wellingborough, England: Thorsons Publishers, Ltd., 1978.

Austin, Mary. *Acupuncture Therapy.* New York: ASI Publishers, Inc., 1980.

Barton, John E. *How To Take Care of Yourselves Naturally.* Shady Cove, Oregon: The Biokinesiology Institute, 1980.

_____. *Muscle Testing Your Way To Health.* Shady Cove, Oregon: The Biokinesiology Institute, 1980.

_____. *Which Vitamin, Which Herb?* Shady Cove, Oregon: The Biokinesiology Institute, 1979.

Beijing College of Traditional Chinese Medicine, et al. *Essentials of Chinese Acupuncture.* Beijing: Foreign Languages Press, 1980.

Bell, Frederick. *Death of Ignorance.* Laguna Beach, California: New Age Holistic Publishers, 1979.

Boericke, William. *Homeopathic Materia Medica.* Calcutta: Sett Dey & Co., 1976.

Clarke, J. H. *A Clinical Repertory to the Dictionary of Materia Medica.* New Delhi: Jain Publishers, 1977.

Cohen, Kenneth. "Channeling the Breath of Life: An Inside Look At Little-Known Taoist Healing Practices." *Yoga Journal,* March/April 1986, Issue 67, pp. 37-39, 60-63.

Cummings, Stephen, & Dana Ullman. *Everybody's Guide to Homeopathic Medicines.* Los Angeles: Jeremy P. Tarcher, Inc., 1984.

Hay, Louise L. *Heal Your Body: Metaphysical Causations For Physical Illness.* Santa Monica, California: Louise Hay, 1982.

Joy, Brugh W. *Joy's Way.* Los Angeles: J. P. Tarcher, Inc., 1979.

Kent, James Tyler *Lectures on Homeopathic Materia Medica.* New Delhi: Jain Publishing Co., 1980.

Seidman, Maruti. *Like a Hollow Flute.* Santa Cruz, California: Elan Press, 1982.

Smith, Trevor, *Homeopathic Medicine.* New York: Thorsons Publishers, 1982.

Steiner, Rudolf. *Geographic Medicine: Two Lectures.* Spring Valley, New York: Mercury Press, 1979.

Thakkur, Chandrashekhar G. *Ayurveda: The Indian Art & Science of Medicine.* New York: ASI Publishers, Inc., 1974.

Vithoulkas, George. *The Science of Homeopathy.* New York: Grove Press, Inc., 1980.

Spiritual Guidance and Growth (Selected)

Alper, Frank. *An Evening With Christos, Vols. I-V.* Phoenix, Arizona: Arizona Metaphysical Society, 1978-84.

_____. *Moses & The Bible: The Story of Creation, Vols. I-IV.* Phoenix: Arizona Metaphysical Society, 1980-82.

The Holy Bible, King James Version. New York: The American Bible Society, 1934.

Hurtak, J. J. *The Book of Knowledge: The Keys of Enoch.* Los Gatos, California: Academy for Future Sciences, 1982.

Keyes, Ken, Jr. *Handbook to Higher Consciousness,* 5th Edition. Coos Bay, Oregon: Living Love Center, 1975.

Prather, Hugh. *There Is A Place Where You Are Not Alone.* Garden City, New York: Doubleday & Company, Inc., 1980.

_____. *The Quiet Answer.* Garden City, New York: Doubleday & Company, Inc., 1982.

Spangler, David. *Revelation: The Birth of a New Age.* Elgin, Illinois: Lorian Press, 1976.

_____. *Reflections on the Christ.* Forres, Scotland: Findhorn Publications, 1978.

_____. *The Laws of Manifestation.* Marina Del Rey, California: DeVorss & Co., 1979.

_____. *Emergence: The Rebirth of the Sacred.* New York: Dell Publishing Co., 1984.

Tolkien, J.R.R. *The Lord of the Rings, Vols. I-III.* New York: Ballantine Books, 1965.

_____. *The Silmarillion.* Boston: Houghton Mifflin Company, 1977.

White Eagle. *Spiritual Unfoldment, Vols. I-II.* Liss, England: The White Eagle Publishing Trust, 1961.

_____. *The Gentle Brother.* Liss, England: The White Eagle Publishing Trust, 1968.

_____. *The Quiet Mind.* Liss, England: The White Eagle Publishing Trust, 1972.

_____. *The Still Voice.* Liss, England: The White Eagle Publishing Trust, 1981.

_____. *The Way of the Sun.* Liss, England: The White Eagle Publishing Trust, 1982.

Young, Alan. *Spiritual Healing.* Marina Del Rey, California: DeVorss & Co, 1981.

Subtle Anatomy and Related Topics (Selected)

Alper, Frank. *The Universal Healing Rays.* Phoenix: The Arizona Metaphysical Society, 1983.

Bailey, Alice. *Esoteric Healing.* New York: Lucis Publishing Company, 1953. Titles of this series of books may be obtained from: Lucis Publishing Company, 866 United Nations Plaza, Suite 566-7, New York, N.Y. 10017.

Jameison, Bryan. *Explore Your Past Lives.* Van Nuys, California: Astro-Analytics Publications, 1976.

Powell, Arthur E. *The Etheric Double.* Wheaton, Illinois: The Theosophical Publishing House, Ltd., 1979.

_____. *The Astral Body.* Wheaton, Illinois: The Theosophical Publishing House, Ltd., 1978.

_____. *The Mental Body*. Wheaton, Illinois: The Theosophical Publishing House, Ltd., 1975.

_____. *The Causal Body*. Wheaton, Illinois: The Theosphical Publishing House, Ltd., 1978.

Steiner, Rudolf. *The Spiritual Hierarchies & Their Reflection in the Physical World*. New York: Anthroposophical Press, 1970.

_____. *The Evolution of Consciousness*. London: Rudolf Steiner Press, 1979.

Steiner, Rudolf, *An Occult Physiology*. London: Rudolf Steiner Press, 1983. The list of Steiner titles is very long in all or nearly all categories we have listed in this bibliography. A complete list of these titles along with purchase order form may be obtained from:

St. George Book Service
P.O. Box 225
Spring Valley, New York 10977.

Tansley, David V. *Subtle Body: Essence and Shadow*. New York: Thames & Hudson, 1978.

Other Inspirational Sources (very selected)

Collette. *My Mother's House*. New York: Farrar, Straus and Giroux, Inc, 1981.

Hollander, Nicole. *I'm In Training To Be Tall and Blonde*. New York: St. Martin's Press, 1978.

_____. *Hi, This Is Sylvia*. New York: St. Martin's Press, 1983. And many others from the same author.

The Complete Grimm's Fairy Tales. New York: Pantheon Books, 1972.

Selected works of John Lennon, Paul McCartney and George Harrison. (Take your pick.)

The author and his wife, Alayna, teach and work as a team in Boulder, Colorado. They are currently writing together two further volumes of *Patterns of the Whole:*

Volume II:
Subtle Body Anatomy
(Who and What We Are)

and

Volume III:
Alignment With Life.

To arrange for workshops and individual consultations, please contact the author and his wife at the following address:

1272 Bear Mt. Ct.
Boulder, Colorado 80303